DOWN AND OUT
IN AMERICA

DOWN AND OUT
IN AMERICA

The Origins of Homelessness

Peter H. Rossi

The University of Chicago Press
Chicago and London

PETER H. ROSSI is the Stuart A. Rice Professor of Sociology and acting director, Social and Demographic Research Institute, University of Massachusetts.

The University of Chicago Press gratefully acknowledges the contribution of the Jensen Lectureship and the American Sociological Association toward publication of this book.

The University of Chicago Press, Chicago 60637
The University of Chicago Press, Ltd., London

98 97 96 95 94 93 92 91 90   5432

Library of Congress Cataloging-in-Publication Data

Rossi, Peter Henry, 1921–
    Down and out in America : the origins of homelessness / Peter H.
Rossi.
      p.   cm.
    "Annotated bibliography of the combined homeless studies and
studies of the extremely poor": p.
    Bibliography: p.
    Includes index.
    ISBN 0-226-72828-5 (alk. paper)
    1. Homelessness—United States—History.   2. Urban poor—United
States—History.   1. Title.
HV4504.R67   1989
362.5′1′0973—dc20   89-31598
                                                      CIP

For America's extremely poor and homeless

Contents

Preface

Although I have been poor, I have never been extremely poor or homeless, for which I am thankful. As I will show in this book, neither condition is pleasant, healthful, or comfortable. To be extremely poor or homeless is to be outside the American mainstream: it is unpleasant, unhealthful, and full of pain. But lack of direct experience does not dictate an absence of either understanding or sympathy. I wrote this volume out of concern for the plight of the extremely poor and homeless of America and in the conviction that we must have good knowledge about both groups before we can devise effective means to alleviate their condition and adjust our institutions so that their numbers will eventually decline and, we hope, diminish to zero.

This book had its immediate origins in a survey I designed and directed on the homeless population of Chicago, but it is rooted in a lifelong concern for those on and outside the margins. My work as a sociologist has consistently centered on the policy concerns of social programs dealing with problems of the less advantaged of our society. My most fervent wish is that this book will help those who are homeless now and prevent others from falling down and out to the fringes of our society.

I owe a debt to George Orwell for paralleling the title of his insightful and sensitive *Down and Out in London and Paris,* one of the best descriptions of living close to destitution.

I wish I could say I had been following in Stuart A. Rice's footsteps in studying the homeless and the extremely poor. In point of fact, at the time I chose his name for the chair I occupy at the University of Massachusetts I did not know that Rice had published several important studies of homeless men in New York during the First World War, stemming from his experience during a short term as the superintendent of New York's Municipal Lodging House. It was a great surprise to discover that the man whose name I had chosen out of admiration for his technical contributions to social research had also done important early work on homelessness.

My labors on this book have been lightened by the help, kindness, and generosity of many people. First, the Robert Wood Johnson Foundation and the Pew Memorial Trust provided funds so we could undertake the Chicago Homeless Study, upon which I draw heavily in this book. The Illinois Department of Public Aid also underwrote a portion of the costs. Funding the Chicago Homeless Study meant taking risks, and I admire its benefactors. It was not clear at the time they funded this research that my colleagues and I had the right solutions to the problems of studying a population whose members had no fixed abode.

Second, I have been blessed with the best possible set of colleagues and collaborators. The staff of NORC: A Social Science Research Institute were true partners in the design of a data-collection strategy that solved the knotty problem of how to reach, count, and interview homeless persons. I am especially indebted to Dr. Martin Frankel, Dr. Mary Utne O'Brien, Dr. Sara Siegal Locvy, and Ms. Ann-Sofi Roden of the NORC staff. At the Social and Demographic Research Institute (SADRI), I was fortunate to have Professor Gene A. Fisher as a working colleague. His contributions to the measurement of mental illness among the Chicago homeless are the basis for much of chapter 6. In addition, he undertook most of the task of preparing estimates of the size of the homeless population of Chicago. Ms. Georgianna Willis, an advanced graduate student at SADRI, worked prodigiously to prepare the Chicago data tapes for analysis, always with great energy and care. Professor James D. Wright also made many contributions to both the design and the analysis and was always ready to read and discuss anything I wrote.

Third, a special feature of this book is that it benefits greatly by drawing upon a variety of data sources; I was given access to them all in the true spirit of scientific collegiality. I would not have been able to enrich this work in that fashion without the extraordinary cooperation of a number of people who gave me access to their raw data. I am particularly grateful to Mr. Matthew Stagner and Dr. Harold Richman of the Chapin Hall Center for Children of the University of Chicago, who gave me copies of data from their studies of clients of Chicago General Assistance and Aid to Families with Dependent Children. Professor Charles Hoch also was gracious in providing data from his study of Chicago SRO (single-room occupancy) hotel residents. Perhaps the most unusual generosity was shown by Professor William J. Wilson of the University of Chicago, who gave me copies of data from his Chicago Urban Family Life Study before he himself had had time to analyze them.

Writing this book was made far easier by a half-year sabbatical granted by the University of Massachusetts. A gracious grant from the Rockefeller Foundation made it possible for me to take a full-year sabbatical and to entice Mr. Jeffry Will as a research assistant whose skill and dogged persistence helped speed the task. I am deeply indebted to the Rockefeller Foundation's support and to Mr. Will's valuable help.

A quick start on the book was made possible by my being appointed to the Jensen Lectureship in Sociology and Social Policy at Duke University. The set of lectures I prepared for presentation at Duke early in my sabbatical served as a detailed outline for the manuscript that took me the rest of the leave to finish.

My tender comrade and wife, Alice S. Rossi, helped me along at every step, ready to listen to my problems and to offer advice that materially improved the book. There is no way I can overstate the value of the steady warmth, friendship, and intellectual excitement that surround me in her presence.

I have been helped by so many. May the virtues of this volume do honor to their kindness. Its faults are due to my inability to take full advantage of their help.

ONE

On the Bottom and Out on the Fringe

Portraits of the Down and Out

Extreme poverty and homelessness are useful abstractions that only dimly reflect the concrete human details of the extremely poor and the homeless. Most of this book concerns those abstractions. Some intimate knowledge of the people described by the terms extremely poor and homeless can be gleaned from this handful of composite case histories.

JOSEPH FISHER

Joseph Fisher, a black man, was thirty-three years old in 1986 when he was interviewed in a Chicago shelter. He was born in Chicago and had lived there all his life except for a two-year enlistment in the navy. His parents, now divorced, still live in that city, as do his older brother and a younger sister. Mr. Fisher did not graduate from high school, although he did qualify for a GED (general equivalency diploma) in the navy. He was employed for a short time "doing factory work" after his discharge in 1976 and has not worked steadily since. Mr. Fisher has been homeless this time for about eighteen months but has been homeless before for shorter periods.

Mr. Fisher looks considerably older than his age. He is thin and seems undernourished. He rates his health as very poor and says he has problems with his kidneys and heart, both conditions that impair his ability to work.

Before becoming homeless, he lived with his mother and younger sister in their apartment, but his mother asked him to leave. He would like to go back with his family but does not believe they would take him in again. He has never been married, although he fathered a child with whom he currently has no contact. He phones his mother every month or so and sometimes sleeps at her apartment.

Mr. Fisher earns ten to fifteen dollars a week hawking newspapers to drivers stopped at downtown traffic lights. Occasionally he receives some day work through a labor contractor. He was on General Assistance but somehow lost his eligibility. Mr. Fisher would like to have steady work but no longer even tries to find regular employment.

Mr. Fisher sleeps most nights in a shelter run by evangelical missionaries, lining up with several hundred others in the late afternoon to be signed in

1

and receive a bed assignment. In the mornings the shelter turns him out. Some days he can get a batch of newspapers from a circulation truck that comes to the shelter looking for men to peddle them. Most days he spends wandering around within a few blocks of the shelter, getting lunch from a local food kitchen. Sometimes he panhandles.

Mr. Fisher is an alcoholic: when he has money, he often spends it on cheap wine, sometimes sharing his fifth with other homeless men. When he has no money, he sometimes gets drinks from friends who happen to have cash.

When interviewed, he was sober, clean, and neatly dressed, though in shabby, unpressed clothing. According to the interviewer he was coherent and articulate in his answers. However, he shows the clinical signs of major depression: he sees no hope for the future, often has no appetite, and thinks about suicide several times a month.

WALTER JOHNSON

Walter Johnson was interviewed while waiting in line to receive a meal at a Chicago food kitchen set up for homeless persons. He was thirty-five at the time and lived in a room in a nearby SRO (single-room occupancy) hotel, for which he paid $200 a month.

Mr. Johnson works twenty to thirty hours a week as a busboy in a downtown restaurant, earning $80 to $150 depending on the hours. His earnings allow him to pay his rent regularly but do not give him much leeway for other expenses. Once or twice a week when his cash is low, he joins the food lines. Buying a new pair of shoes forces him to show up regularly in the food lines for a week or so.

He went to work in a metal fabricating plant when he finished high school and worked there more or less steadily until the plant closed four years ago. Since then the only jobs he has been able to pick up have been at slightly more than minimum wage. He has tried repeatedly to get steadier employment at higher wages. Despite high-school graduation, Mr. Johnson does not read or write with any ease. Indeed, one of his major problems is that he cannot fill out an employment application without help.

He has a few friends, mostly fellow residents in his SRO. Occasionally he goes to a local bar with them. He does not drink heavily, saying he cannot afford to.

Mr. Johnson has never married. He lived with his parents until he was twenty-five but moved out when his mother died. He is not sure where his father is now living, nor does he know the addresses of his brother and two sisters.

Mr. Johnson seems very depressed about his future. He worries about what may happen if he loses his job, fearing he might have to resort to the shelters.

PHOEBE COTT

Phoebe Cott, a white woman, was thirty-eight when she was interviewed in 1985. Born in Chicago, she lives with her mother and several younger brothers and sisters in a small apartment. She was interviewed because she is a General Assistance recipient, receiving a monthly check of $154 from the Illinois Department of Public Aid. She gives her mother $75 each month to help pay living expenses. Occasionally she works, usually as temporary help in local stores.

Ms. Cott married at eighteen and was divorced after two years. She had no children. Since finishing high school, she has been employed fairly steadily, mostly at low-level clerical jobs—receptionist, retail sales clerk, data entry, and such. None of the jobs lasted long, but until 1983 she was able to rent small apartments by herself or occasionally with a live-in partner.

In 1983 she was injured seriously enough in a car accident to require several weeks in the hospital and a long period of recovery. When she left the hospital, she went to live with her mother while she recovered. She has not worked steadily since. After exhausting her unemployment benefits, she applied for General Assistance and has been on the rolls for about six months.

Ms. Cott hopes to find work soon. She has looked consistently, prodded somewhat by the General Assistance requirements for job search. When she finds steady work, she would like to have her own apartment.

DENNIS CALDER

Dennis Calder was interviewed standing in line at a food kitchen in downtown Los Angeles in 1986. He was then thirty-two years old and had lived in that city since early childhood, when he arrived from Texas with his parents and siblings.

Mr. Calder was married for a few years in his early twenties and is now divorced. He has not been in touch with his ex-wife or his two children for several years. Since the breakup of his marriage, he has lived by himself, mostly in rented apartments. For some of the time he lived with his parents, usually for the few weeks between his employment episodes. His parents moved back to Texas in 1980.

Mr. Calder has been intermittently employed since he left high school in his junior year, working in low-paying jobs such as parking attendant, busboy, and wallboard installer. In 1980 he was convicted of breaking and entering and sentenced to a year in a minimum-security California prison. This was his fourth arrest on felony charges; the previous arrests had led to dropped charges or probation. With time off for good behavior, he returned to Los Angeles in 1981. Since his release he has had a hard time finding and keeping employment and has worked less than six months out of every year.

In 1986 he was on California's General Relief rolls, receiving $212 a month. He lived in an SRO hotel most of the time, but the benefits were not

3

enough to cover a full month's rent, food, and other expenses. Mr. Calder got along by sleeping in shelters for about one-fourth of the nights each month and by frequently patronizing food kitchens, clothing depots, and other services set up for homeless people in the downtown area.

Mr. Calder does not consider himself an alcoholic, although he does drink moderately heavily. His health is good, and he is neat and clean. Scars from an old facial injury mar his looks. He is not a sanguine person and believes he has little future. Although he looks for work every week, he doesn't have much hope that he can find steady employment. "Something always goes wrong with me," he replied when asked why he had trouble finding work.

RUTH CORONOD

Ruth Coronod was interviewed in 1985 in a Chicago South Side shelter for homeless families, where she had been living for a month with her two daughters, aged two years and six months. She is a slight black woman who was then twenty but looked sixteen or seventeen.

Ms. Coronod has never been employed. In her last year of high school she became pregnant with her older daughter and dropped out. After the baby was born she lived in her mother's home, supported by an AFDC grant. The child's father initially contributed small sums for his daughter's support but has not done so for more than a year. Her younger daughter was fathered by another young man.

A month before the interview her mother asked her to move out, and she found that the shelter would keep her for two months while she looked for an apartment. Although her AFDC benefits will increase when she finds a place to rent, those benefits plus other programs do not provide enough funds for any but the cheapest apartments. She expects to find a place soon and to leave the shelter. Shelter housing counselors are helping her search.

Ms. Coronod would like to work but has only a vague notion of how to find a job and even vaguer ideas about what kind of work she might do.

HENRY KUBILIK

Henry Kubilik, a white man, was fifty-five years old in 1985 when interviewed in his room in a Chicago SRO hotel. He has been living in SRO hotels since the breakup of his marriage in 1975.

Mr. Kubilik worked in a South Chicago steel mill from high-school graduation until 1974, when he suffered a heart attack. After recovery he needed a less physically demanding occupation and took a job as a salesman for a home-renovation firm. His income declined and became erratic. He tried to go back to the steel mills, but by that time the company had cut back production severely and could find no place for him except in very poorly paying positions. His marriage began to go to pieces as his earning ability declined. He left his wife and three adolescent children in 1975 and was divorced in 1980. His wife has remarried.

He sees very little of his children, who are now married. He occasionally visits his widowed mother and his married siblings but does not consider his relationships with these relatives very close.

Since leaving sales, he has held a number of low-paying, low-skill jobs. When interviewed he was working as a guard for a private security firm, earning $100 to $300 a week depending on how often he was called to work. He would like to find steadier employment.

Mr. Kubilik has been homeless several times for short periods when his bouts of unemployment exhausted his cash reserves. During his homeless episodes, he lived in shelters while he looked for work.

He is worried about his health, in particular how he would survive a second heart attack. Without health insurance, he fears he would not get proper care.

EUGENE SNAPPS

Eugene Snapps is a slight white man of twenty-five with a strong regional accent. He is a recent arrival in the Sun Belt city where he was interviewed, having traveled from the small rural market town one hundred miles away where he grew up.

A high-school dropout, Mr. Snapps has held a succession of low-paying jobs in construction, gas stations, fast-food restaurants, and retail stores. The jobs have never lasted more than a few months; most he has simply left. In his hometown, employment has become harder and harder to find.

He came to the city to find work. After exhausting the $200 his father gave him as a stake, Mr. Snapps came to the Salvation Army for shelter. Under shelter rules, he is allowed to stay five days, then he must find a bed elsewhere for ten days. When barred from the Salvation Army shelter, he sleeps in public places—parks, vestibules, bus stations, and so on. He has been in the city for the three summer months.

Mr. Snapps was interviewed in a local park, where he was sitting on a bench talking to several other men. He was dressed in blue jeans and a T-shirt, both reasonably clean. At the time he had heavy facial stubble and needed a haircut. Mr. Snapps says he has trouble filling out employment forms and doing arithmetic.

He hopes to find a job soon and makes the rounds of construction companies weekly. If he doesn't find work soon, he intends to go back to his hometown. He hopes his father and mother will make a place for him in their home.

JOHN DORE

John Dore[1] was interviewed in 1986 as he huddled in a sandwichlike arrangement of cardboard over a steam grate in Washington, D.C. He was

---

1. This account is based on a homeless man I interviewed in the Foggy Bottom area of the District of Columbia. I had seen Mr. Dore several times on my visits to Washington, and I struck

5

unkempt, wearing soiled and ragged clothing, and his face and hands were dirty. He had difficulty understanding the questions, and they often had to be repeated. His answers were confused and sometimes contradictory.

Mr. Dore is forty-five years old but looks in his sixties. He has been homeless in the District for more than four years. He never graduated from high school, leaving when he was sixteen. When younger he worked primarily as a warehouse laborer for the General Services Administration, running a forklift that shuttled paper supplies into and out of inventory, loading and unloading trucks. He lost his GSA job in 1970 for repeated absences and being incapacitated on the job.

Mr. Dore is an alcoholic and claims to have undergone half a dozen detoxification sessions. He drinks whenever he can get the money to buy pints of cheap wine. His only source of income is panhandling, and he averages a dollar or two a day. He was sober when interviewed, or so he claimed. Indeed, the interviewer promised him a fee of $5, which he planned to spend on wine.

Mr. Dore has never married, nor does he claim to have children. Until 1980 he lived with his parents, who provided food and lodging. When he worked, he gave them some money for room and board. In 1980 his father died and his mother moved to Pittsburgh to live with his married sister. For a year he rented rooms in cheap hotels using money his mother sent him. After she stopped sending money he slept in one shelter or another, but as each shelter came to recognize him as a chronic alcoholic, he was refused admission because his behavior upset other clients. Except when he admitted himself to a detoxification unit or was taken to a hospital, he slept on the streets, usually on the same steam grate.

Mr. Dore's decades of heavy drinking have probably impaired his mental functions. He claims to hear voices that constantly urge him to drink. He is certain FBI agents are trying to kidnap him and send him to Cuba or Russia. He is subject to alcoholic seizures and has been injured several times when he fell in traffic. He was not sure what year it was or who was the current president of the United States.

Ida Madigan

Ida Madigan was thirty-five years old when interviewed in a woman's day shelter on New York's West Side, but she looked fifty. Although she seemed freshly washed up, her overall appearance was of unkempt frowsiness. Although it was a hot day in July, she sat on a bench in the shelter wearing a ragged winter coat over a wrinkled rayon dress. Her hair was uncombed and straggled across her face.

Ms. Madigan has been homeless for several years. In 1982 she committed

---

up a conversation when he came into a fast food restaurant for a cup of coffee while I was having breakfast. After that contact I often met him on the streets and talked with him further.

6

herself to a psychiatric hospital out of fear that she would commit suicide and stayed six months. After her discharge, she lived for a time in an SRO hotel, supported by Social Security disability payments. She does not understand why her eligibility was terminated in 1984, but since then she has lived in shelters and on the streets.

Ms. Madigan held a number of clerical jobs after finishing high school, the longest being four years as a billing clerk for a department store. She lost that job when she began to have severe depressive episodes and could not get to work. Subsequently she held a series of short-term clerical jobs. Since her discharge from the hospital Ms. Madigan has not worked, and she does not believe she has the strength to hold a job because of her "nerves."

Before her hospitalization she shared a small apartment with her sister and several other women, each contributing a share of household expenses and rent. During Ms. Madigan's periods of unemployment, her sister would pay her share. While she was in the hospital her sister married and moved to Atlanta. She does not know what happened to the other women.

Ms. Madigan has never married and has no children. Her parents are both dead. She has not been in touch with her only sister for a number of years.

JOHN DEIRING

John Deiring, a forty-seven-year-old white man, now dead, came to a medical clinic for the homeless in Birmingham, Alabama, in 1986 for treatment for severe bruises and a slight cut on his arm, received when he "fell on the streets."

He claimed to have been homeless since he was twenty, when his parents asked him to leave their home because of his heavy drinking and irregular work habits.

In his younger years Mr. Deiring worked as a construction laborer, usually day to day. For the past few years he had made a living as a scavenger, collecting discarded cans, bottles, and cardboard and anything else of value that could be found in the garbage. He had fashioned a high-sided cart from the chassis of an old baby carriage and scrap lumber. Wheeling the cart through the back alleys behind stores and offices, he collected enough salvage to earn up to $10 a day. He paid $20 a week for a small basement room beneath a store whose owner believed his presence was a security measure.

Mr. Deiring was an alcoholic. When he finished his early morning rounds of scavenging, he was one of the first customers at a package liquor store. He claimed to drink several pints of wine a day.

In the course of his several visits to the medical clinic he was found to be suffering from a variety of debilitating conditions, including leukemia and chronic pulmonary obstruction, in addition to the injuries that brought him there.

The last entry on his medical chart is a report from the hospital on his death. A final mugging had left him with a lung punctured by broken ribs as well as brain injuries from a blow that fractured his skull. He apparently was killed for the proceeds from the thirty pounds of aluminum cans he had collected that day.

The vignettes are composites, made up from the life experiences of many of the people who have been interviewed in one or another of the studies undertaken since 1980. Some are homeless, living in shelters or sleeping in public places. Others live in the cheapest housing available or stay with relatives or friends.[2]

All share the condition of extreme poverty, with incomes that are very small and often erratic. Most have disabilities that make it hard to obtain and hold steady employment. Severe skill deficiencies, chronic mental illness, physical disabilities, and serious criminal records are common.

Although most are well into adulthood, they are alone in life. Some have never married, and the others' marriages had broken up some years ago. Except for those living with parents or siblings, ties to immediate family and other relatives are characteristically tenuous. These are not people at the centers of strong networks of family and friends.

In many ways the extremely poor, those with homes and the homeless, are off the margins of our society. The homeless are especially afflicted, unconnected to the worlds of work and family and subsisting at levels far below an acceptable minimum.

The Connections between Extreme Poverty and Homelessness

This book started out to be entirely about the homeless of America. But the more I looked into homelessness the more it appeared to be misstated as merely a problem of being without shelter: homelessness is more properly viewed as the most aggravated state of a more prevalent problem, *extreme poverty*. As the cases described above illustrate, it is difficult to distinguish consistently between those with homes and the homeless among the extremely poor. There are many points at which the two groups are indistinguishable. A recent study (Sosin, Colson, and Grossman 1988) showed that more than half the people waiting in Chicago food kitchen lines or using medical clinics for the homeless were living in conventional dwellings. A respectable minority of shelter users also have homes.

As a consequence, the scope of the book soon expanded to include all those Americans who get along on close to no income, people with a precarious hold on the basic amenities of life that most of us take for granted. The extremely poor constitute the pool from which the homeless are drawn; they are at high risk of becoming homeless and from time to time find themselves in

2. Detailed and lengthy excellent case studies can be found in books or monographs by Kozol (1988), Baxter and Hopper (1981), and Hope and Young (1986).

that condition. Some become homeless for long periods, although fortunately they constitute only a small proportion of the extremely poor. Most are homeless for a few months at a stretch, but many have had several episodes of homelessness over the years.

This is not to make homelessness trivial. There can be no doubt that *literal homelessness*,[3] as I have come to call having no home to go to, is a condition of extreme deprivation; but it is only a step away from being *precariously housed*—having a tenuous hold on housing of the lowest quality. Like the literally homeless, those with precarious homes are extremely poor. It is the major thesis of this book that extreme poverty is at the root of both literal homelessness and being precariously housed.

Although there is clearly a line between those with homes and the literally homeless, that line is easily crossed. A life of extreme poverty is one of extreme vulnerability. For most Americans it is easy to roll with all but the major punches life can give; most of us can absorb the shocks of illness and unemployment up to a point. A few months of unemployment or a week in the hospital are serious, but most people have enough financial and psychological reserves to survive either without becoming destitute or deeply depressed. Among the extremely poor, however, the many untoward events that the rest of us absorb can be major shocks catapulting them across the blurred line between having a home and being homeless. For the extremely poor, with no reserves of savings, no safety net of entitlements, and no credit cards, losing a few days' wages or catching a severe cold can mean losing a job, going without adequate food, or getting evicted. Events of this sort can trigger an episode of homelessness. Being homeless is a considerable notch below having a home although being extremely poor. And getting back among the domiciled population is not easy for someone with essentially zero resources.

Homelessness as the Major Focus

Although the broad concern of this book is extreme poverty,[4] for practical reasons the emphasis will be most heavily on the homeless—the most disadvantaged of the extremely poor—since there is much more information about them than about the larger population of the extremely poor. For reasons I will give later, the bulk of the extremely poor, both homeless and with homes, are precisely those elements in the United States population that are least likely to

3. For convenience, throughout this book I will use the terms "homeless" and "literally homeless" interchangeably.

4. The term "extreme poverty" as I use it is definitely not equivalent to "underclass," which covers those who are persistently poor, are long-term unemployed, and engage in behaviors at variance with those of mainstream America, particularly economic crime and drug abuse. The underclass is defined by both poverty and behavior. In contrast, the extremely poor are defined primarily by income. Surely some extremely poor persons also fit the definition of the underclass, but most do not.

be reached by the information-gathering agencies of the federal government and by social scientists. The extremely poor are not invisible, but they are not neatly packaged into traditional households, the units most amenable to study. As a consequence, it is much more difficult to find firm information, especially statistical data, on the extremely poor. In contrast, there is much more information on the homeless, much of it recent.

Because homelessness has become a well-recognized social problem in recent years, the homeless segment of the extremely poor has been studied fairly extensively. The attention of the public, elected officials, agency personnel, and the media has made the homeless a topical subject for social researchers. As of the beginning of 1988, close to sixty social science studies of the homeless had been published in one form or another.[5] These are mainly local studies of specific urban places. The aim of most of these local studies has been to describe the conditions of the homeless; only a small minority have attempted to estimate the size of the homeless population. My colleagues and I undertook one of these local studies in Chicago (Rossi, Fisher, and Willis 1986). I will give special emphasis to the findings of this study, partly out of pride of authorship, but mainly because ours is among the most thorough technically. Fortunately for our purposes, Chicago was the site of several recent studies of extremely poor persons and families and was also the subject of an excellent study done in the late 1950s, by Donald Bogue (1962), of the homeless of that time. The rich findings of these studies amply justify the attention this book gives to Chicago.

Defining Homelessness and Extreme Poverty

It is a prime contention of this book that extreme poverty and homelessness are adjoining segments at the bottom of the American standard-of-living continuum. To be homeless is clearly to be on the bottom rung in living standards, but the line between homelessness and having a home is fuzzy, as is the line between extreme poverty and being simply poor. Consequently it is easy to obtain agreement on the extreme cases of poverty and of literal homelessness, but there is much disagreement on where boundaries should be placed between those with homes and the literally homeless, and between the poor and the extremely poor.

Homelessness, at its core, means not having customary and regular access to a conventional dwelling; it mainly applies to those who do not rent or own a residence. Thus people we find sleeping in abandoned buildings or on steam grates who do not have an apartment or house they could go to are clearly among the literally homeless. At the other extreme, those who own houses clearly do have homes. But there are many instances where disagreements may arise.

5. These studies are listed in appendix A.

The ambiguities of homelessness center on two critical components of the definition given above: What is a "conventional dwelling"? And what is "customary and regular access"? Conventional dwellings surely include apartments, houses, and mobile homes in a mobile home park, but does the concept include hotel rooms (especially SROs),[6] rented rooms in private dwellings, beds in dormitorylike accommodations, cars, trucks, vans, tents, or shacks made of scrap materials? Similarly, those who own or rent their own homes surely have "customary and regular access," as do current members of a household in which someone owns or rents a home. But what about someone who has been given temporary permission to share a conventional dwelling? What period constitutes "temporary"? For example, if a divorcing adult child is provided temporary shelter by parents "for as long as you like," does that constitute having a home or being homeless? In a sense, all these ambiguous cases are ones where those involved do not have a regular dwelling to which they can go consistently and regularly or where the right to do so is tenuous.

Additional ambiguities are easily encountered: for example, some of the shelters for the homeless ask for a small payment but may forgo it if a homeless person claims not to have the money. Does that payment constitute rent, and hence should paying occupants of such shelters not be considered homeless? Comparable questions center on people in other institutional settings. Should general or mental hospital patients who do not have conventional dwelling arrangements to return to when discharged be considered homeless? What about the inmates of jails and prisons in comparable circumstances?

It is easy to get bogged down in academic exercises in definition. I will resist the temptation. Instead, I will use a definition of homelessness that covers the essence of that term and is also practical to use in actual research. Although my ultimate conception is that homelessness is a matter of degree, I am constrained to use the definition most common in the social science studies of homelessness that I rely on for grounded knowledge of the homeless. This common definition is toward the narrower end of the range. Most of the studies used here address literal homelessness, defined as not having customary and regular access to a conventional dwelling. They also center mainly on the most accessible of the homeless, clients of agencies that provide services, such as shelters, food kitchens, and medical clinics set up to serve the homeless.

I further recognize "conventional dwellings" as including homes, apartments, mobile homes, and rented rooms (in hotels, rooming houses, or private homes). An unconventional dwelling is any structure that is not intended to be used as a sleeping place, including public areas such as bus stations or

6. "Single-room occupancy" or SRO hotels are places that rent single rooms, usually by the week or the month, at very low rents. SRO rooms usually do not have private bathrooms or cooking facilities. Maid service is skimpy and erratic.

lobbies, abandoned buildings, dormitory arrangements (as in shelters),[7] cars, vans, trucks, and scrap-material shacks.

Thus any current member of a household who occupies a dwelling rented or owned by someone in that household can be said to have a home. Any person who does not own or rent a dwelling and is not a regular member of a household that does so is homeless. Note that this definition covers one-person as well as multiperson households. The definition of literal homelessness also excludes the inhabitants of hospitals, jails, prisons, and nursing homes.

There are some very persuasive logistical reasons why most studies of the homeless have adopted this definition in practice. Most important, this definition can be given a practical operational form. It is relatively easy to determine whether a given person is or is not literally homeless; for reasons I will discuss in chapter 3, it is very difficult in practice to employ a definition that includes marginally housed persons and families.

This definition of homelessness may be controversial. A number of influential commentators on homelessness argue for a definition that would include those I have called "precariously housed," who may live in a conventional dwelling but whose hold on that home is precarious. There is clear merit to that viewpoint, especially since the precariously housed are from time to time among the literally homeless.

As with other social problems, disputes over definitions are not simply about scholastic issues. They involve defining the goals of social welfare policies and hence engage central political values. In the broadest sense, the issue is what constitutes the floor of housing adequacy and decency below which no member of our society should be permitted to sink without being offered[8] some alternative. If we set the standard that every household—including one-person households—should have the opportunity to live in an apartment or house of its own, and that anyone whose living arrangements do not meet those standards is homeless, then the definition of homelessness is considerably enlarged to include many of the ambiguous instances listed above. If we accept a lower standard, the definition of homelessness narrows. My position is that I have not ignored the precariously housed by accepting a fairly narrow definition of homelessness. Rather I include the latter in the broader category of the extremely poor.

Considerable difficulties also surround the definition of extreme poverty. No one could deny that anyone whose income, in cash or in kind, is zero is extremely poor. But what should be the upper boundary? Surely it should be set below the current official poverty line, but how far below? The 1987 poverty line defined as poor any single person who has less than $5,250 in annual income, with higher poverty thresholds for families. The poverty line is an

7. I also decided not to consider as rent payments or "donations" asked of shelter occupants.
8. Note that the emphasis in this statement is on "being offered" better housing opportunities, ruling out coercing people to accept such opportunities.

arbitrary one that is current only because it has been in heavy use for official purposes since the 1960s, corrected annually for inflation.

Despite its usefulness, the official poverty level has come under heavy criticism.[9] Liberals say it is set too low, making the near poor appear better off than they actually are; conservatives object because it counts only cash income and not the many benefits in kind—for example, food stamps and Medicaid—that some of the poor receive through one benefit program or another.

The history of controversy surrounding the poverty line is instructive for our efforts to develop a definition of extreme poverty. There can be little doubt that whatever definition we may propose will be subject to much the same objections, as would be any arbitrary cutoff on a continuum. If we could have any information we might want, my preference would be for a definition of extremely poor that would measure how far cash income and benefits in kind fall short of basic subsistence needs. Unfortunately for our purposes, the concept of subsistence needs is neither clear in theory nor practical to measure.

In the end we are forced to resort to a certain arbitrariness. As a working definition, I propose that the extremely poor consist of households whose annual incomes are three-quarters or less of the current official poverty line, or below $4,000 (in 1988). The term "household" in this definition covers single persons who are living alone as well as groups of persons who share a dwelling, pool their incomes to some extent, and consume basic commodities jointly.[10] This means that a single person earning up to $4,000 in 1988 dollars is one of the extremely poor. (Extremely poor multiple-person households would have higher boundaries for their total household income.) Although there is some virtue to such seeming precision, that precision is useful only if the definition is easy to operationalize. That is, if we have no way to identify persons who fit, then the definition is not very useful. We will find that we must use this definition in a fairly imprecise fashion, since income data on those below the poverty level are often lacking and many extremely poor people are missed by conventional social science data-collection methods.

For all practical purposes, under these definitions almost all homeless people are also extremely poor. Keep in mind that when I refer to the homeless I am also referring to a subset of the extremely poor. Since there are many more extremely poor persons and families than there are homeless ones, most of the former have homes. As a convenient shorthand, I will use the term "extremely poor" to mean domiciled extremely poor persons and families.

9. See the report of the United States General Accounting Office (1987) for a discussion of the difficulties of "cashing out" the benefits in kind received by the poor.

10. There are fuzzy components to this definition. A person renting a room in an apartment who does not share any other expenses is by this definition not part of the renting household but a single-person household. An adult child who pays nominal room and board to parents is marginally a household member, but adult children who pool most of their income should be considered members of the household. Of course most of these niceties in definition are not useful in practice, since most data sources do not contain enough information to apply them.

Homelessness and Extreme Poverty as Social Problems

A societal condition becomes a social problem when it draws the attention of a significant portion of the public. In that sense there can be little doubt that homelessness is currently a social problem in the United States. Since the early part of this decade, our country has become increasingly aware of and concerned about homelessness. Articles about homeless people are to be found every week in our local newspapers, clips about the homeless appear on the television news, and articles on the topic abound in popular periodicals. Media attention increases around major family-centered holidays such as Thanksgiving and Christmas. As the severe weather of deep winter approaches, more articles appear in the newspapers, and television news camera crews seek out spots where the homeless congregate.

As a concrete measure of media attention, articles about the homeless listed in the *Readers' Guide to Periodical Literature* rose from zero in all of 1975 to thirty-four in 1984 and forty-eight in 1986. Several television documentaries have been devoted to the homeless. "Hands across America," the mixed-media event of 1987, raised millions in donations for the homeless. Homelessness throughout the world has also come into the limelight: in 1982 the United Nations declared 1987 the International Year of Shelter for the Homeless. At the time, few Americans would have thought the year applied to conditions in the United States as well as in those developing nations where millions went unhoused and even more millions were inadequately housed. In short, at present there is no dearth of popular interest in or sympathy for the homeless.

On the surface it is not surprising that so much attention has been paid to the plight of the homeless in the 1980s. Our ideas of creature comforts are bound up with the concept of home. The Oxford Unabridged Dictionary devotes three pages to definitions of the word *home* and its derivatives: Almost all stress the close association with the themes of safety, family, love, shelter, comfort, rest, sleep, warmth, affection, food, and sociability.

Robert Frost provided a marvelous definition in his poem "The Death of the Hired Man": "Home is the place where, when you have to go there, / they have to take you in." To be without a home is to be without some or all of the valued things the dictionary alludes to. Not to have a place where "they have to take you in" would for most of us mean being close to the bottom of existence. It is surely no mystery why Americans shudder empathically at the idea of being without a home and easily extend sympathy to those so afflicted.

Although direct empathy with the plight of the homeless is certainly one root of the current concern, it would not be an explanation were the homeless not so visible. Hardly anyone visiting the downtown areas of our major cities can avoid direct sight of homeless people. The incongruity of a shabby person rummaging through a trash can in front of a modern office building while

14

well-dressed and well-fed professionals and clerks go in and out the doors can be shocking.

If direct experience is not enough, a social movement to help the homeless and advocate on their behalf has arisen, complete with its own organizational framework, and this also raises public consciousness. The National Coalition for the Homeless, headquartered in New York, holds together a loose framework of local coalitions in our major cities. The National Coalition and the local coalitions are composed of persons who want to institute social changes aimed at improving the condition of the homeless and lowering their numbers in American cities. The coalitions have yet to articulate a coherent set of programs, nor have they begun to press for specific legislation or other social action. Rather, their main aim at present seems to be consciousness raising—heightening public awareness of widespread homelessness and its rapid growth.

In contrast, extreme poverty among those with homes has not surfaced as a widely recognized major social problem in America today. There are few articles on extreme poverty, hardly any vignettes showing the grinding conditions of life on little or no income. There are understandable reasons for the comparatively high level of attention to the homeless and the lack of attention to the extremely poor. The domiciled extremely poor are comparatively invisible: when a homeless person sleeps on a downtown steam grate, hundreds of people will see the bedraggled figure wrapped in cardboard. When an extremely poor person goes to sleep in a shabby SRO room, no one will see the huddled shape under the dirty bedclothes. When a poor family takes in one of its adult children who cannot find a job, that person is also invisible. Homeless people concentrate around the shelters, food kitchens, and clinics set up to serve them. The extremely poor may use the food kitchens and clinics, but if so they become identified as simply part of the homeless. They are dispersed more widely throughout the city and are less identifiable. No social movement has arisen on their behalf.

The Plan of This Book

The chapters that follow deal with a number of topics. Mindful that every social problem has a historical setting, in the next chapter I will briefly review the history of homelessness in the United States, concentrating on the transformation of the problem that has occurred over the past three decades. I will show that today's homeless are different in many important respects from the inhabitants of the pre-1960s Skid Row.

Chapter 3 examines the problems encountered in gathering data on the size of the homeless and extremely poor segments of our population and evaluates some of the resulting estimates. Chapters 4 and 5 provide data on the conditions of the extremely poor and the homeless as found in the contemporary studies of these two groups; in chapter 4 I describe the demographic composition of these groups, their dire employment status, and the resulting economic deprivations. In chapter 6 I attempt to explain why some extremely poor people become homeless and most do not, concentrating on the disabilities that make some of them vulnerable to becoming homeless.

Chapter 7 brings together the findings of the previous chapters through a general interpretation of the social problem of homelessness and extreme poverty and also presents concrete steps that I believe our nation can take both to ameliorate the condition of these groups and to lower their numbers.

The point of the book is not to startle and amaze, though many readers may have such reactions, but to explain why these problems plague our nation and to propose remedies.

TWO

The New Homeless and the Old

If there is no mystery about the sympathetic attention paid to the problem of homelessness in America over the past decade, there certainly *is* a mystery concerning why comparable attention and sympathy were not extended to the homeless in the past. Homelessness has waxed and waned throughout our history, but America has always had a goodly complement of homeless people.[1] Nevertheless, compared with the scale of contemporary popular concern, throughout most of our history the homeless have been regarded at least with indifference and often with contempt, fear, and loathing (Hopper 1987).

Homelessness in Colonial and Early America

Concern about homelessness can be discerned in the minutes of seventeenth-century New England town meetings. Under the Elizabethan poor laws that governed colonial New England towns, each town shouldered responsibility for the care of its own poor. A critical distinction was made between what must be done for "settled" persons, whose households were members of the town, and everyone else, especially newcomers. Those with settlement rights, acquired by being accepted by vote as a town member or by being born into an accepted family, were entitled to help from the town when in adversity. The town had no responsibility for nonmembers.

Newcomers could petition the selectmen and the town meeting for permission to settle in the town. Many of the applicants for membership considered at town meetings were by definition homeless and often without resources, raising a concern whether they would mean additional tax burdens for the town. As a consequence, those who had some promise to be self-supporting stood a better chance of being accepted. Nonmembers likely to become town charges, especially widows and children as well as disabled or aged adults, were often "warned" to leave town. There thus arose a kind of transient poor, shunted from community to community because in place after place they were denied settlement rights.[2]

---

1. In this respect our history is no different from those of other countries. Literal homelessness has existed throughout the world and is especially prevalent now in the large cities of developing countries.

2. This raises the question how such people managed to survive. Some hint of coping methods can be gleaned from the town meeting minutes. Many became squatters, living on unused land

Local responsibility for the unfortunate may have benefited town members and their families when misfortunes fell, but it must have made life miserable for those not on town rolls. The town meeting minutes are silent about what happened to the men, women, and children who were warned out of town: Did some community take them in, or did they wander endlessly from place to place?

The colonial preoccupation with rights of settlement and the benefit entitlements accompanying them has persisted throughout most of our history, placing a good proportion of the indigent and needy who were migrants in a kind of geopolitical limbo where no jurisdiction was responsible for their care. Throughout the nineteenth century and most of the twentieth, in most states welfare legislation made clear distinctions between the settled and the transient poor, with benefits reserved mainly for the former. Some states even distinguished between county and state settlement rights, with different benefit schedules for those who qualified as residents of each. Settlement rights were dependent on length of residence (usually one or more years of uninterrupted time).

Correspondingly, the "local" homeless were treated in a variety of ways ranging from receiving small support payments to being settled in poorhouses. The transient homeless were either left in limbo or urged, sometimes forcibly, to move on. As in colonial times, those who did not have settlement rights (or could not document uninterrupted residence of the required duration) were often transported to the jurisdiction boundary. Indeed, during the early years of the Great Depression, in some years more money was spent in New York on "Greyhound relief" (bus tickets to bordering states) than on direct benefits (Crouse 1986).

The settlement issue in public welfare was ended only twenty years ago by a 1969 Supreme Court decision that declared unconstitutional the length-of-residence restrictions that states and local communities ordinarily placed on eligibility for benefits.[3]

Nineteenth-century Americans were no more sympathetic to the homeless than were their ancestors. The post–Civil War period saw a considerable increase in homelessness and transience. The construction of the railroads, their subsequent continual maintenance needs, and the rise of large-scale commercial agriculture created a strong demand for transient workers who could supply seasonal and episodic labor. The skills needed were often based on

---

and hoping the town would not notice them. In addition, some must have found their way to the larger settlements, such as Boston, where their presence might be more easily overlooked. Most historical studies on the treatment of the poor in colonial New England have concerned small communities that were primarily rural: it may well be that larger places were more tolerant of outsiders.

3. Voting privileges in most jurisdictions are still predicated on establishing some minimum period of residence, thus disfranchising a sizable number of voters, perhaps as many as the 20 percent who change residence over a year's time.

strength and endurance. The demand was met by restless discharged Civil War veterans, immigrant laborers, and other young males, often recruited by labor agents—middlemen commissioned to recruit workers. These transient homeless of the post–Civil War period were predominantly young, unattached men with low levels of education and job skills. Their employment took them all over the country: some settled far from where they started as recruits.

A bit more can be learned about the local homeless of the nineteenth century because of the records kept by local community relief officials. Katz (1986) provides a detailed account of how the indigent poor were treated in New York State. Policies vacillated between providing small monetary stipends (outdoor relief) and maintaining poorhouses (indoor relief), and there was a protracted debate over which was less expensive. Alongside this controversy was another debate over whether outdoor relief encouraged the lazy and immoral to look to the public treasury for support rather than to earn their living, a point that favored poorhouses, since they were unlikely to attract those seeking subsidized loafing. You may recognize this last theme as a variant on the perennial issue of how best to help the "deserving poor" without subsidizing the undeserving.

In the second half of the nineteenth century there were several severe economic downturns, each accompanied by surges in homelessness and the demand for public relief. Homelessness per se was not so much the central concern as was the general need for food, fuel, and clothing.

The relief burdens of counties and municipalities also varied seasonally: when wintry conditions reduced the demand for unskilled labor, the need for poor relief grew. How frequently indigence led to literal homelessness is not discussed, although the literature is full of references to using police station lockups and local jails as temporary housing for the poor. For example, anyone could approach a New York City police station and be given lodging for the night without being arrested and booked for any offense. The New York City police reported in 1890 that over the previous decade the department had provided lodging in jails and lockups to 150,000 persons annually (making it the largest lodging supplier in the city).[4] How many of the homeless people they housed were transient and how many were local is not known. There are also references to the nineteenth-century shantytowns that grew up on the periphery of settled urban areas.[5] Building houses on unused land out of scrap materials has always been one of the solutions the poor resorted to before the time of zoning laws and when much vacant land was held by absentee owners speculating on price increases. Indeed, the impetus for many of the urban monuments of today came out of nineteenth-century urban renewal efforts to

4. In the 1890s the major police departments were relieved of their role as housing supplier of last resort. Most cities established municipal lodging houses, charging token sums for beds in dormitory arrangements to all who applied.

5. The term "shanty Irish" undoubtedly had its origins in the shantytowns built by poor Irish immigrants on the urban fringes.

remove the eyesores of shantytowns. Such motives played a part in the construction of New York's Central Park, Chicago's Grant Park, and the filling in of Boston's Back Bay, all built on land that had been occupied by shantytowns built by poor squatters.

Despite the important role they played in constructing the infrastructure of late nineteenth-century industrial development, the transient homeless scarcely had any respected place in American society. These transient workers were characterized as tramps, hoboes, and bums and were often warned to leave town when there was no demand for their labor. Police departments solved many crimes by attributing them to tramps and bums. Mark Twain ended one of his stories by advertising to medical schools that he had the bodies of several tramps in his basement to sell as teaching cadavers.

The prevailing lack of sympathy in the nineteenth century for the homeless and the transient is all the more puzzling because the absence of any significant safety net of social welfare programs meant that almost every household had a good chance of suffering catastrophic declines in standard of living through unemployment, illness, and death and hence of becoming impoverished and homeless. Katz's (1975) detailed longitudinal study of the census records of Hamilton, Ontario, found many families that plummeted from middle-class, homeowning status to indigence when catastrophic illness struck down a main breadwinner. The imposing sizes of nineteenth-century orphanages also testify how frequently death broke up families. That a widespread fear of the economic consequences of illness persisted into the 1930s is shown in the Lynds' classic studies of Muncie, Indiana (Lynd and Lynd 1929, 1937).

The Rise of Skid Row

It was in the nineteenth century that transient homelessness became institutionalized and segregated in American cities. Toward the last quarter of the century, Skid Row areas were established in each of our major cities, sections inhabited mainly by homeless men. These familyless transient laborers supplied muscle power for industries—such as large-scale agriculture, lumbering, and railroad and highway construction and maintenance—offering highly seasonal employment in out-of-the-way places. In the large urban centers similar activities—such as loading and unloading ships or railroad freight cars, paving and maintaining streets, and constructing water supply and drainage systems—also required unskilled labor, with highly seasonal demand.

The Skid Rows that grew up consisted of a concentration of enterprises catering to the needs of transient, poor, familyless workingmen. The core businesses that defined Skid Row were hotels, lodging houses, and restaurants providing inexpensive housing and food, where meals and a bed for the night could be had for pennies. Bars, brothels, pawnshops, and cheap clothing stores also served the men who ate and slept on Skid Row. Urban missions of

evangelical denominations found plenty of work to do among the inhabitants, and they located churches and dormitories in the Skid Row neighborhoods in the hope of welcoming some men back into Christian respectability.

It was also in the late nineteenth century that transient homelessness became masculinized. The transient workers were almost all men, mainly because the transient labor market was concerned primarily with muscle power. Apparently the same trend occurred with the local homeless as well. The proportion of women among those sent to the Philadelphia House of Correction for vagrancy dropped from 40%–50% in pre–Civil War years to 15% in 1899 (Clements 1984).

The height of Skid Row populations was reached in the early decades of the twentieth century. By the 1940s technological changes, especially the development of earth moving and materials handling equipment, had drastically reduced the demand for casual unskilled labor. The hobo and the tramp were gradually disappearing as a major component of our labor supply as demand for their labor dropped. For example, in unloading freight trailers and railroad cars, forklifts could accomplish in a few hours what would take teams of laborers a whole day.

More detailed information on the transient homeless in the first part of the twentieth century is available from early social research. One of the studies that helped define the "Chicago school" of sociology, conducted about 1920 by Nels Anderson, is reported in *The Hobo: Sociology of the Homeless Man* (1923). Anderson, a former transient worker who became a sociologist, drew upon his own experiences as a hobo supplemented by interviews with homeless men on Chicago's Skid Row. By current social research standards, Anderson's work is only marginally different from standard investigative journalism.[6] There is no main thesis, nor are there any firm descriptive materials: his main purpose was to show that hoboes and tramps fulfilled a role in the economy by supplying labor that was needed only intermittently. He carefully distinguished the seasonal casual workers who made up the hobo and tramp contingents from the "bums," who got by as much as possible without working, preferring to beg or steal rather than earn a day's wages. Anderson devoted a good portion of his monograph to exotic details of life among the homeless; for example, he provided a detailed description of their (then) current argot.

The title Anderson chose uses the term homeless with a different meaning than I outlined in the first chapter. Indeed, until very recently the term covered more than the literally homeless I identified as my focus. The hoboes and tramps were transients who had intermittent housing. They may have been without conventional shelter when they traveled from place to place in freight

---

6. Indeed, that was Anderson's own judgment in his preface to the second edition, published in 1961. He regretted having made the life of homeless people seem more romantic and attractive than it really was.

cars, but they often rented accommodations in cheap hotels and flophouses. It was not their housing conditions that rendered them homeless so much as their not participating in a life that gave them homes in the larger sense of that term. To Anderson and all the other commentators on homelessness up to the most recent times, homelessness marked off persons who were living transient lives outside conventional family contexts. A man was not homeless if he stayed with his parents or with other relatives or lived permanently in a rooming house. He was certainly not homeless if he was married and living with his wife and children. The homeless, in short, were those who were not embedded in more or less permanent quarters and were not in enduring contact with a set of kin and friends. The men Anderson studied on Chicago's Skid Row were sheltered, but they did not live in homes.

Homelessness in the Great Depression

With the advent of the Great Depression in the 1930s, local and transient homelessness increased drastically. Although no definitive counts were made during the Great Depression, we can get some notion of the magnitude of homelessness from the activities of federal relief agencies: in 1933 the Federal Emergency Relief Administration (FERA) housed 125,000 people in its transient camps, and a 1934 survey of social agencies in seven hundred towns and cities estimated 200,000 homeless. Other estimates went as high as 1.5 million in the worst years of the Great Depression (Wickendon 1987).

Writing in the 1930s at the peak of the Great Depression, Nels Anderson (1940) described the changes that period brought to the composition of the homeless. Anderson claimed that the transient homeless he had studied in the early 1920s were on the decline. In their place had grown up a new homeless population that was quite different in composition from the hoboes and tramps of the earlier period. The homeless population of the depression was made up of people he thought would be permanently unemployed, men who had virtually no chance of ever finding steady work. These relatively young men, he believed, would grow old as surplus to the labor market.

As described in the social research of the time, the transient homeless of the Great Depression consisted mainly of young men (and a small proportion of women) moving from place to place in search of employment. Many left their parents' homes because they no longer wanted to be burdens on impoverished households and saw no employment opportunities in their depressed hometowns. Others were urged to leave by parents struggling to feed and house their younger siblings. In either event, many returned home when their job search failed.

Although large-scale social research was in its toddlerhood in the 1930s, a few studies were published on the depression-period homeless. The most detailed study of the transient homeless was undertaken by a psychologist, Herman J. P. Schubert, employed by the Transient Center established in

Buffalo, New York. His assignment at the center was to administer aptitude tests to those applying for aid under New York's Temporary Emergency Relief Administration, that state's counterpart to the federal agency set up to administer the Federal Emergency Relief Act of 1933. Taking good advantage of his position, he systematically collected data on those who applied for aid. The resulting monograph (Schubert 1935) contains detailed statistical descriptions of the applicants for aid over a year's time. The data were collected and hand processed with the help of a few transients who had the requisite white-collar skills.

The Buffalo Transient Center was set up to provide temporary shelter and meals to "transients," defined as those who had not been resident in a New York county for more than a year (and therefore did not have settlement rights under New York law). Because Buffalo is a Great Lakes port, the center also served seamen, a special category under FERA legislation who were defined as persons who had no permanent settlement. The Transient Center supplied beds and food to single persons for a few days, sending them back where they came from when that period was up. Homeless families were allowed to stay longer.[7]

Most of the data presented derive from intake interviews, laboriously hand tabulated by Schubert's white-collar transients, and describe almost 20,000 persons applying for aid in 1934. The overall portrait of the transient homeless that resulted shows them as predominantly young (median age was thirty), unattached (89% single) white (82%) males (98%). The majority (59%) arrived in Buffalo on freight trains. Most had been on the road looking for work for a few months (median was two months) and originated in Ohio and Pennsylvania. The transient homeless had slightly below average[8] educational levels (median was 8.5 years) and had been unemployed for 1.5 years (median). Their previous employment had been as semiskilled or unskilled workers. Many had been to other cities, notably Cleveland and Pittsburgh, on their job searches before coming to Buffalo. On the average they had been in Buffalo for five days before applying to the center.

There is no way we can evaluate, at this time, how usual or unusual were the transient men Schubert described. However, it is difficult to imagine some special characteristic of Buffalo compared with, say, Cleveland or Milwaukee that would have produced markedly different results had Schubert been appointed to a transient center in another city. On the reasonable assumption of generalizability, Schubert's monograph strongly suggests that the increased

7. Schubert (1935) reports that from twenty to thirty transient homeless families applied for assistance every month, with about two hundred persons from homeless families being in the Buffalo Transient Center at any one time.

8. Schubert considered this median to indicate low levels of education. The median years of educational attainment for United States males aged twenty-one to thirty-five was 10.5 in the 1940 census, indicating that the Buffalo homeless had a level about two years below what was typical for males in a comparable age group. (The 1940 census was the first to collect data on education.)

transient population of the Great Depression consisted of large groups of young men from small and medium-sized places who made relatively short-term excursions to nearby large cities in search of employment. These were men of below-average education and meager job experience, if any, largely without marital or parental responsibilities, who were freer than their married counterparts to explore opportunities in the world beyond their home communities. Judged by the average time length of their excursions, it appears that many went back home after their job search failed in Buffalo and other urban labor markets.

During the Great Depression those who came to the largest cities were too numerous to be accommodated in the established Skid Rows of the nation. In addition, the depression transients were also too poor: the Skid Row flophouse hotels were not charitable trusts; they charged for their accommodations. Even though the rent for a night was typically about 25¢ and often as low as 10¢, that was more than many of the depression homeless could afford day after day.

In the worst early years of the depression, many of the penniless transients were taken care of in urban emergency shelters like the Buffalo Transient Center. Typically, accommodations were available for less than a month. In addition, the Federal Emergency Relief Administration[9] in its brief two-year existence also set up camps for transients, usually in rural areas far from the few jobs that were available, safely out of sight of city dwellers. The federal transient centers allowed men to stay longer, employing them on public works such as road maintenance in national parks, flood-control projects, and similar tasks requiring mainly hard physical labor.

As described by Schubert, applicants to the Buffalo Transient Center were offered the opportunity to enter a nearby federal transient center. He reported that those who agreed to go to the federal camp were largely "discouraged" workers, usually men over forty who had given up hope of gaining a foothold among the employed. Crouse (1986) reported that the federally supported transient camps in New York State were reserved primarily for "old" men—defined as forty and over[10]—whose employment prospects were regarded as

9. For its time, the FERA legislation was unusual both in recognizing that settlement issues left a large proportion of the poor in limbo, since local and state residence requirements could not be met by those who migrated in search of work, and in setting up a program to meet their needs. The FERA program explicitly for "transients," defined in the legislation as those not eligible for local and state relief, provided for federal subsidies to states that would set up emergency shelters. FERA also directly ran camps for the transient homeless.

10. Note how the definition of "older worker" has changed in the past half-century. In the 1920s and 1930s, both industry and the workers defined old age as starting at forty. The Lynds in their famous Muncie, Indiana, studies (Lynd and Lynd 1929, 1937) frequently refer in both studies to the expressed fears of blue-collar workers that their employment and reemployment chances dropped drastically after age forty. They were afraid they were vulnerable to being let go at that age and would be unable to obtain any other employment.

virtually hopeless. From this distance the federal camps appear to have been rural warehouses for those considered unemployable.

What happened to the transient homeless when the FERA was succeeded by the Works Progress Administration (WPA), a program that provided no coverage for that group, is a mystery. Some cities operated their own shelters without federal or state subsidy. Police departments resumed the nineteenth-century practice of opening their jails and precinct lockups as overnight shelters.

In the 1930s not much sympathy was accorded transient homeless unattached men and women. The welfare departments of states and local communities often solved the problem by literally escorting transients to their borders. Only one homeless category garnered public sympathy—the families in the Dust Bowl states who packed up their meager belongings, loaded their dilapidated cars, and drifted westward to California to become the Okies Steinbeck wrote about so eloquently in *The Grapes of Wrath*. Homeless *families* evoked more sympathy than the more usual homeless unattached person.

Not much is known about how the local homeless fared. Presumably they built the shantytowns of the depression. Some must have been absorbed into local relief programs, especially families. The only study of the local homeless of any quality is one that two young University of Chicago sociologists, Sutherland and Locke (1936), conducted in emergency shelters for local homeless men set up by the Illinois Emergency Relief Commission and funded by the commission. Presumably local homeless families were taken care of through cash relief payments.

Sutherland and Locke contend there were 20,000 homeless persons in Chicago sheltered by the state of Illinois in 1933 and 1934. They defined homeless persons as unemployed, destitute local Chicago residents who had no family or others who would take responsibility for them. The commission rented or obtained donations of vacant industrial or commercial buildings, primarily in the vicinity of Chicago's Madison Street Skid Row, and converted them to dormitory shelters. Each building was divided into large rooms in which twenty to fifty men slept on cots. Toilet and bathing facilities were supplied. Sparsely furnished "assembly" rooms were provided for lounging and recreation, open from 9:00 A.M. to 7:00 P.M. Access to sleeping accommodations was allowed only after 7:00 P.M. Basement rooms were used for men who were drunk or otherwise disruptive.

Men who applied for shelter had to certify that they were Illinois residents who had no resources and no possible support from family members. Those accepted were given passes that entitled them to sleep in the dormitories and to obtain two meals a day at central kitchens. In fact the emergency shelters of the 1930s, as described by Sutherland and Locke, were very much like the emergency shelters of the 1980s as I will describe them in a later chapter.

The Sutherland and Locke study was based on data from a sample of 1,882 residents, using administratively collected personal records supplemented by informal interviews. Structured tests were given to subsamples. In addition, staff members lived in the shelters for short periods as participant observers.

The data showed that the local homeless of Chicago were men on their way down from the flophouse hotels and surrounding room house areas, their previous residences. When employment in Chicago became tight, these were the men who lost the intermittent low-skilled employment that had furnished their income.

The Chicago local homeless were all men[11] and considerably older than the transient homeless Schubert studied in Buffalo, with forty-five as their average age. Three out of five had never married, and the marriages of the others had been broken up by death or, more often, by divorce or separation. (The authors did not give the racial composition of the local Chicago homeless.) Educational attainment was also characteristic, the average being eight years, lower than but not much different from typical education levels of the time. A subsample was given the Army Beta intelligence test, on which 80% were shown to be deficient in intelligence. Their places of birth mirrored Chicago of the 1930s: 50% were foreign born, 20% were born in Chicago, and 30% had migrated from other states. Psychiatric examinations given to another subsample disclosed a fair amount of disturbance: 18% were judged by psychiatrists to show psychotic or disordered mentality. Sutherland and Locke mention widespread alcoholism among the homeless men but do not estimate prevalence. The local Chicago homeless were not short-term homeless: average length of shelter residence was 1.6 years. Average time totally unemployed was 2 years.

If the findings of this Chicago study are at all representative, the local homeless were the older unattached men whose previous hold on the labor market was tenuous. When the casual and intermittent jobs they were dependent on became scarce with the depression, these men became superfluous, joining the "permanent unemployed." When their incomes became too small for them to rent cubicles in the flophouses or cheap hotels on or near Skid Row, the local and state relief agencies stepped in to provide minimal dormitory accommodations.

The local homeless described by Sutherland and Locke contrast strongly with the transient homeless Schubert studied, who were considerably younger and had been homeless and unemployed for much shorter periods. The transient homeless were seeking employment in labor markets that looked more promising than their hometowns. The local homeless of Chicago had been marginally employed and appeared similar to the older, discouraged transient workers that the federal government admitted to the rural camps. In both the federal camps and the urban emergency shelters for the local homeless, unem-

---

11. Sutherland and Locke were silent on whether Chicago had any emergency shelters for homeless women. The shelter studies were restricted to men.

ployable older men apparently were being maintained indefinitely at a minimum level of subsistence.

Although all the sources consulted mentioned the plight of homeless families during the Great Depression, special housing arrangements for them were not ordinarily set up, possibly because they were not needed. The cash relief available to local homeless families must have been sufficient to provide them with housing on depressed local housing markets.[12] Transient homeless families were another story; their plight was aggravated by residence rules that made them ineligible for local relief funds, the migrant "Okie" families in the West and Southwest being cases in point.

The outbreak of World War II drastically reduced the number of the homeless, absorbing them into the armed forces and into mushrooming war industries. The permanent unemployed that worried Nels Anderson virtually disappeared, almost within months. The WPA public works employment projects were terminated after 1943 and relief programs were drastically reduced as employment opportunities increased and men went into the armed forces. Municipal lodging houses and emergency shelters were closed; what remained of the local and transient homeless were apparently left to forage on Skid Row, the bottom tier of the private housing market.

We can speculate that the casual labor market also must have improved as the labor market generally became tighter, bettering the employment prospects of the clientele of the municipal lodging houses of the sort studied by Locke and Sutherland.

Skid Row in the 1950s and 1960s

When the war was over and employment rates remained high, both homelessness and Skid Row areas declined sharply compared with the 1930s. But neither disappeared. In the first two decades of the postwar period, the Skid Rows of the nation remained as distinctive neighborhoods, collections of cheap hotels, cheap restaurants and cheaper bars, and casual employment agencies. The religious missions that had been dedicated to the redemption of Skid Row residents since the nineteenth century were still operating. Business may not have been brisk, but it was enough to keep them going.

With the major exception of New York's Bowery, the Skid Rows of our large cities were originally close to the railroad freight assembly yards, warehouses, and trucking terminals that provided much of the casual employment for their inhabitants. Changing their locations was made difficult by zoning and building codes, even though their presence depressed building rents and land prices. When the changing structure of transportation and the relocation

12. Sutherland and Locke cite several interviews in the Chicago shelters in which homeless men expressed regret that they did not marry when the opportunity arose. Had they married, they would have become eligible for relief payments and could have been living in conventional dwellings.

27

of major industries removed transient jobs and casual labor opportunities, the Skid Rows remained anchored to urban sections where they had been established in the early twentieth century: Seattle's Skid Row still borders the street that has long since superseded the "Skid Road" along which lumber was skidded to the loading docks. In today's Chicago, labor contractors use secondhand school buses to take day laborers from their employment offices out to jobs on the periphery of the city.

Since the early 1900s, the rest of the city typically had undergone major changes. Freight railroads were supplemented and later partially supplanted by long-distance trucking lines. Unloading freight cars for local transshipment was obviated by long-distance trucks traveling over the postwar interstate highway system and pulling up to factory and warehouse loading docks, as well as by "piggyback" rail freight cars carrying fully loaded trailers that are hitched to tractors at a terminal and driven directly to their destinations. Freed of dependence on fixed railroad tracks, factories and warehouses moved out to the periphery. Offices and luxury apartments expanded their holdings in the downtown center.

In time the Skid Row that had once been a decent and respectful distance from downtown stores and offices became a next-door neighbor. The physical distance between Chicago's West Madison Street and the corner of State and Adams had not changed, but the commercial and administrative activities that were once concentrated at those crossroads had spread west and south up to the borders of Skid Row. Urban decay now rubbed elbows with modernity and progress.

In the 1950s, as our urban elites turned to renovating the central business districts, the problem of what to do about the collection of unsightly buildings, low-quality land use, and unkempt people in the Skid Rows of the nation sparked a revival of social science research. Undertaken between 1958 and 1964 and financed under grants from the Housing and Home Finance Agency, the predecessor of the Department of Housing and Urban Development (HUD), these studies provide us with considerable detailed information on the Skid Rows of several major cities and their inhabitants, based on fairly modern social research methods. Taken together, the studies of the 1950s and 1960s can be used to show whether the homeless of today are different from those of the past, thereby furnishing important clues to why today's homeless are at the center of public attention.

Especially important for our purposes were studies of New York's Bowery by Bahr and Caplow (1974), of Philadelphia's Skid Row by Blumberg, Shipley, and Shandler (1973), and of Chicago's Skid Row by Donald Bogue (1963).[13] All these studies had much the same set of objectives—to find out who was on Skid Row and determine what to do about them when the area was demolished. Note that the motivation for funding these studies was to

13. Other major studies were undertaken in Minneapolis and Sacramento.

learn what to do about Skid Row neighborhoods, not what to do about homelessness.

All the studies emerged with much the same findings, with slight local variations. The title of Bahr and Caplow's volume on the Bowery in the early 1960s, *Old Men: Drunk and Sober*, provides a succinct summary of their findings as the authors perceived them. Donald Bogue's *Skid Row in American Cities* promises to tell about all the homeless in America, but mainly it provides a very thorough description of the homeless of Chicago in 1958.[14] Indeed, for that reason I will rely on Bogue's monograph more than on any other study in the discussion that follows. In addition, since I will also depend heavily on my own study of the Chicago homeless conducted in 1985 and 1986, Bogue's data provide a more relevant contrast.

Using 1950 census data, Bogue estimated that there were approximately 100,000 homeless persons on the Skid Rows of our forty-one largest cities in 1950,[15] basing his estimates on the 1950 census counts showing at least that many people living outside households in the Skid Row census tracts. Since there is some ambiguity concerning whether his numbers include all the Skid Row population and exclude persons living in those areas but not in Skid Row conditions, it is difficult to regard his estimates as definitive even for the forty-one cities studied.

Bogue's estimate of Chicago's Skid Row homeless population is more precise: by actual count, Bogue found about 12,000 homeless persons on Chicago's Skid Row; almost all were men.[16] In 1964 Bahr and Caplow estimated that about 8,000 homeless men lived in New York's Bowery district (and possibly as many as 30,000 additional homeless persons lived in the rest of the

14. Although all three studies used one variant or another of modern sample survey techniques, Bogue's study was based on more precise delimitations of both the universe and the measurements used and, in addition, includes a census of all those living in cubicle hotels and SROs in the traditional Skid Row areas of Chicago.

15. In preparation for his study, Bogue wrote to officials in all cities having 50,000 or more residents in 1950, asking them to identify the areas occupied by the city's Skid Row. Usable replies were obtained from forty-one, enabling him to identify the Skid Row census tracts in each of these cities. The 1950 census data on unattached persons living outside households in census tracts in Skid Row areas constitute the basis for his estimate. This estimate must be regarded as only an approximation: since in 1950 there were more than two hundred cities with populations of 50,000 or more, the forty-one providing data cannot be regarded as an unbiased sample without knowing more about why some cities responded to Bogue's request and some did not. Furthermore, some of the people counted as homeless may have been living in places that did not fit reasonable descriptions of cubicle or SRO hotels, since the census is silent on what kinds of accommodations were involved.

16. Obtaining a special tabulation from the 1950 census of all persons in Chicago living in hotels, rooms, or motels, Bogue reports that there were about 20,000 in all of Chicago. The discrepancy between his count and the census count may have reflected (1) a 1950 to 1958 decline in the number of homeless persons, (2) measurement error arising because people living in comfortable circumstances in luxury residence hotels are included in the census tabulations, or (3) some dispersion of homeless persons in areas outside the identified Skid Rows. I suspect it is a function of all three, with the dispersion factor being the major reason.

city).[17] In 1960 Blumberg and his colleagues found that about 2,000 homeless persons lived in the Skid Row area of Philadelphia. In each of the studies cited, actual counts were made of residents of hotels and rooming houses within delimited areas of the cities in question.[18]

Clearly, despite the postwar economic expansion, homelessness persisted. The American Skid Rows may have been dying out: if so, the death was prolonged.

Note that the meaning of homelessness as used by Bahr, Blumberg, and Bogue was somewhat different from the current usage of the term. In their studies, homelessness was equated with living outside family units. Today the meaning of homelessness is more directly tied to absolute lack of housing or to living in shelters expressly provided for homeless persons. Almost all of the Chicago homeless men Bogue studied in 1958 had shelter of some sort: four out of five rented windowless cubicles in flophouse hotels. The cubicles they rented for 50¢ to 90¢ a night hardly fit any definition of home. They were called rooms by the hotel managers, but in fact were partitioned-off spaces in former factory lofts, typically measuring five feet by seven, that could hold a cot and little more. Light was minimal: each cubicle was lit by a dim bulb. The partitions did not extend to the ceiling or to the floor, and wire mesh filled the gaps to provide security and ventilation. Most of the other homeless men lived in cheap SRO hotels that had private rooms or in the mission dormitories. Bogue reported that about 110 of the homeless men lived out on the streets, sleeping in doorways, under bridges, and in other somewhat protected places.[19]

Similarly, Blumberg found that most of Philadelphia's 2,000 homeless people lived in cubicle hotels and in the mission shelters. Only 64 persons were found sleeping in the streets in his survey that searched the streets, hotels, and boardinghouses of Philadelphia's Skid Row area in 1960.[20]

On any given night, many of the Skid Row homeless were given shelter in police stations and local jails after arrests for public drunkenness or other status crimes. Before the decriminalization of public drunkenness in 1966, large proportions of the total arrests in large cities—over 25% in New York—

17. The estimate of the homeless living outside the Bowery was made by extrapolating from the deaths of homeless persons living in non-Bowery areas of the city. There are serious problems with this estimate, since it was apparently based on assuming unrealistically low death rates for homeless persons.

18. For the Philadelphia census Blumberg enlisted the entire junior class of Temple University's Hahnemann Medical School. Medical students dressed in their white coats, dangling stethoscopes, knocked on every door in Philadelphia's Skid Row neighborhood and conducted the census.

19. Based upon interviews with homeless men in the local public library reading room, where men sleeping out on the streets were reputed to congregate during the day.

20. The Temple University medical students canvassed all the streets and residential structures in Philadelphia's Skid Row over a twenty-four-hour period, interviewing everyone they encountered. Token payments of 25¢ or 50¢ were given to those who responded, the larger sum going to those submitting to a longer interview.

were for this and related offenses. Chicago's jails and police stations accommodated several hundred Skid Row residents each evening.[21]

The median age of Chicago's homeless as described by Bogue was close to fifty. More than 90% were white. About a quarter were Social Security pensioners, making their $30 to $50 minimum Social Security payments last through the month by renting the cheapest accommodations possible. Another quarter of the Skid Row inhabitants were alcoholics.[22] The remaining half suffered from physical disability (20%), chronic mental illness (20%), or what Bogue called "social maladjustment" (10%).

Aside from those who lived on their pension checks, most Skid Row inhabitants earned their living through menial, low-paid employment, mostly intermittent. The mission dormitories and municipal shelters provided food and beds for those who were out of work or could not work. Skid Row residents considered the mission dormitories the least desirable living conditions available, lacking privacy and safety and usually requiring they attend evangelical religious services.

The social scientists who studied the Skid Rows in the postwar period all remarked on the social isolation of the homeless (one of Bahr's books is called *Disaffiliated Man*). Bogue found that virtually all the homeless men were unmarried, and most had never married. Although many had families, kinship ties were very tenuous, and few of the homeless maintained contact with family and kin. Most had no one they considered a good friend. While there may have been some camaraderie among the homeless, both the researchers and the homeless remarked on the superficiality of such ties.[23]

Much the same portrait emerged from Caplow and Bahr's study of the Bowery and other Skid Rows throughout the country. All presented the same picture of three dire conditions: extreme poverty, arising out of low earnings and low benefit levels; disability through advanced age, alcoholism, and physical or mental illness; and disaffiliation—absent or tenuous ties to family and kin and few or no friends.

21. Bogue's count is about 400 persons in jails, in hospitals, and sleeping out on the streets. Since he later estimates about 100 sleeping on the streets nightly, the remaining 300 were apparently found in hospital or in jails. Researchers on the Skid Rows before the decriminalization of public drunkenness remark that it was the custom of the police to cruise Skid Row streets, arresting men sleeping outside or acting visibly intoxicated. An arrest meant at least one night in jail and possibly a sentence of a week or more, especially for repeat offenders. As in the nineteenth century, urban police departments functioned as a major provider of housing for the homeless.

22. All the social scientists writing of Skid Row found about the same proportion of alcoholics. Yet all wrote as if these alcoholics were clearly in the majority among the Skid Row population. This interpretive emphasis is manifested in Bahr and Caplow's title, *Old Men: Drunk and Sober,* and in Blumberg's title, *Liquor and Poverty,* and is shown in Bogue's monograph by his breaking down each descriptive statistic by the drinking status of his respondents.

23. This is not the only view: several researchers relying on more qualitative data claim that the homeless men on the Skid Rows formed a community characterized by considerable mutual aid and camaraderie. See Jacqueline O. Wiseman, *Stations of the Lost: The Treatment of Skid Row Alcoholics* (1970).

The uniform emphasis in each of the three studies on the prevalence of alcoholism among the Skid Row residents is somewhat puzzling. Granted that rates of alcoholism among the homeless were several magnitudes above that among American adults generally, all the studies found alcoholism to be a problem among a minority—from 20% to 35%—of the homeless, and hence not a problem for the majority. Nevertheless, the researchers wrote as if it affected almost all Skid Row inhabitants.[24]

It may be that the overemphasis on alcoholism a provided a rationale for the relatively neutral stance that all three monographs took toward the homeless men studied. However seriously alcoholism may affect health, it does not elicit much sympathy. After all, alcoholism is easily seen as the outcome of bad judgment rather than of bad luck or oppressive institutional arrangements: alcoholics choose to drink. Few of the social scientists extended much compassion to the alcoholic "bums" and "derelicts," and that lack of concern colored assessments of the other inhabitants of Skid Row.[25] The only residents to receive much sympathy were impoverished aged pensioners, seen as the victims of an ungenerous pension system.

Moreover, at the time there were strong signs that whatever social problems Skid Rows represented were disappearing. Most of the social scientists studying the old Skid Rows thought they were declining in size. Caplow and Bahr claimed that the population of the Bowery had declined from 14,000 in 1949 to 8,000 in 1964, a trend that would lead to its disappearance by the middle of the 1970s. Bogue cited high vacancy rates in the cubicle hotels as evidence that Chicago's Skid Row was on the decline; in addition, he claimed its economic function was fast disappearing. With the mechanization of many low-skilled tasks, the spot labor market was shrinking.

Indeed, for quite a while it looked as if the forecast decline was occurring. Studying population trends in the Skid Row areas of forty-one cities through successive censuses,[26] Barrett Lee (1980) found that the Skid Row populations had declined by 50% between 1950 and 1970. Furthermore, in cities where the market for unskilled labor had shrunk the most, the Skid Row populations had declined the most.

Bogue proposed a plan that would remove Chicago's unsightly flophouses and cheap SROs over a five-year period through acquisition by eminent do-

24. There is an interesting parallel between the role alcoholism is given by the researchers of the 1950s and 1960s and that attributed to chronic mental illness among the current homeless. As I will show, alcoholism among the homeless is now about at the level found in the earlier studies, with perhaps as much as a 50% increase in the prevalence of chronic mental illness.

25. The researchers of the 1980s, following the lead of advocates for the homeless, have turned the emphasis completely around, underemphasizing the fact that among today's homeless about the same proportion have been found to be alcoholics as in the 1950s and 1960s in a seeming attempt to downplay the prevalence of a condition that arouses little public sympathy.

26. These were the same cities Bogue studied, and Lee used the same definitions of Skid Row areas.

main and demolition under urban renewal. The land so released was to be used to expand the central business district with more office buildings and downtown apartments. To provide housing for the homeless, he suggested that the flophouses and cheap SROs be replaced by scattered subsidized housing for familyless men and that social services be provided for alcoholics and the physically or mentally disabled. The result would be a beautified downtown, better housing for the homeless, and better care for the disabled.

The New Homeless of the 1970s and 1980s

By the middle of the seventies, striking changes had taken place in city after city. Indeed, it looked as if at least part of Bogue's advice to Chicago had been followed in every large city. Many of the flophouse cubicle hotels had been demolished, replaced initially by parking lots and later by office buildings and apartment complexes for young professionals. The collection of cheap SRO hotels, where the more prosperous of the old homeless had lived, also had been seriously diminished.

Although the long-established Skid Rows had shrunk and in some cases had been almost obliterated, urban Skid Rows did not disappear altogether: in most places the missions still remained,[27] and smaller Skid Rows sprouted in several places throughout the cities where the remaining SRO hotels and rooming houses still stood.

In the 1960s and 1970s the need for very cheap accommodations for old age pensioners documented by Bogue and by Caplow and Bahr diminished. The number of elderly extremely poor had declined as the coverage of the Social Security old age pension system increased to include more of the labor force and Congress in the 1960s voted more generous benefits for those who had been working all their lives under its coverage. In 1974 Social Security old age benefits were pegged to the cost-of-living index, ensuring that the high inflation rates of the 1970s would not wipe out their value. In addition, subsidized senior citizens' housing, our most popular public housing program, began to provide affordable accommodations to the elderly. This increase in the economic well-being of the aged is most dramatically shown in the remarkable decline in the proportion of those sixty-five and over who were below the poverty line: from 25% in 1968 to less than 13% in 1985, with the most precipitous decline of 9% in the three-year period between 1970 and 1973. The consequence of these changes was that a large portion of those who might otherwise have been residents of the 1950s-style Skid Row disappeared in the

27. Pacific Garden Mission, one of Chicago's oldest and largest missions, is still at the same address as in 1958. When studied by Bogue, it was surrounded by exceedingly shabby buildings housing cubicle hotels, pawnshops, and cheap restaurants and bars. When I visited there in 1987, it was in the midst of a considerably upgraded neighborhood with only one of the SROs still functioning.

1970s into the more general housing stock.[28] Higher benefits and subsidized housing made it possible for the aged pensioners successfully to obtain modest housing. In addition, more generous benefits were available for the physically disabled and the chronic mentally ill through an expanded Supplemental Security Income (SSI) and Social Security Disability Insurance (SSDI) program, enabling this group to move up in the housing market.

The "old" homeless may have blighted some sections of the central cities, but from the perspective of urbanites they had the virtue of being concentrated on Skid Row, which one could avoid and hence ignore. Also, most of the old homeless had some shelter, although inadequate by any standards, and very few were literally sleeping on the streets.

Indeed, in those earlier years, if people had tried to bed down on steam grates or in doorways and vestibules anywhere in the city, police patrols would have bundled them off to jail. The subsequent decriminalization of many status crimes, such as public inebriation and vagrancy—and the decreased emphasis on charges such as loitering has enlarged the turf homeless persons can claim.

Homelessness began to take on new forms by the end of the 1970s. Although all the researchers found some homeless people sleeping out on the streets or in public places in the 1950s and 1960s, the homeless by and large were familyless persons living in very inexpensive (and often inadequate) housing, mainly cubicle and SRO hotels. Toward the end of the next decade, what had been a minor form of homelessness became more prevalent: literal homelessness began to grow and at the same time to become more visible to the public. It became more and more difficult to ignore the evidence that some people had no shelter and lived on the streets. The "new" homeless could be found resting or sleeping in public places such as bus or railroad stations, on steam grates, in doorways and vestibules, in cardboard boxes, in abandoned cars, or in other places where they could be seen by the public.

With the decriminalization of public drunkenness and relaxed enforcement of ordinances concerning many status crimes, police patrols no longer picked up people sleeping out on the streets or warned them away from downtown streets or places with nighttime public access. In addition, whatever bizarre behavior may have characterized the old homeless of the 1950s and 1960s, that behavior was acted out on Skid Row.[29] Now the public could observe firsthand shabbily dressed persons acting in bizarre ways, muttering, shouting, and carrying bulky packages or pushing supermarket carts filled with junk and old clothes.

---

28. The age structure of the 1950s and 1960s Skid Rows made changes rapidly evident. The elderly residents of those times were mostly dead by the end of the 1970s. The changes in the Social Security system primarily benefited those who retired after 1970.

29. Bahr and Caplow mention that 1960s bus tours of New York advertised as visiting New York's famous "sights" regularly included a visit to the Bowery, with the tour guide pointing out the "scenes of depravity" that could be viewed safely from the bus.

Even more striking was the appearance of significant numbers of women among the homeless. Shabby and untidy women could now be seen shuffling along the streets with their proverbial shopping bags or nodding sleepily in bus stations. What few homeless women there were in the 1950s and 1960s must have kept out of sight.

Although homeless families rarely were seen walking streets, they started to appear at welfare offices asking for help in obtaining shelter. When homeless families began to come to the attention of the mass media and to show up in television clips and news articles, public attention grew even stronger and sharper.

Reminiscent of the Dust Bowl migration of the Great Depression, stories began appearing in the newspapers about families migrating from the Rust Belt cities to the Sun Belt. The resemblances were striking. The family breadwinner has lost his job in a factory and, after weeks of fruitless search for employment in one or another mid-American city, had loaded household possessions and family into an old car, driving to Houston or Phoenix in search of the employment reputed to be found in the booming Sun Belt.

Popular response to the new homeless grew with the evidence of homelessness. In a celebrated 1979 New York case,[30] public interest lawyers sued the city, claiming that New York had an obligation to provide shelter to homeless men. Their victory in New York led to an expansion of a network of "emergency" municipal shelters in that city, which currently provides 6,000 beds nightly, almost entirely in dormitory quarters. Subsequent court decisions have extended New York City's shelter obligations to include homeless women.

The new "emergency shelters" that have been provided in city after city are certainly better than having no roof at all over one's head, but a case can be made that in some respects the cubicle hotels were better. The men's shelters established in New York in the past decade resemble in physical layout the dormitory accommodations provided by the missions in the old Skid Row, which the homeless regarded as last-resort alternatives to sleeping outside. In social organization these shelters most closely resemble minimum-security prisons whose gates are open during the day.

As reported in a survey of New York shelter clients (Crystal and Goldstein 1982), the shelter residents rated prisons *superior* to shelters in safety, cleanliness, and food quality. The shelters were regarded clearly superior only in freedom—meaning the right to leave at any time. The new homeless were clearly worse off in regard to shelter than the old homeless.

---

30. The case in question, *Callahan v. Carey*, was filed in the New York State Supreme Court in 1979 by Robert Hayes, then director of the New York Coalition for the Homeless. The suit claimed that the state constitution and municipal charter stated that shelter was an entitlement. Shortly after the case was filed, the court issued a temporary injunction requiring the city to expand the capacity of municipal shelters. When the case came to trial in 1981, it was settled by a consent decree in which the city agreed to provide shelter upon demand.

The housing for homeless single women was somewhat better than that supplied to men. The single-women's shelters most closely resembled the cubicle flophouses with their cramped individual accommodations.

New York is exceptional in that the municipal government has directly provided most of the shelters for the homeless. In most cities, private charities with government subsidies usually provide the shelters. The long-established religious missions—for example, the Salvation Army, the Volunteers of America, and the Society of Saint Vincent de Paul—expanded their existing shelters and in some instances undertook to run shelters under contract to municipalities or states. Other charities provided shelters for the first time.

In Bogue's 1958 study, the four or five mission shelters provided only 975 beds for the homeless of Chicago, in contrast to the forty-five shelters we found in that city in the winter of 1985–86, providing a total of 2,000 beds. Several commentators have observed that the shelters provided by private charities are superior in many respects to those run by municipalities.[31]

To accommodate the influx of family groups into the homeless population, new types of shelter arrangements have come into being. Some specialize in quasi-private quarters for family groups, usually one or two rooms per family with shared bathrooms and cooking facilities. In many cities welfare departments have provided temporary housing for families by renting rooms in hotels and motels: for example, in 1986 New York City housed 3,500 homeless families a month in "welfare hotels" (Bach and Steinhagen 1987).[32]

On a scale that was inconceivable earlier, considerable funds for the new homeless have been allocated out of local, state, and federal funds. Private charity has also been generous; most of the "emergency" shelters for the homeless are organized and run by private groups with subsidies from public funds. Foundations have given generous grants. For example, the Robert Wood Johnson Foundation in association with the Pew Memorial Trust supports medical clinics for the homeless persons in nineteen cities. The states have provided funds through existing programs and special appropriations.

In the spring of 1987, after a prelude media event in which congressmen and advocates for the homeless slept overnight on the Capitol steps, Congress passed the McKinney Homeless Assistance Act, which appropriated $442 million for the homeless in fiscal 1987 and $616 million in 1988. The money was channeled through a group of agencies, providing some housing for the homeless, subsidies for existing shelters, and subsidies for a variety of re-

31. At least part of the difference in quality arises because most privately run shelters restrict whom they admit, usually excluding those who are drunk, appear aggressive or behave bizarrely. Municipal shelters ordinarily have to admit everyone and hence find it difficult to exclude anyone on such grounds.

32. An ironic feature of the use of welfare hotels is that the rents paid by the welfare departments for these accommodations are clearly far greater than current rents at the lowest end of the housing market. Welfare payments are not enough to pay market rents for apartments, but the welfare departments find it possible to pay much higher hotel rents for homeless clients!

habilitation programs including vocational training, medical care, and services for the chronically mentally ill. The funds authorized in the McKinney Act were in addition to those available from existing programs that have supported homeless persons through welfare benefit programs and federally supported medical services.

Reversing the decline discerned in the 1960s, there can be little doubt that homelessness has increased over the past decade and that the composition of the homeless population has changed dramatically. There are ample signs of these changes. In the few cities where data over time exist, there is clear evidence that the number of homeless people is increasing in at least some localities. In New York City, shelter capacity has increased from 3,000 beds to 6,000 over a five-year period. In the same city, the number of families in the welfare hotels has increased from a few hundred to the 3,500 of today. In addition there are many homeless people who do not use the shelters, though the number is not known with any precision.

Nevertheless, for the country as a whole no one knows for sure how much of an increase there has been over the past decade, let alone how many homeless people there are in the United States today. There are many obstacles to obtaining this knowledge. (Detailed discussion of existing estimates and procedures is postponed until chap. 3.) Some of the major obstacles are technical. For example, conventional censuses and surveys proceed on the assumption that nearly everyone in the United States can be reached through an address, an assumption that is clearly violated in the case of the homeless. Hence we cannot look to the 1980 census (or likely to the 1990 census)[33] or the Current Population Survey for credible estimates of homelessness. Other obstacles are more ideological, as discussed in chapter 1; a central one centers on whether the concept of homelessness should be restricted to those who are without conventional housing or extended to cover all who are inadequately housed. Depending on whether one adopts a narrow or a more inclusive definition, the number of homeless will differ by several magnitudes.

These difficulties notwithstanding, several estimates have been made of the size of the homeless population. The National Coalition for the Homeless, an advocacy group, "guesstimates" anywhere between 1.5 and 3 million. A much maligned report of the United States Department of Housing and Urban Development (1984), using four different estimation approaches, put the national figure at somewhere between 250,000 and 300,000 in 1983. A more recent estimate by Freeman and Hall (1986) comes closer to the HUD figures

---

33. Current plans for the 1990 census include enumerations late at night in public places, such as bus stations, where homeless persons are known to congregate, as well as full coverage of emergency shelters. If carried through as currently (1988) planned, the 1990 census will provide a better count of the literally homeless than now exists. Nevertheless, the improved tally will still not include homeless people in locations other than those best known to the local experts on whom the census will rely for information on where to count.

with an estimate of 350,000 in 1986. All the existing estimates are vulnerable to criticism, since they all rest on heroic assumptions that challenge credibility.

Although the issue of how many homeless people there are in the United States is a contentious one, it does not really matter which of these estimates is most accurate: homelessness is obviously a major social problem. By any standards, all the estimates point to a national disgrace, clearly unacceptable in a rich, humane society.

Since 1980, there have been approximately forty reasonably well-conducted social science studies of the homeless whose results are available to the diligent and patient researcher.[34] As in the late 1950s and 1960s, the purpose of funding and carrying out these studies is to provide information on which to base policies and programs to alleviate the pitiful condition of the American homeless. Research funds have been provided by private foundations and government agencies, among which the National Institute of Mental Health has been a major contributor.

The cities studied range across all regions of the country, including all the major metropolises as well as more than a score of smaller cities. One study even attempted to study the rural homeless but had little success in locating them. The cumulative knowledge about the new homeless that can be acquired through these studies is impressive and hardly contentious. Despite wide differences in the definitions of homelessness used,[35] approaches taken, methods, and degree of technical sophistication, there is considerable convergence among their findings. A fairly clear understanding is now emerging concerning who the new homeless are, how they contrast with the general population, and how they differ from the homeless of the 1950s.

Some of the important ways the current homeless differ from the old homeless have already been mentioned. Bogue estimated that in 1958 only about 100 homeless men slept out on the streets of Chicago. Caplow and Bahr make some passing mention of the Bowery homeless sleeping out on the streets or in public places in 1964, but their lack of attention to this feature implies that the number was small. Blumberg's study of Philadelphia uncovered only 64 homeless persons living on the streets in 1960. In contrast, my own studies of homelessness in Chicago found close to 1,400 homeless persons out on the streets in the fall of 1985 and 528 in that condition in the dead of winter in early 1986. Comparably large numbers of street homeless, proportionate to community size, have been found over the past five years in studies of, among other cities, Los Angeles, New York, Nashville, Austin, Detroit, Baltimore, and Washington, D.C. A major difference between the old and the new homeless is that the old homeless routinely managed somehow to find shelter in-

34. Many of these studies are privately published in reports that are not circulated through the publications market.

35. The definitional differences are mainly on the nominal level. Although many of the studies include the precariously housed as homeless in principle, in practice almost all deal with the literally homeless.

doors, while a majority of the new homeless in most studies are out on the streets. As far as shelter goes, the new homeless are clearly worse off. In short, *homelessness today means more severe basic shelter deprivation.*

There is also some evidence that those housed in emergency shelters may be worse off than the homeless who lived in the cubicle hotels of the 1960s. Whatever the deficiencies of the cubicle hotels, they were a step above the dormitory arrangements of the 1980s and considerably better than sleeping on the streets or in public places.

Furthermore, the new homeless, sheltered or out on the streets, are no longer concentrated in Skid Row. They can be encountered more widely throughout the downtown areas of our cities. Homelessness today cannot be easily ignored as in the past. In the expectation that homeless were on the decline, the traditional Skid Row areas were demolished and homelessness was decentralized. In addition, the liberalization of police patrol practices in many cities has meant that the homeless can wander more freely through our downtown areas. Thus the public receives more direct exposure to the sight of destitution.

A second major contrast is the presence of women among the homeless. In Chicago's Skid Row, Bogue estimated that women may have constituted up to 3% of the residents, and he thought that many were not homeless but were simply living in the Skid Row areas.[36] As reported by Bahr and Garrett (1976), homeless women on the Bowery in the 1960s constituted only a handful—64 over a period of a year—of alcoholics housed in a special shelter for homeless women.[37]

In contrast, we found that women constituted 25% of the 1985–86 Chicago homeless population, close to the average of 21% for studies of the homeless conducted during the 1980s. All the studies undertaken in the 1980s have found that women constitute a much larger proportion of the homeless than in research done before 1970. The proportion female among the homeless varies somewhat from place to place: if women living in the New York welfare hotels are counted as homeless, then women constitute close to one-third of the homeless population of New York. In contrast, a study of the homeless of Austin, Texas, found that only 7% were women, certainly a smaller proportion than in New York, but clearly greater than was found in any of the older Skid Row studies.

A third contrast with the old homeless is in age composition. There are very

36. Bogue did not interview any women in his sample of cubicle hotel and SRO residents. His estimate of 3% comes from a special tabulation from the 1950 census of persons living outside households in Skid Row census tracts. Bogue believed some of the women were live-in employees of the hotels and others were simply renting rooms in households that lived in conventional dwellings in the Skid Row areas.

37. In their study of homeless women, they took as subjects every person admitted to a Bowery treatment center for alcoholic women. It took an entire year's set of admissions to supply sixty-four subjects for their study.

few persons over sixty among today's homeless and virtually no Social Security pensioners. Instead, today's homeless are concentrated in their twenties and thirties, the early years of adulthood. This is clearly shown in the median age of today's Chicago homeless, thirty-nine, in comparison with the median age of fifty found in Bogue's study. In the forty studies of the homeless conducted in the past few years, the average median age recorded was thirty-six, with a range running from twenty-eight through forty-six. Among the homeless populations throughout the country, most people are in the middle and lower thirties. Where we have data over time, as in the New York City men's shelters, the median age has been dropping rapidly over the past decade.

A fourth contrast is in employment status and income: except for aged pensioners, over half of the Chicago homeless studied in 1958 were employed in any given week, either full time (28%) or intermittently (25%), and almost all worked for some period during a year's time. In contrast, among the new Chicago homeless, only 3% reported having a steady job, and only 39% had worked for some time during the previous month.

Correspondingly, the new homeless have less income than the old. Bogue estimated that the median annual income of the 1958 homeless was $1,058. Our Chicago finding was a median annual income of $1,198. Correcting for inflation, the income of the current homeless is equivalent to only $383 in 1958 dollars. The new homeless are clearly farther out on the fringe of the American economy: their income level is less than one-third that of the old homeless! Similar levels—average median was $1,127—were found in the nine other studies that attempted to measure income.

A final contrast is presented by the ethnic composition of the old and new homeless populations. The old homeless were predominantly white—70% on the Bowery and 82% on Chicago's Skid Row. But the new homeless are recruited heavily from among ethnic minorities: in Chicago 54% were black, and in New York's shelters more than 75% were black, a proportion that has been increasing since the early 1980s. Similar patterns are shown in other American cities, with the minority group in question changing according to the ethnic mix of the general population. In short, we can generalize that minorities are consistently overrepresented among the new homeless in ratios that are some multiple of their presence in the community. The old homelessness was more blind to color and ethnicity than the new homelessness.[38]

There are also some continuities from the old to the new homeless. First of all, they share the condition of extreme poverty. Although the new homeless are lower on the economic ladder, there can be little doubt that both groups' incomes are far too low to support any reasonable standard of living. In Chicago in 1985 and 1986, we found abysmally low incomes among the home-

---

38. Blumberg speculated that the black homeless men in the Philadelphia of 1960 were kept out of Skid Row by the discriminatory practices of cubicle hotel landlords and had to be absorbed into the black ghetto areas in rented rooms and boardinghouses. He predicted that the proportion black would rise.

less. With median incomes of less than $100 per month or about $3.25 per day, even trivial expenditures loom as major expenses: for example, a round trip on Chicago's bus system in 1986 cost $1.80, more than half a day's income. A night's lodging at even the cheapest hotel costs $5.00 and up, more than a day's income. And of course, a median income figure simply marks the income received by persons right at the midpoint of the income distribution: half of the homeless live on less than the median, and close to one-fifth (18%) report no income at all. In addition, the income of the homeless is not a steady stream of $3.25 every day; it is intermittent and unpredictable, meaning that for many days in the week, weeks in the month, and months in the year many homeless people have no income at all.

Given these income levels, it is no mystery why the homeless are without shelter; their incomes simply do not allow them to enter effectively into the housing market. Indeed, the only way they can get by is to look to the shelters for a place to sleep, to the food kitchens for meals, to the free clinics and emergency rooms for medical care, and to the clothing distribution depots for something to put on their backs.

The new and the old homeless also are alike in having high levels of disability. The one change from the 1950s to the 1980s is that fewer have the disability of age. As I mentioned earlier, few of the new homeless are over sixty. The current homeless suffer from much the same levels of mental illness, alcoholism, and physical disability as the old homeless.

Much has been written asserting that the deinstitutionalization of the chronically mentally ill during the 1960s and 1970s is a major cause of the recent rise in homelessness. Almost as much has been written denying it. At this time it is almost pointless to try to determine which side in this controversy is correct, largely or in part. The decanting of the mental hospital population occurred throughout the 1960s, so its current effects have in any event long since been diluted by time. What is important right now are the current admissions policies of our mental hospitals. Many of the chronically mentally ill homeless would have been admitted two decades ago under then-existing practices. The shelters and the streets now substitute in part for the hospitals of the past.[39]

Remember also that the old Skid Rows were not free of the chronically mentally ill. All the researchers of the 1950s and 1960s remark on the presence of clearly psychotic persons in the flophouses of Chicago and New York.

39. In 1958 the municipal court that had jurisdiction over Chicago's Skid Row area had a psychiatrist on its staff whose function was to recommend commitment to mental hospitals for Skid Row residents judged psychotic who were brought before the court. Bogue suggests that this screening process lowered the proportion of Skid Row residents he found to be psychotic. A 1934 study by Sutherland and Locke of emergency municipal shelters for homeless men describes a psychiatric screening process in admission that shunted the clearly psychotic men to mental hospitals. Shelters in Chicago now often refuse admission to persons who behave bizarrely. The clearly psychotic are left to sleep on the streets.

Bogue estimated that about 20% of Skid Row inhabitants were mentally ill. Blumberg found that among the 1960 Philadelphia homeless, 16% had been hospitalized at least once in a mental institution. Chronic mental illness seemingly has always been a significant presence among the homeless. Skid Row, with its easy acceptance of deviance of all sorts, certainly did not draw the line at chronic mental illness.

Because of the attention paid to deinstitutionalization as a possible contributory factor in homelessness, research on the new homeless almost invariably attempts to estimate the prevalence of chronic mental illness among them. A variety of measures have been employed, with the surprising outcome that they tend to converge: a fair summary is represented by the following averages; 25% of the homeless report previous episodes as mental hospital patients, and 33% show signs of current psychosis or affective disorders. Although the reported current prevalence of chronic mental illness appears to be more than 50% higher among the new homeless than among the old, measurement procedures may account for that difference. In any event, compared with the general population both levels are extremely high.

Physical disabilities also are prevalent among the new homeless. The best evidence on this score comes from the records of medical clinics for the homeless supported by the Robert Wood Johnson Foundation, which document high levels of both chronic conditions, such as hypertension, diabetes, and circulatory disorders, and acute conditions, some integrally related to homelessness, such as lice infestation, trauma, and leg ulcers. The few studies that looked into mortality rates among the new homeless reported rates ten to forty times those found in the general population. Unfortunately, none of the studies of the older homeless give comparable detail on medical conditions, although all the researchers remark on the presence of severe disabilities. Bogue did judge that close to half of the 1958 Skid Row inhabitants had moderate to severe disabilities that would substantially reduce their employability. His studies found much the same mortality levels as have been found among the new homeless—more than ten times higher than among comparable age groups in the domiciled population.

All the studies of the old homeless stress how widespread alcoholism was. Bogue found that 30% were heavy drinkers, defined as persons spending 25% or more of their income on alcoholic beverages and drinking the equivalent of six or more pints of whiskey a week. Using a comparable measure, Bahr and Caplow found 36% to be heavy drinkers. Similar proportions were found in Minneapolis and Philadelphia about the same time.

Studies of the new homeless show similar degrees of prevalence of alcoholism. In our Chicago study, 33% had been in a detoxification unit, indicating that one in three had had serious problems with alcohol. Studies in other cities produced estimates of current alcoholism averaging 33%, with a fairly wide range. The consensus of the studies is that about one in three of the new homeless are chronic alcoholics.

A new twist is drug abuse. None of the studies of the 1980 homeless has attempted to measure drug abuse in any satisfactory way, but all point to the significant presence of drug abuse, past and present, among the new homeless. Recent studies of the homeless in New York men's shelters claim that about 20% of the homeless men were current hard drug users or had been addicted in the past.

Although only large minorities of the new homeless are afflicted with any one of the disabilities of chronic mental illness, debilitating physical conditions, or chronic alcoholism, their effects are additive. A substantial majority have at least one and sometimes several disabling conditions. About two-thirds of the Chicago homeless had physical health problems, mental health problems, substance abuse problems, or some combination of them.

Another point of comparability between the old and the new homeless concerns the heterogeneity of both populations. Both comprised some persons who remained homeless for only short periods and others who were homeless for a long time. The Skid Rows were points of entry for poor migrants to urban centers, who rented cubicles until they had established themselves and could afford conventional dwellings. The short-term new homeless are somewhat different—poor persons whose fortunes have temporarily taken a turn for the worse and who find the shelters a good way to cut back on expenses until they can reestablish themselves.[40] A large portion of the temporary new homeless population consists of young female-headed households in transition from one household (often their parents') to another, using the shelters as a resting place until they can establish a new home on their own, often while waiting for certification as AFDC recipients.

A final point of comparability between the old and the new homeless is that both are relatively isolated socially. The new homeless report few friends and intimates and little contact with relatives and family. There are also signs of some friction between the homeless and their relatives. So extensive was the absence of social ties with kin and friends among the old homeless that Caplow and Bahr define homelessness as essentially a state of *disaffiliation*, without enduring and supporting ties to family, friends, and kin. Disaffiliation also characterizes the new homeless, marking this group off from other extremely poor persons.

The contrasts between the homeless of the 1950s and 1960s and the homeless of the 1980s offer some strong clues to why homelessness has become defined as a social problem. First, there can be no doubt that more Americans

---

40. In many housing markets a prospective renter must have enough cash to put down a month's rent in advance plus a security deposit in order to rent an apartment. Thus one may need as much as $800 simply to make an offer for an apartment renting for $400 a month. If we also consider that some minimum of furniture is necessary, setting up a new household in a rental apartment may take more than $1,000 in cash. Although few researchers have provided any firm numbers, several have remarked on shelter dwellers who are employed full time and using the cheap accommodations while they accumulate the cash necessary to enter the conventional rental market.

are exposed to the sight of homelessness because homeless persons are less spatially concentrated today. Second, homelessness has shifted in meaning: the old homeless were sheltered in inadequate accommodations, but they were not sleeping out on the streets and in public places in great numbers. Literal on-the-street homelessness has increased from virtually negligible proportions to more than half of the homeless population. Third, homelessness now means greater deprivation. The homeless men living on Skid Row were surely poor, but their average income from casual and intermittent work was three to four times that of the current homeless. The emergency shelter housing now available is at best only marginally better than the cubicle rooms of the past.

Finally, the composition of the homeless has changed dramatically. Thirty years ago old men were the majority among the homeless, with only a handful of women in that condition and virtually no families. The current homeless are younger and include a significant proportion of women. Finally, advocate organizations and groups have arisen to speak on behalf of the homeless and to raise public consciousness of the problem.

This combination of changes helps explain why there is so much interest in the homeless today compared with a few decades ago.

THREE

Counting the Homeless and the Extremely Poor

In the classic formulations of how to apply social research to social policy and program issues, the earliest steps are to assemble existing data and to obtain new intelligence. This first stage includes developing adequate conceptual and empirical definitions of the problem and gathering sufficient data to identify its scope, social location, and spatial distribution. This dictum applies to the issues of homelessness and extreme poverty as much as to any social problem.

Describing the nature of the social problem and its extent is important in developing social programs. To identify a social problem, as discussed in chapter 1, such elaborate knowledge is usually not needed; it may be enough to know that there are homeless people in our society, to recognize that homelessness lies below the threshold of minimum decent living conditions, and to be quite certain that the homeless population is steady or increasing. However, to devise effective programs and policies and to allocate appropriate amounts and kinds of resources to them, it is essential to know with some confidence the total number of the homeless and how fast it is changing. In addition, before we can begin to design adequate social policies and programs addressing the needs of the extremely poor and the homeless, we clearly must have a valid understanding of the size, distribution, and composition of those populations. It is also obvious that we must have quantitative information: a judgment that a problem is "large" may arouse concern and interest, but actual numbers are needed in policy planning and program design. Although exquisite precision is probably unnecessary, we must estimate magnitude.

The necessary information at sufficient precision is almost totally lacking for the United States as a whole. Although it is abundantly obvious that there are enough homeless people to justify defining a social problem, it does make a considerable difference to social policy and programs whether the number of homeless people in the United States is 350,000 (HUD 1984) or 1.5 million or higher, as many advocates suggest (Hombs and Snyder 1982). Knowing the distribution and social characteristics of the homeless is also crucial, for to finance programs adequately we must know how many homeless or extremely poor people there are. Since programs should probably be tailored to identifiable subgroups of the homeless—women and children present a different problem from the mentally ill—it does make a difference whether the sex ratio is 100 or 300, what proportion are substance abusers, whether the homeless are primarily long-term unemployed, and so forth. What kinds of ameliorative programs to design, how best to reach potential clients, and how much the programs would cost are all questions that require firm quantitative information.

With respect to the problem of homelessness, this classic formulation of the first steps for applied social research simply has not been possible to implement. In particular, awareness of and concern for the homeless have far outstripped our knowledge. As is often the case, both the private and public sectors—private philanthropy and federal, state, and local public officials—have moved quickly to put into place policies and programs designed to ameliorate the lot of the homeless without waiting for an adequate knowledge base to be developed.

This is not atypical: often enough policies and programs are in place long before we know the details of the problem. Nor would anyone want it entirely otherwise. In natural disasters, not only is it unnecessary to know the full extent of the damages before sending in emergency aid, but it would be heartless to wait until that detailed knowledge became available. However, when it comes to planning and implementing long-term measures to reduce the risks of damage from earthquakes or floods, it is best, if not essential, to have accurate knowledge about the extent and location of risk.

Much the same considerations apply to homelessness. Surely we must provide food, shelter, and medical care as soon as any need becomes obvious, but to devise long-term measures that can reduce homelessness, we need to know the extent of the problem and what social forces produce it.

Extreme poverty as a social problem is in a different stage. Concern for the poor has been strong for a long time. Federal programs have addressed poverty for more than fifty years, and state and local programs have been in place since colonial days. Certainly extreme poverty is included, though it is not a well-defined target. The consequence is that, compared with homelessness, we know much more about poverty in general, but there is neither specific concern for the extremely poor nor special knowledge about this group. The main issue with respect to knowledge about extreme poverty is a conceptual one. Good data of high reputation exist, but they have not been examined from the proper perspective, as I will explain later.

The rest of this chapter will explicate the technical and substantive issues involved in estimating the size and composition of the extremely poor and homeless populations. A final section will gather the several estimates of the size of each and identify what I consider the "best" ones.

Measuring Homelessness

Let us start with the more difficult of the two tasks, measuring the size and composition of the homeless population of the nation and of particular places within it. Not only do conventional censuses and samples by design typically miss the homeless, but special technical difficulties stand in the way of developing empirically grounded knowledge about homelessness on any level. These obstacles, described in detail below, have seriously impeded our gathering reasonably precise data on the prevalence and distribution of homelessness through surveys or censuses. Indeed, several commentators on the problem claim that the extent of homelessness, especially on the national level, is essentially "unknowable." Governor Mario Cuomo's report for the governors' conference states the problem as "counting the uncountable" (Cuomo 1983).

Of course, the difficulties that all agree upon have not prevented everyone from voicing "estimates" of the size and composition of the national homeless population. In the absence of authoritative data, "guesstimates" and conjectures flourish, often bolstered by dramatic anecdotal accounts and fervent personal testimony. Driven by their avid appetite for the startling and counterintuitive, journalists provide a strong market for such guesses, with the strongest demand for extreme estimates. (Later in this chapter I will review some of the better-known attempts to estimate the size of the national homeless population.)

In addition to national "estimates," there are many estimates of the homeless populations of specific cities. Indeed, most of the national estimates are based on compilations of and extrapolations from local estimates. On the surface it may seem easier to estimate the number of the homeless in specific cities or states, but the task is plagued by many of the same problems as developing national estimates. The methods used in preparing local estimates are also reviewed in this chapter.

The Problem of Definition

A primary obstacle to developing credible data is the absence of a widely accepted definition of homelessness. Indeed the range of definitions currently in use is very wide, running the gamut from highly inclusive ones that cover all those who are inadequately housed—including doubled-up households, persons living in (by some standards) poor housing, and persons temporarily housed in hospitals or other institutions, as well as those who do not rent or own conventional dwellings. More restrictive definitions focus primarily on the last group.

As with many social problems, definitional issues are not simply technical ones but include political and value questions centering on the level of housing no one should be allowed to sink below. Clearly, more inclusive definitions imply a higher floor for the concept of decent housing, but they also enlarge the size (and change the composition) of the homeless population. More inclusive definitions also expand and considerably complicate the task for researchers; they set very fuzzy boundaries for homelessness, allowing guesstimates to range more widely.

Often bound up with more inclusive definitions is the concept of the "hidden homeless," who have managed to hide so effectively—for example, in the subbasements of buildings or in concealed rooms in abandoned buildings—that they can never be located. Since the number of "hidden homeless" is by definition unknowable, the true size of any homeless population is also unknowable.

The idea of "hidden homeless," as often used, comes close to being an oxymoron. Persons who are so completely concealed that they cannot be found no matter how hard one tries are persons whose existence no one can affirm. Although there undoubtedly are homeless persons who conceal themselves so thoroughly that they can be located only with great difficulty, the more radical interpretation of "hidden homeless" defines the measurement issue as unsolvable.

In all the homeless research, operational definitions tend to be less inclusive, focusing primarily on what I called in chapter 1 the "literally homeless," as opposed to the "precariously housed." As I stated in that chapter, the "literally homeless" are those who sleep in shelters provided for homeless persons or in places, private or public, not intended as dwellings. The "precariously housed" are those who live in conventional dwellings but run a high risk of becoming literally homeless for shorter or longer periods.

The more restricted definition tends to be used in practice because the more inclusive ones are extremely difficult to implement, except at prohibitive costs. The "hidden homeless," by definition, cannot be studied. Studying the precariously housed involves working with very broad sampling frames including most impoverished households and entails both high costs and severe measurement problems. Of course, it is possible to estimate the size of at least some portion of the "precariously housed," as I will do later in this chapter, using data from comprehensive censuses or sample surveys.

Sampling Frames

Social science research has made considerable strides in the past half-century. As a consequence, modern censuses are considerably more accurate and precise than those taken in the early decades of this century. However, conventional social research methods are largely useless for studying the homeless because most are based on the assumption that every person or household has an address and may be reached there by an interviewer's visit, through a telephone call, or by mail.

Modern censuses and sample surveys start with the development of lists of geographic areas and the residential structures within them. A population census is conducted by approaching each residential unit in the area being studied and enumerating the persons living within it. Sample surveys of human populations differ from censuses only by approaching members of carefully picked samples of residential units rather than visiting every dwelling.[1]

Of course the critical assumption that a human population can be enumerated by querying residential units simply does not hold for the bulk of homeless persons. Even for those homeless found in a shelter, their stay may be so temporary that the address is meaningless as a place where they can be counted or reached. Especially puzzling is how to reach people who are on the streets twenty-four hours a day or in other places that are not conventional dwellings.

This means that sampling frames for surveys of the homeless must be quite different from sampling frames for the domiciled population. A sampling frame for the homeless has to be concerned with nondwelling units and a plan for studying a homeless population has to be like a photographic negative of the conventional survey research design, based on nondwellings.

Statistical Rarity

Any appreciable amount of homelessness is a national disgrace. Nevertheless, under even the most inclusive definitions it is still a rare condition that affects at most 1.5% of the adult population and most likely less than 0.10%. Studying rare populations is not impossible, but it is expensive. For example, if we undertook a random sample of any urban area to obtain a sample of homeless persons, we might have to approach anywhere from 70 to 500 adults to encounter one homeless person.

To study rare populations efficiently, one must devise strategies that will reduce the screening problem—that is, the many observations needed to reach a person or household that is part of the rare population. Clearly, as I indicated earlier, simple random sampling is very inefficient. Studying rare populations usually involves developing strategies that reduce the costs of screening by what is technically termed prior stratification—in the case of the homeless, identifying those places where their destiny is high.

Identification

Whatever definition of homelessness one may adopt, there remains the problem of how to apply it in specific instances. Since homelessness is not immediately observable, applying most definitions requires asking people di-

---

1. For most structures, residential units can be easily discerned and defined. However, should hotel rooms, army barracks, school and college dormitories, and convents be included? The answer is probably yes for a census but is not so clear for a sample survey concerned primarily with employment status. Indeed, as I discussed earlier, the Current Population Survey includes only conventional dwellings within its sampling frames.

rect questions. Although many of the homeless are shabbily dressed, many are not. In addition, some people with homes also dress shabbily.

The problem of identification plagues the use of client data in the study of homelessness. For example, none of the Robert Wood Johnson Foundation–Pew Memorial Trust medical clinics for the homeless attempt to determine whether people who present themselves for medical services really are homeless. (This is a very sensible strategy; whether homeless or not, most of the people in the clinic lines need medical care and cannot afford to obtain it in conventional ways.) I surmise that some portion of their clients, perhaps as many as half, are not homeless by my definition. Indeed, a 1987 survey of persons in food kitchen lines in Chicago (Sosin, Colson, and Grossman 1988) found that more than half were not literally homeless but were living in conventional dwellings.

The identification problem means that any survey approach has to develop means of reliably identifying whether a person is homeless, and this usually involves some interviewing.

Transience and Turbulence

An important characteristic of the homeless population is that the individuals it comprises change frequently, moving into and out of the homeless condition. As I have repeatedly asserted, among the extremely poor the line between the homeless and those with homes is often crossed, in both directions.

As later chapters will show, only a minority of the homeless appear to be permanently in that condition. Significant subgroups include: (1) One-time momentary (or very short-term) homeless, who are homeless for less than a week and only once or twice over a few years. Examples include runaway or "throwaway" young people, who usually rejoin their families within a few days, and new arrivals coming to a city to seek employment, who may be homeless until they establish themselves. (2) Part-time or periodic short-term homeless, who are repeatedly homeless in a somewhat regular pattern—for example, the last few days before their benefit checks arrive. These are persons whose hold on their homes is so precarious that they resort from time to time to shelters and food kitchens because they do not have the resources to maintain them continuously. The significant number of part-time homeless testifies to the heavy housing costs some poor people bear. (3) Transitional homeless, who are in transition between one living arrangement and another but who have the long-term potential to connect with the conventional housing market—for example, young mothers and their children leaving a previous housing arrangement, households burned out or evicted, or persons migrating to a new community. The size of this component reflects the current high cost of entering the conventional housing market: advance rent, security deposits, and other up-front costs can be serious obstacles to finding rental housing, even at its lowest levels. And finally (4) Long-term homeless, persons without the ability to connect with the conventional housing market because their potential for employment is severely impaired or because they have not qualified for benefit programs.

This distribution means that the homeless population is quite heterogeneous in duration,[2] so it is very important to make a variety of prevalence and incidence estimates as measures. The homeless population at any given point in time includes only some fraction of all the people who are ever homeless. This means there are a variety of interpretations of the question of how many homeless there are (and correspondingly many answers). For example, we can expect to find many more persons homeless over the course of a year than at any one time.

To make a useful estimate of the size of the homeless population we must find out how long people have been homeless, usually by asking them.

Geographical Concentration

The homeless are not distributed uniformly throughout a community but tend to be concentrated in particular localities. In part this geographical concentration makes it easier to do research on the homeless, but it is also an obstacle. The concentration of homeless people occurs because the institutions that serve their needs are also concentrated, but in turn that institutional concentration reflects the distribution of the homeless (McMurry 1988). This means that optimal sampling requires some prior knowledge of spatial distribution. If those areas of concentration can be identified in advance, we can devise an efficient sampling strategy that minimizes screening. Of course, some of the major clumps are easily identified. The shelters for the homeless can be easily enumerated, since most of them are known—there are no "hidden shelters."[3] In particular, that most shelters are subsidized to some extent by local, state, and federal governments means that local public officials often maintain up-to-date lists of currently operating shelters.

The locations of the street homeless present more difficulties, although the most-used gathering points of the homeless are well known; for example, bus and train stations, food kitchens, and clothing depots. Other common locations usually can be identified by relying on the occupationally derived knowledge of those who deal with the homeless—social workers, managers of shelters, advocates for the homeless, and the like. In short, with some effort we can assemble lists of locations where there is a high probability of finding homeless people.

2. This heterogeneity in duration also makes it difficult to employ capture/recapture estimation methods.

3. This statement applies only to formally established shelters that are subsidized by public funds. "Informal" shelters may exist, as when a building manager lets homeless people bed down in an unused basement or storage room.

Communications Problems

In addition to the usual problems encountered in surveying poorly educated persons, the homeless, by reputation, are more difficult to interview because of disabilities—including substance abuse and mental illness—that make communication difficult. In addition, some are reputed to be hostile and suspicious, unwilling to talk to people they do not know.

Why do the homeless have this reputation as hard to talk to? Many researchers have remarked that they were warned it would be close to impossible to get any information from the homeless that would conform to standards for reliable data. The same researchers remarked that it was much easier than they expected. This has been my own experience: among the close to 800 homeless persons we tried to interview in Chicago, in fewer than half a dozen instances was it impossible to obtain any information.[4] Nevertheless, the reputation of the homeless as hard to reach has undoubtedly discouraged research.

Approaches Used in Research on the Homeless

Since starting research on the homeless, I have collected as many as possible of published and unpublished empirical studies of homelessness— approximately sixty. Using fairly minimal quality standards,[5] nearly forty studies survived after I rejected those that did not conform: these studies will be used extensively in the chapters that follow.

The approximately sixty studies conducted since 1980 have used variations on the five research strategies described in the next few pages. Some studies have used several approaches. Most have not tried to estimate the size of the homeless population, realizing that their approaches were not appropriate to that purpose.

Key-Person Surveys

The first approach consists essentially of asking "key persons" (defined as those with some knowledge of homelessness, usually acquired through occupations dealing with homeless people) to estimate the size and composition of this group. There are many attractive features to this approach. First, a key-

4. Among the few studies that reported the information, seven reported an average response rate (completed interviews as a proportion of total persons approached and eligible) of 78% in interviewing the street homeless. The larger number (twenty-four) of studies based on interviewing sheltered homeless samples reported even higher average response rates, 85%. Clearly the difficulties reported, usually by persons responsible for services to the homeless, are highly exaggerated or possibly experienced primarily by human services workers who deal with the homeless as clients.

5. The standards used included the following: having an explicit sampling plan; providing quantitative data summaries; and being based on direct interviewing or administrative records.

person survey can be conducted quickly and inexpensively. Second, this method appears on the surface to have some validity; after all, the men and women who run shelters, food kitchens, and drop-in centers or administer public welfare programs have had considerably greater direct experience than anyone else in their communities. Certainly the administrator of a shelter for the homeless ought to have a fairly accurate understanding of the number of persons served by that facility and others. At least on the face of it, querying such experts ought to yield reasonably good data on the extent and character of homelessness.

Perhaps the best example is the key-person survey[6] that was the basis of one of the three estimates of the national homeless population published by the United States Department of Housing and Urban Development (HUD 1984). Estimates of the number of the homeless people in each locality were obtained from telephone interviews with about five hundred local experts in a national sample of sixty metropolitan areas. Experts were chosen from among local government representatives, public housing officials, advocates for the homeless, social researchers, and administrators of social agencies such as the Salvation Army or Travelers Aid. To improve accuracy, the several estimates for each area were combined into an average, after weighting each for its "validity."[7] In addition, the definition of homelessness was standardized and estimates were gathered for the same period (any given night, winter 1984). The number of estimates obtained in each city ranged from three to five for smaller cities to eight to twelve for large metropolitan areas.

A national estimate of homeless in all metropolitan areas (210,000) was then calculated from these data. Making the assumption that the rate of homelessness in small towns and rural areas was the same as for the small metropolitan areas, HUD researchers multiplied the population outside metropolitan areas by this rate and came up with an estimate of 44,000 for rural areas. This figure was combined with the estimate for metropolitan areas for a total estimate of 254,000.

The HUD key-person survey is to be commended for the care taken in sampling and in weighting each item of information according to its credibility. In contrast, the estimates offered by the Committee on Creative Non-Violence in congressional testimony (Hombs and Snyder 1982) apparently were arrived at much more casually. Hombs and Snyder claim that their national estimate of 1.5 million homeless was also based on extrapolations from local estimates by knowledgeable persons. But, how such persons were chosen—or why certain cities were used—was not revealed. Nor can we learn how many key persons

6. The HUD report also reflects two additional approaches to be discussed below.

7. Each of the local city estimates was weighted in terms of the respondent's knowledge and the source of the information. For instance, an estimate from a street count throughout a city was weighted 4, while an estimate based on police records and observations received a weight of 2. Weighted estimates for each city were averaged to produce a single city estimate.

were approached or how the local estimates were projected to the national level. Not enough information is given about the Hombs and Snyder estimates to let us evaluate their worth.

The key-person approach has been used by several state commissions, including ones in California, Florida, and Maryland (California Department of Housing and Community Development 1985; Florida Statewide Taskforce on the Homeless 1985; Maryland Department of Human Resources 1986), in their reports on the homeless in their states. The most recent key-person survey was used by the United States Conference of Mayors (1988) to estimate changes in the demand for services for homeless persons in twenty-six of the larger central cities.

The point of this considerable detail is to show that many questionable assumptions have had to be made in using data obtained through a survey of key persons. Nevertheless, the main problem is that such surveys are of unknown validity—probably better than no information at all, but how much better no one knows. The validity of this approach rests upon the ability of the key persons to integrate their personal experiences and those of their agencies into quantitative estimates that usually go beyond direct experience—a difficult task even for persons trained and experienced in making such calculations. For example, a shelter operator may be fairly accurate in estimating typical nightly numbers of homeless persons in that shelter but not as knowledgeable about other shelter operators' experiences and even less so about the number of homeless people who live on the streets.[8]

In addition, if key persons are selected in some haphazard way from an equally haphazard sample of cities, even less credible national or state estimates will result. There may be an unwitting upward bias from using knowledgeable persons whose agencies have a stake in showing that the homelessness problem is "bigger than one would think" and hence worthy of increased support.

Partial Counts

The second approach relies on enumerations or surveys of some subset of the homeless population, usually one that is easily identified. Typical ex-

8. A homely example dramatically illustrates this point. My colleague Jim Wright and I walked from our hotel in Manhattan's midtown to the medical clinic for the homeless at St. Vincent's Hospital. When we arrived I remarked that we must have passed at least fifty homeless people on our walk. Jim responded that he had taken the trouble to count the seemingly homeless persons we encountered. There were fifteen. Besides proving that I am not very good at subliminal counting, the point is that unsystematic observation can lead to estimates that are wide of the mark.

Another illustration also shows how variable such key-person estimates may be: Hamilton, Rabinowitz and Alshuler, Inc. (1987) asked eight service providers in the Los Angeles Skid Row area to estimate the total homeless population in that fifty-block area. The estimates obtained were as follows: provider 1, 6,000 to 10,000; provider 2, 200,000; provider 3, 30,000; provider 4, 10,000; provider 5, 10,000; provider 6, 2,000 to 15,000.

amples of partial counts include surveys of persons in shelters, in the lines of soup kitchens, or at well-known gathering places for the homeless. These are partial counts because they clearly miss important components of the homeless population, usually those who do not use shelters and do not congregate in these other places.[9]

Partial counts may be conducted very systematically, providing a good basis for estimating the size of the subset in question, or they may be done carelessly, with little regard for proper sampling or interviewing practice. Among the best of the partial count surveys was one conducted in 1985 in the downtown Skid Row area of Los Angeles (Farr, Koegal, and Burnham 1986). The researchers undertook a systematic sample of persons sleeping in shelters, supplemented by samples of persons on food lines and in day shelters who did not use shelters for sleeping. The partial character of the Los Angeles survey is due to the intentional omission of the homeless found outside the overnight shelters, food lines, and day shelters in the Downtown area.[10]

Other partial counts have been far less systematic. Brian Hall (Freeman and Hall 1986) interviewed people who looked as if they were homeless because of their dress, their behavior, or their use of food kitchens. Aside from his dividing Manhattan into four districts and distributing his time among them, Hall's selection process can best be described as "catch-as-catch-can."

A final example of partial counting is the attempt by the Census Bureau during the 1980 census to undertake what was called a "casual count," presumably a description of its object, not its style. The census counted people residing in shelters and also sent enumerators into bus stations, all-night theaters, and other places where casuals (homeless persons) were likely to be found. The census never widely publicized the casual counts they undertook in sixteen cities, apparently not having enough confidence in their findings.[11]

These partial surveys may be far better than sheer guessing, but they are again of unknown validity for estimating purposes because the extent of bias is unknown. The main problem with partial counts is that no one knows what proportion of the total homeless population is being omitted or how frequently homeless persons use the places sampled.

Heroic Extrapolations from Partial Counts

Because some portions of the homeless population are more easily counted and interviewed, it is tempting to extrapolate from a partial count to the total

9. It is also likely that some homeless persons use such services more consistently than others. The less frequent users will tend to be underrepresented in any one sample.

10. Indeed, it is because of the partial nature of their survey that the authors made no attempt to estimate the total size of the homeless population either in their subset or for the city or county of Los Angeles.

11. Plans for the 1990 census constitute a considerable improvement. Shelters will be visited systematically in all places. In addition, congregating places for the homeless, as identified by local key persons, will be visited in the dead of night.

homeless population. Of course the validity of such estimates rests heavily on a valid relationship between a partial population and the total.

Perhaps the best known "heroic" extrapolation from shelter enumerations is that in the 1984 HUD report (HUD 1984). A national sample survey of shelters providing overnight housing to homeless persons was chosen in order to estimate the total shelter population of the United States.[12] The results were used to estimate the number of homeless people found in shelters on any given day (average of 69,000). Assuming that the sample was picked correctly, the resulting estimates are based on sound procedures.

To estimate the number of homeless people on the streets, HUD relied on shelter-to-street ratios derived from several sources: data from the 1980 census casual count and from four locally conducted studies (Phoenix, Boston, Pittsburgh, and Boston) in which separate counts were made of shelter and street homeless populations.

A more recent attempt to extrapolate based on street-to-shelter ratios was made by Freeman and Hall (1986). Using data from the interviews Hall conducted (described above), the authors used the proportion of nights the New York homeless spent in shelters to arrive at a street-to-shelter ratio, applying that ratio to the earlier HUD estimates of the homeless population in shelters, adjusted upward to take into account the growth in shelter population since 1983.

The main difficulty with such heroic extrapolations lies in the critical street-to-shelter ratio. There is extensive evidence that the ratio varies from city to city and has strong seasonal variations. The lowest ratio, 0.10, was found in Nashville and the highest, 2.73, in Phoenix. In the Chicago Homeless Study I conducted, the ratio was 1.44 in the milder weather of the fall survey but 0.35 in the winter survey. About the best that can be said of the recorded ratios is that none of them would sustain heroic extrapolations that could come anywhere near the estimates of 1 million seen frequently in the press.

"Windshield" Street Surveys and Censuses

Windshield surveys identify and count homeless persons by sight while canvassing streets and other open places in a city. They have been undertaken in Washington, D.C. (Robinson 1985) and in Boston (Boston Emergency

---

12. A two-stage sampling plan was used: first, selecting a sample of metropolitan areas to represent all metropolitan areas in the nation; second, selecting a sample of shelters to represent the universe of shelters in metropolitan areas. Briefly, the first stage sampled 60 out of the 394 Rand McNally metropolitan areas (RMAs) over 50,000 in population, each city being chosen with probability in proportion to the size of the RMA in which it was embedded. In the second sampling stage, the shelters in each of the 60 sampled places were listed and then sampled, also with probability proportionate to shelter size. The 60 sampled cities contained 679 shelters out of an estimated 1,811 nationwide. The desired sample size was 200. Thirty-eight shelters were selected with certainty (capacities of over 200 persons per night, or weighted shelter capacities of over 300 persons); the total number of shelters in the sample was 206.

Shelter Commission 1984). (Both studies actually included shelter, hospital, and jail counts as well in arriving at their estimates of the total homeless population.)

In the Washington, D.C., study teams of researchers, each assigned an area of the city, drove through at night counting everyone they saw who appeared to be homeless. These counts were adjusted for missing persons (the "hidden homeless")[13] to arrive at an overall enumeration of persons homeless in the city on the night of 31 July 1985. Similar procedures were used to count homeless persons in Boston.

Windshield surveys have some very attractive features—they are relatively inexpensive and bypass the communication problem. However, there are also drawbacks. First, because there is no communication between the enumerators and the homeless, only the most obvious demographic features—gender and race—can be reliably recorded, and in some cases even those may be ambiguous. Second they are biased to the extent that homeless persons are not out in plain sight. (In all fairness to the Washington study, the researchers did attempt to adjust for this bias, as discussed in the note 13.) Finally, windshield surveys are subject to severe identification difficulties: it is not at all clear that homeless persons can always be identified by their appearance or that people with homes never resemble them. As I will show in chapter 4, many of the Chicago homeless were neat and clean, and most were not sleeping when we encountered them on the street or in public places. Granted that homeless persons who match the common stereotype would likely be correctly identified and counted, the proportions of those with homes incorrectly counted as homeless and vice-versa are unknown and possibly large.

Adaptations of Area Probability Designs

The last approach modifies conventional survey designs to take into account the special obstacles in studying the homeless, described earlier in this chapter. As I said before, conventional surveys and censuses are based on strategies designed to draw unbiased samples of dwellings. The modifications need to draw unbiased samples of nondwellings—shelter for the homeless and locations on the streets and in public places where the homeless can be found.

---

13. The adjustment took into account the findings of an intensive count of the "hidden homeless" undertaken in two areas in ward 1 by one of the twenty-nine teams. (Ward 1 is close to the central business district of downtown Washington and is a place where many homeless people congregate.) The team was composed of an experienced social worker, a policeman in plain clothes, and two shelter residents. The shelter-resident assistants led the team to such places as vacant buildings, parking garages, and rooftops. The assistants reported that 280 homeless people were spending the night in these areas. The intensive examination searching for the "hidden homeless" yielded an estimate of the homeless for ward 1 considerably greater than the count obtained by the unaided observer team. The researchers proceeded to make citywide adjustments based on the intensive count. The ratio of 1:2.5 open homeless to concealed homeless was used to extrapolate to a citywide estimate of 1,785 concealed homeless.

So far the only study that has employed a sampling strategy covering both the sheltered and the street homeless in a major city is the Chicago Homeless Study, which I conducted (Rossi, Fisher, and Willis 1986). A Los Angeles study (Hamilton, Rabinowitz and Alshuler, Inc. 1987) sampled the street homeless in 1986, using a very similar approach in the fifty-block area that constitutes that city's traditional Skid Row.

The Chicago Homeless Study was conducted under a program jointly initiated by the Robert Wood Johnson Foundation and the Pew Memorial Trust that provided grants to support medical clinics for the homeless in nineteen cities throughout the country. Any assessment of those city projects was badly handicapped by the absence of firm information on the characteristics of the intended client group. In 1984 there were a few studies of the homeless, but each was flawed to some major degree by the absence of a technically acceptable plan for sampling and interviewing. At the time, we had too little background information about the homeless to judge the coverage and adequacy of the Johnson-Pew clinics. Furthermore, the conventional social research approaches were patently inappropriate. For example, most methods used in the quantitative study of modern societies assume that people can be enumerated and sampled within their customary dwelling units, an assumption that fails by definition in any study of the literally homeless.

The foundations asked the Social and Demographic Research Institute at the University of Massachusetts to design a survey that would come as close as possible to fulfilling the technical demands of sampling theory, producing an unbiased sample of homeless persons. The strategy we proposed departed from the traditional approach in that persons were to be sample apart from dwelling units and interviews were to be conducted at times when the separation between those with homes and the homeless would be at a maximum. We also proposed that the foundations support a demonstration survey that would show the feasibility of the proposed approach and the costs involved. Chicago was suggested as a site because a major survey research organization, NORC: A Social Science Research Center,[14] was situated at the University of Chicago and because the Illinois Department of Public Aid was willing to supply additional funds. The foundations agreed to this proposal, jointly providing the funds to test the plans we had drawn up. (A fuller description of the Chicago Homeless Study is found in appendix B.)

We defined our target population as residents of the city of Chicago who did not rent or own (or have rights of customary access to) a conventional dwell-

14. NORC staff had independently been developing plans very similar to those devised at the Social and Demographic Research Institute (SADRI). Indeed, the final study design and fieldwork strategy were as much a product of the NORC staff as of my own work. Principal contributors on the NORC staff include Martin Frankel, who worked out the final sample design, Mary Utne O'Brien, who worked out an effective fieldwork strategy, and Sara Siegal Loevy and Ann-Sofi Roden, who skillfully managed the very difficult fieldwork operation.

ing unit—an apartment, a house, a mobile home, or a room or rooms in a hotel, an SRO, or a rooming house. Our definition was meant to cover the "literally homeless," which did not include those who were doubled up, living in inadequate quarters, or resident in hospitals, jails, or prisons. In relation to a conventional sampling frame, the one used in this study is like a photographic negative—it taps places that are *not* dwellings.

Our survey divided the homeless universe into two portions, each the subject of a separate survey operation:

1. The sheltered homeless were surveyed in a sample of shelters meant primarily for homeless persons, each chosen with probability proportionate to shelter size. To draw the shelter sample we enumerated the total universe of shelters, using local agency lists and asking experts to establish their inclusiveness. Within each sample of shelters, we took a systematic sample of shelter residents, amounting to an overall one-in-three sampling ratio. Interviewing in the sampled shelters was undertaken in the evening after their clients had signed up for beds or in the morning before they left for the day. On the night of interviewing, NORC staff members collected rosters of residents from shelter operators and systematically sampled those rosters. The sample of shelter residents constitutes a probability sample of persons using the shelters on the nights when interviewing took place.[15]

2. The street homeless were surveyed by searching a probability-based sample of Chicago blocks as defined by census conventions. In each of the blocks chosen, nonresidential areas were searched by NORC staff, who interviewed each person encountered using a short screening questionnaire to determine whether that person was homeless. Those who were homeless were interviewed further, using the same twenty-minute schedule employed for shelter residents.

To make the sample of blocks more efficient, the 19,400 blocks of Chicago were grouped into strata based on the number of homeless persons one could expect to find there in the dead of night. We obtained what we hoped were expert ratings of the expected numbers from persons who were concerned with the issue and whose working routines led them to cover the entire city in detail. There are just a handful of such wide-coverage organizations—the police and fire departments and some of the public utilities. After some high-level negotiation, NORC was able to obtain the cooperation of the Chicago Police Department. In each precinct the community relations officer, in consultation with patrol officers, classified each block in the precinct into one of

---

15. We took it for granted that all persons sleeping in the shelters were homeless, that is, that none had customary access to a conventional dwelling unit, at least on the night they were at the shelter. Unfortunately we should have tested that assumption, however reasonable it may have appeared. NORC interviewers learned from two or three shelter residents who were interviewed that they also rented quarters elsewhere but stayed in the shelters on the survey night because of quarrels with fellow residents or for some other reason.

three strata, defined by the expected density of homeless people. This massive task grouped the blocks of Chicago into three categories: high, medium, and low probability of finding homeless persons there.

The stratification was reviewed by several groups of experts, including the staff of the Chicago Planning Department and members of the Chicago Coalition for the Homeless, primarily to determine whether the high-density blocks were chosen correctly. We then added other blocks and deleted some the police had classified as high density. Random samples of blocks were then drawn from each of these three strata, chosen randomly with probabilities proportionate to the expected numbers of homeless persons in each of the three strata.[16]

To minimize the identification problem, the street survey was undertaken between 1:00 A.M. and 6:00 A.M., when the separation between the domiciled and the street homeless would be at a maximum, hence enhancing the probability that those encountered would be homeless. Even so, of the 607 persons encountered on the streets, fewer than one in ten (9%) were determined to be homeless.

To respond to the problem of the "hidden homeless," the interviewer teams were instructed to search every nonresidential place on each sampled block, defined as any area one could enter without encountering a locked door or its social equivalent. ("Social equivalents" included managers of all-night restaurants, security guards, and so on.) Places that were routinely searched included streets and sidewalks, alleys, doorways, hallways, garages, abandoned buildings, and open basements or roofs. In addition, interviewers were to examine parked cars, trucks, boxcars, dumpsters, packing cases—in short, anything that could contain a person.[17]

Chicago (or any other city) is not safe in the dead of night. To protect our interviewers, we hired off-duty policemen to escort them on their rounds of the streets and shelters.[18] The interviewers operated in teams of two, each accompanied by two off-duty policemen (in plain clothes but carrying their police revolvers, as required by law). The police advised the interviewers on any safety measures to be taken, and they preceded them into any building.[19]

To compensate people for the time spent in interviews and to increase coop-

16. In other words, we chose high-density blocks with a higher sampling ratio than those used for the lower-density blocks. Technically this strategy should reduce the sampling variance and hence lead to lower standard errors than would a random sample of blocks. An additional benefit was that we were able to interview more homeless persons and thereby enrich our description of their characteristics and condition.

17. Although we were apprehensive about waking people up, most of those encountered during these searches were awake and either sitting or in motion (see chap. 4). In the few cases when we had to arouse people, we took great care not to frighten or upset them.

18. Incidentally, the physical danger to interviewers was presented not by the homeless but by the nighttime predators found in the same areas.

19. Fortunately we had no incidents where the policemen had to intervene to protect the interviewers. Apparently their presence was enough to discourage predators. The police were also entrusted with judging whether it was prudent to enter any building. That prerogative was exer-

eration, we paid each person screened on the streets $1. If the longer interview followed, we paid another $4—a total of $5 for a complete interview. Shelter residents also were paid $5.

A good deal of effort went into measuring how long those interviewed had been homeless and whether they had been homeless before. In addition, the twenty-minute interview covered a variety of other topics that will be discussed in the chapters to follow.

The one other recent survey of the homeless that also used a probability sampling strategy, explicitly modeled after the Chicago Homeless Study, was a 1986 survey of the fifty-square-block Skid Row area in downtown Los Angeles (Hamilton, Rabinowitz and Alschuler, Inc. 1987). Because it concerned only a few square miles of the total Los Angeles area, it must be considered a "partial survey." All the shelters in the Los Angeles Skid Row section were approached; counts of residents were taken, and a sample of residents was interviewed with a short questionnaire. In addition, a sample of "block faces" (one side of a block) was drawn randomly. Teams of interviewers accompanied by off-duty Los Angeles policemen searched the block faces in the dead of night. Respondents were paid $2 for answering the questions on the interview schedule.

The initial plan for the Chicago Homeless Study was to undertake three surveys at different seasons over the year, so we could investigate seasonal differences in homelessness and collect enough observations over time to estimate the flow of persons into and out of the literally homeless state.[20] Unfortunately, each of the surveys turned out to be more expensive than anticipated,[21] and we were not able to conduct one during the summer. We did do a fall survey over a two-week period spanning 1 October 1985, and a two-week winter survey spanning 1 February 1986.

The Preferred Approach to Studying the Homeless

The five approaches described above vary considerably in cost and also in credibility—how far social researchers would rely on the results. Unfortu-

cised only once, when the police escort made the decision not to enter a high-rise public housing project of national notoriety that fell into our block sample.

20. We originally planned to base some of our population estimates on a "capture/recapture" strategy, using the overlap among persons sampled at different times to estimate the total size of the population in question. Using "capture/recapture" information from three independently drawn samples, one can also estimate with greater precision the flow into and out of the population.

21. Funds were obtained through grants from the Robert Wood Johnson Foundation, the Pew Memorial Trust, and the Illinois Department of Public Aid. NORC spent approximately $450,000 on the fieldwork, and SADRI an additional $130,000 to support the direction of the study and the analysis of the resulting data. NORC expenditures included much of the development work involved in devising approaches to shelters and to the stratification of blocks. Given that designing a new study would be made considerably easier by experience gained in Chicago, comparable studies could be undertaken in other cities for between $100,000 and $200,000 (in 1988 dollars).

nately, these two characteristics are strongly correlated: the most credible approaches are also the most expensive. In addition, within each approach there are alternative ways to proceed that affect both credibility and cost.

Also, the opinions of social scientists do not necessarily rule in judging research. The least credible (to social researchers) of the national estimates of the size for the homeless population are those advanced by the National Coalition for the Homeless. Yet these estimates are the ones most cited in the mass media and by legislative bodies.

On scientific grounds there can be no question that the modified area probability strategy employed in the Chicago Homeless Study is the preferred approach to estimating the homeless population in any jurisdiction. The strategy resolves most of the technical difficulties described earlier. To the extent that the problem of the hidden homeless can be addressed, it does so. Identification is possible through face-to-face screening. And so on. Of course no research strategy can obviate the definitional issue: about the best one can do is to be clear and explicit about the definition used. But the most important positive feature is that the estimates derived from this strategy are based on sampling theory and thus have a rational foundation. Another important feature is that the approach is general and not confined to any particular locale. (In a later section, I shall propose extending the strategy to support national estimates of the homeless.)

Estimating the Chicago Homeless Population

One of our major goals was to estimate the average nightly prevalence of homelessness for each of the two seasons involved. Another was to estimate incidence and prevalence over a longer period. The first goal was easier to achieve, requiring only a straight projection of the average number of homeless persons found on the blocks we searched plus the count of those in the shelters. Since the fieldwork lasted about ten nights in each survey, we had to subtract any overlap that might have occurred because a person interviewed in one shelter on one night could have been found in another shelter or on the street on some other night.[22] In fact there was some overlap, mainly among shelters, as was to be expected.

Using just the sample counts consisting of two sets, one for each of the two surveys, we calculated unbiased estimates of the average nightly sizes of the literally homeless populations of Chicago, as shown in table 3.1. Note the much larger standard errors for the fall 1985 sample, in which we did not have a large enough sample of blocks to counter the heterogeneity of block estimates. The winter 1986 block sample is considerably larger, with correspondingly smaller standard errors.

---

22. Homeless persons interviewed were identified by Social Security numbers, names, and date of birth, information obtained in the interview.

Chicago Prevalence and Incidence Estimates for 1985 and 1986

The size of a transient population such as the homeless needs to be described in a variety of ways that together are more fully descriptive. From some points of view the "point prevalence" of homelessness—the number of persons found homeless on any given night—is of greatest interest, measuring as it does the daily potential demand for shelter and other services. But other prevalence measures based on different periods may also be relevant. For example, annual prevalence measures consist of the unduplicated number of persons who are homeless over the period of a year. Measures of incidence, the number of persons who become homeless over a given period, indicate turnover in the population, especially in conjunction with the prevalence measures discussed earlier. The two Chicago surveys formed the basis for estimates of all three kinds.

Table 3.1 presents the point prevalence estimates from each of the two surveys. The two nightly prevalence estimates were close in size, 2,344 derived from the fall survey and 2,020 from the winter survey. Given the standard errors involved, it is safe to say that the number of literally homeless persons in Chicago was somewhere between 1,600 and 3,000 and most likely was about 2,300.

When first released in August 1986, these average point or nightly prevalence estimates were greeted with dismay by advocates for the homeless in Chicago (Rossi 1987). In their discussions with the press and public officials, they had been fixing the size of the city's homeless population between 15,000

Table 3.1   Fall 1985 and Winter 1986 Point Prevalence Estimates of the Chicago Homeless Population

Survey Component	Estimate	Standard Error
A. Fall 1985 Estimates (22 September to 4 October 1985)		
Shelter residents	961	±13
On streets or in public places	1,383	±735
Total homeless	2,344	±735
Range ± 1 SE = 1,609–3,079		
B. Winter 1986 Estimates (22 February to 7 March 1986)		
Shelter residents	1,492	±55
On streets or in public places	528	±269
Total homeless	2,020	±275
Range ± 1 SE = 1,745–2,295		

Note: Point prevalence estimates are the average daily number of persons homeless during the relevant survey period.

Table 3.2   Fall and Winter Annual Chicago Homelessness Incidence and Prevalence Estimates

	Estimate	Standard Error
A. Annual Incidence (Number of Persons Newly Homeless Each Year)		
Fall 1985[a]		
Method alpha[b] (conservative)	5,907	±1,852
Method beta[c] (liberal)	2,953	±926
Winter 1986[a]		
Method alpha[b] (conservative)	3,719	±475
Method beta[c] (liberal)	3,752	±479
B. Annual Prevalence (Number of Persons Ever Homeless in a Year)		
Fall 1985[a]		
Method alpha[b] (conservative)	6,962	±1,881
Method beta[c] (liberal)	4,624	±1,064
Winter 1986[a]		
Method alpha[b] (conservative)	5,051	±505
Method beta[c] (liberal)	5,147	±511

[a] Annual estimates were made using data on reported lengths of time currently homeless obtained in interviews. These estimates assume that the population is stationary and that there are no multiple entries into the homeless state during a year.
[b] Estimates made using only data from street and shelter sample cases.
[c] Estimates made using all data, including pretests and extrasample interviews.

and 25,000. When challenged on these counts, the advocates typically referred to the 1984 HUD report that reported much the same estimates. The estimates shown in table 3.1 are many magnitudes smaller than the lowest prevailing ones. Advocates were concerned that our figures would undermine their efforts to obtain more funds and support for the homeless in Chicago.[23]

Estimating annual incidence and prevalence, as shown in table 3.2, was much more difficult, requiring knowledge of the annual turnover of the Chicago homeless population. From interview data on the length of each person's current episode of homelessness, we could plot the distribution of time homeless and thus estimate the annual flows into and out of the homeless population.

Data on the length of time homeless in the current episode are not the best basis for such estimates, because this episode of homelessness had not yet been completed. Furthermore, we quickly realized (but too late to change the questionnaire) that this measure was too coarse: many short-term homeless persons averaged a week or two homeless but the shortest time the measure could detect was one month. Compensating to some degree for errors of measurement in time homeless was that the population in total appeared to be stationary from survey to survey, which simplified estimates of inflow and

23. Of course, citing the 1984 HUD report was more than a little disingenuous, since it had simply printed the estimates given to HUD by the key informants interviewed in Chicago, possibly the advocates themselves.

outflow by constraining them to be identical. Depending on which of the several equally convincing assumptions one makes about the shape of the distribution of time homeless, we arrived at a "family" of annual prevalence estimates that ranged 3,000 to 4,000 around the annual prevalence estimates shown in table 3.2. (Greater details on the prevalence estimation procedures used are given in appendix B.)

Mindful that homeless persons move into and out of institutions fairly frequently and that estimates based on the number of persons in shelters and on the streets necessarily omit this institutionalized component, we also tried to estimate the number of homeless persons in prisons or jails, in hospitals, or temporarily living in conventional dwellings. These estimates were also based on information gathered in the questionnaires. For example, we asked the respondents where they spent each of the seven nights before the interview, providing the basis for estimating how many persons ordinarily homeless were temporarily domiciled. The estimates for institutionalized homeless people were more shaky, resting on the proportions who reported ever being in prison or jail or hospitalized. The resulting figures are shown in table 3.3. In summary, our final estimates were as follows:

Average nightly number of Chicago homeless	2,020 to 2,722
Estimated annual number ever homeless	4,624 to 6,962

Estimates for Washington, D.C., and Boston

Estimates based on windshield counts were conducted in two other cities (Boston Emergency Shelter Commission 1984; Robinson 1985). In Boston and the District of Columbia, observers were sent out on a systematic search of every street, with the mission to count the numbers of homeless persons encountered. The numbers present in shelters on the same nights were also obtained. In Boston on the night of 27 October 1983, a total of 2,767 persons either were in shelters or appeared homeless on the streets and in public places. The comparable number of homeless found in the District was

Table 3.3 Combined Total Point Prevalence Estimate of the Chicago Homeless Population

Average of fall 1985 and winter 1986 estimates	2,182
Average number of homeless dependent children	273
Average in temporary homes[a]	42
Average institutionalized homeless[b]	80
Average homeless in excluded shelters[c]	145
Estimated grand total of Chicago homeless	2,722

[a] Based on proportion of time that homeless persons interviewed claimed they spent in rented rooms or in the dwellings of others.

[b] Based on hospitalization rates of the homeless.

[c] Based on counts of available beds in shelters excluded from the sample because they were primarily shelters for special persons other than the homeless. Includes shelters for battered women, the physically disabled, and so on.

2,562 on the night of 31 July 1985 and was 6,454 when adjusted to take into account the homeless who had sought shelter in places not observable from the streets.[24]

Both these windshield surveys suffer from the limitations of that approach described earlier. It is difficult to judge whether these limitations lead to systematic under- or overreporting. On the one hand, the windshield observers may have missed persons who did not "appear" to be homeless, and on the other, some domiciled persons who looked like the homeless may have been included. In any event, both counts are far below the highest estimates for those cities given in the HUD 1984 report, as gathered by interviewing key persons in those cities—8,000 for Boston and 10,000 for the District—and are slightly higher than the lowest estimates that HUD reported as gathered from key persons in those cities.

National "Estimates" of Homelessness

Almost all items in the popular press cite one estimate or another of the size of the homeless population of the country. Most of the estimates can be traced to one of three sources: the 1984 HUD report on homelessness (HUD 1984), estimates given by national spokespersons of the advocates for the homeless, and estimates prepared by Richard Freeman of the National Bureau of Economic Research (Freeman and Hall 1986). Seemingly, no other source has been bold (or foolhardy) enough to venture into the dangerous waters of national estimation.

Among the citations most frequently encountered is a 1986 estimate of from 2 to 3 million homeless in the United States, whose ultimate source appears to be the Community on Creative Non-Violence. Almost as frequently cited are the considerably lower estimates produced by a Housing and Urban Development task force (HUD 1984). Somewhat less frequently encountered are references to Freeman's estimates.

It is important to keep firmly in mind that there have been no direct counts of homeless persons on a national scale, accomplished by conducting either a census or a sample survey. Accordingly, every national estimate issued to date is based on local estimates, usually from key persons, employing more or less arguable assumptions about how to compile and properly "adjust" them.

In the case of the most widely quoted set of estimates, it is not possible to obtain detailed information on how the calculations were made. The Community on Creative Non-Violence has been distressingly vague in print about how it arrived at its figures. For example, in an earlier report issued by the Community (Hombs and Snyder 1982) the authors note that they based their estimates on information received from "more than 100 agencies and organizations in 25 cities and states. . . . It is as accurate an estimate as anyone in the country could offer, yet it lacks absolute statistical certainty" (p. xvi).

24. See the section on windshield surveys for a description of how this adjustment was made.

They go on to speculate that during 1983 the number of homeless people could reach "three million or more." Subsequent estimates have cited even larger numbers. The authors did not give any details on what information they received from the agencies and organizations and on the distribution of those agencies throughout the United States. Presumably the local figures were compiled in some way and then weighted to produce national estimates. Of course, whether such estimates are worth any attention depends heavily on the validity of the compiling and weighting, procedures that are simply unknown.

The HUD report also relies on information collected from other sources, but it provides specifics on the four approaches used for arriving at estimates. I will describe these four approaches in some detail, because each is typical of approaches used in other studies that do not rely on direct counts.

The first approach involved extrapolating to the nation as a whole from the highest published estimates of the local homeless that claimed to be the total number homeless at one time. No effort was made to assess the accuracy of the estimates used. To calculate the rates of homelessness in thirty-seven cities from which published estimates were available, HUD summed the figures for all the cities involved and divided that sum by the total metropolitan population in those areas.

It should be noted that Rand McNally Metropolitan Areas (RMAs) were the basis for the overall population figures. RMAs consist of an urban center— usually a city of 50,000 or over—plus adjacent urbanized townships and localities.[25] Dividing the RMA population bases into the number of homeless leads to HUD's estimate of a national overall homeless rate of 0.0025 (or 25 homeless persons for each 10,000 Americans). Extrapolating from this rate to the entire nation yields a figure of 586,000 homeless.

The authors of the HUD report characterize the result as an outside estimate because of the means used to calculate it. There are several reasons for believing it is an overestimate. First, published local estimates are likely to come from areas where homelessness is more severe and are less likely for cities with few homeless people. Second, the local estimates are not evaluated as to their ultimate source: the mass media show no particular tendency to publish only verifiable estimates. Finally, the procedure assumes there is a constant rate of homelessness in cities and rural counties, which HUD argues later in the report is not so.

The second approach HUD used attempted to obtain local estimates more systematically by gathering them from local experts in a national sample of

25. This is in contrast to the following alternatives that could have been used by HUD: (1) standard metropolitan statistical areas, consisting of a central urban place of 50,000 or more, plus adjacent urbanized counties. SMSAs tend to be larger areas than RMAs because they include largely rural parts of the adjacent counties. (2) Central city population counts, based on the assumption that the homeless to be found in, say, Boston are largely drawn from among the domiciled within that city. The choice of RMAs as the base for HUD's calculation of homelessness rates has been the focus of considerable criticism.

metropolitan areas and assessing their accuracy. Because I discussed this approach earlier in this chapter, I will not describe it in detail here. This key-persons approach led to an estimate of 254,000 homeless people in the nation, rural and urban areas combined.

The third approach arrived at a national estimate by extrapolating from estimates of the local homeless given by shelter operators as key persons selected in a national shelter survey. The figures gathered from the shelter operators were not assessed for accuracy but were accepted as given. By extrapolating from these estimates, HUD came up with a national figure of 309,000 for all metropolitan areas. The 44,000 estimate for the rural homeless derived from the second approach was then added, giving an overall national estimate of 353,000, represented as the average number homeless on any given night during the winter of 1984 (December 1983 and January 1984).

The fourth approach arrived at a national figure by estimating the number of homeless people in shelters and the number on the streets and summing the two. The results from the national shelter survey were used to estimate the number of homeless people found in shelters on any given day (average of 69,000). This 69,000 figure combined both metropolitan and rural shelter populations. In arriving at the number of homeless people on the streets, HUD used estimates from two sources—the 1980 census casual count and three local studies (Phoenix, Pittsburgh, and Boston)[26] in which separate counts were made of shelter and street homeless populations.

The casual count undertaken by the Census Bureau in 1980[27] was an attempt to count transients on the streets or in other public/private places where they congregate. The count took place in only some census districts; HUD extrapolated from the census figure of 23,237 (based on counts covering cities comprising 12% of the United States population) to a total figure of 166,000 homeless in the nation. They adjusted this figure both upward to account for changes since the census was taken and downward to adjust for large-city bias in the casual count. The final adjusted estimate from extrapolating from the casual count was 198,000.

The second method HUD used to estimate the total number of homeless on the streets nationwide was to extrapolate from three local studies of street and shelter counts, apparently undertaken in systematic ways during mild weather when the homeless were more likely to be on the streets. HUD calculated an average ratio of 1.78 of homeless people on the streets to those in shelters based on these three studies. Using the 69,000 figure for the homeless in shelters, HUD estimated the total number of street people at 123,000. Depending on whether the estimate for street people is taken from the casual count ex-

---

26. It is difficult to regard the Phoenix and Pittsburgh studies as on the same level of quality as the Boston windshield study. In neither Pittsburgh nor Phoenix did the researchers attempt to seek out street homeless in every possible location; they looked only in selected spots—food kitchens, shantytowns, bus stations, and the like.

27. United States Department of Commerce, Bureau of the Census (1984).

trapolation or the extrapolation from the three studies, figures for the total homeless population in 1983 range from 192,00 to 267,000. The range of estimates derived from the four approaches is 192,000 to 586,000. The HUD report (p. 19) concluded that the most reliable estimate for the number of homeless people in the nation on an average night during December 1983 or January 1984 was 250,000 to 350,000.

To sum up, three of the methods—extrapolation from highest published estimates, extrapolation from estimates obtained from local interviews in a national sample of sixty metropolitan areas, and extrapolation from estimates by a national sample of shelter operators—do not deal with actual counts. The fourth approach is the only one that estimates from actual counts of those in shelters and on the streets nationwide. As HUD points out, the shelter-count population was based on a national probability sample and the street count was done by the United States Census Bureau in a nonrandom sample of cities.

Although the HUD report provided more information on how its estimates were calculated and in that sense produced considerably more credible figures than those of the Community on Creative Non-Violence, some of the necessary assumptions stretch that credibility quite thin. The first HUD approach uses unevaluated estimates that simply "happen" to exist. The second approach is somewhat better in that local estimates were solicited in a systematic way, but there was no systematic assessment of the "expert opinions" used.

The third approach simply restricts the opinions solicited to a single type of source, shelter operators, whose guesses about the total number of homeless people in their cities may be better than anyone else's but are still of unknown accuracy.

Finally, the fourth approach makes the simplifying assumption that the ratio of street homeless to shelter homeless is uniform across cities and across seasons. As we will see in chapter 4, the street-to-shelter ratio is highly affected by the season, although the total Chicago homeless population is not. Our findings cast considerable doubt on the use of ratios from any set of cities.

The final national estimates to be discussed are those produced by Richard Freeman of the National Bureau of Economic Research (Freeman and Hall 1986). Although somewhat more sophisticated technically, Freeman's work can be regarded as an extension of the fourth HUD approach, as described above. Using somewhat different estimates of the street-to-shelter ratio, he applied those estimates to the 1983 shelter population, adjusted for an assumed growth in the latter, to come up with national estimate of 254,000 homeless persons in 1986. In a more recent unpublished paper Freeman (1988) suggests that the 1988 national totals may be as high as 500,000, given the average increases reported in the sheltered homeless counts over the years since the 1984 HUD report.

Although the national estimates discussed in this section all leave much to be desired, they can serve as the basis for at least roughly limning out the magnitude of the national homeless population. The firmest figures are those for the portion of the homeless housed nightly in emergency shelters, numbering about 100,000 in 1984. Depending on which estimate of the street-to-shelter ratio is chosen, the street homeless are at least equal in number to the shelter homeless and likely closer to double. Hence, based on available information and reasonable assumptions, the most believable national estimate is that at least 300,000 people are homeless each night in this country, and possibly as many as 400,000 to 500,000 if one accepts growth rates in the past few years of between 10% and 20%.

The discrepancy between the estimates of the last paragraph and the often-cited 2 to 3 million deserves some comment. Given the information available, there are no grounds whatever for regarding the higher estimates as valid. On some level it is surely strange that guesstimates of the sort issued by local advocate groups and the Community on Creative Non-Violence should be cited repeatedly in the press as serious and valid calculations. Although one must sympathize with the journalists' strong need to have some idea of the size of the homeless population and its growth trends, it is difficult to have the same feelings toward their need for ever more sensational figures.

The Case for a National Probability Survey of Homelessness

There is no way to settle how many homeless persons there may be in the United States without making a major data-gathering effort. A strategy for doing so is presented in this section. But there is also a sense in which the issue is moot—no additional evidence or greater precision is needed to establish that homelessness is a serious social problem in our country. However, the argument for a national survey of homelessness is persuasive on other grounds.

The main reason for more precise estimates is that we need the information to design appropriate ameliorative social programs. We need not only size estimates but also data on the composition and location of the homeless population. Both kinds of data can be obtained in the same research operation, much as the decennial census provides information on the size of the American population and also on its composition and geographical dispersion.

The strategy used in the Chicago Homeless Study can be extended to provide the necessary information. In rough outline, the extension would proceed along the following lines. First, a national sample of local areas would be obtained. Using conventional area sampling methods, the strategy would call for a first-stage sampling of counties with probabilities proportionate to population size. The resulting sample would consist of about one hundred counties, whose combined populations would mirror the population of the United States. Note that the strategy of picking counties with probability proportionate to their size usually means that all the largest urban counties—such as Manhattan, Cook, and Los Angeles—would fall into the sample. Any sparsely populated rural county, in contrast, would have a very small chance of being selected.

Second, the counties so chosen would be approached using the subsampling method developed in Chicago. Lists of shelters for the homeless would be collected for each county, shelters would be sampled, and enumerations of shelter inhabitants would be undertaken, along with interviews of samples of shelter clients. The shelter samples, properly projected, would provide unbiased estimates of the number of homeless people who use shelters. Since the objective is to make national, not local, estimates, proportionately fewer shelters would be selected in each county.[28]

The unsheltered homeless would be enumerated by developing samples of small areas within each of the counties, stratified according to informed knowledge concerning the usual haunts of the street homeless. Each of the areas chosen in the sample would be searched, as in the Chicago Homeless Study, and interviews obtained from a sample of the homeless persons encountered. In Chicago we chose several hundred blocks to search: in the national survey the county subarea samples would be much smaller, although many more blocks or comparable areas would be studied all told.

Finally, combining the national shelter sample and the national street sample would provide the basis for firm and precise national estimates of the homeless population. In addition, interview data could be used to develop rich descriptions of the homeless.

Of course this rough sketch of a national study of the homeless skips over several serious fiscal and technical obstacles. First of all, the survey would be expensive. Collecting the data necessary for drawing the subsamples of shelters and of subareas within counties would be a tedious, labor-intensive task. Searches for the street homeless would also consume considerable resources. In current (1988) dollars, it is likely that such a survey would cost close to $10 million. Second, the homeless populations in small cities may not be as concentrated in locations as in a large city like Chicago, requiring technical adjustments in sampling that cannot be fully anticipated in advance.

I believe the main advantages to be gained from launching a national survey effort are as follows. First, we need firm data on the size and composition of the homeless population in order to make decisions on the size and character of the social programs necessary to ameliorate the problem of homelessness. Second, the national survey would establish a set of baseline measures against which to assess the progress of such programs. The final goal of any national program is to reduce the prevalence of homelessness. As someone has put it, "If you don't know where you've been, you can't tell how far you've gone." Second, programs have to be tailored to the diversity of the homeless popula-

28. Indeed, in largely rural counties no shelters may be found at all.

tion. The next few chapters provide ample evidence that the problems of the homeless are multiple, with different needs found among identifiable subgroups. Finally, without the information obtainable from a national survey, it is hard to achieve a firm intellectual understanding of the problem.

Measuring Extreme Poverty

In contrast to the lack of almost any estimates, good or bad, of the national homeless population, poverty and unemployment are measured routinely and richly. Indeed, the monthly briefing of the Bureau of Labor Statistics at which the previous month's unemployment rate is made public provokes comments in all the daily media and often by the president and congressional leaders. Similarly, the annual release of the previous year's poverty rate is a media event that receives wide coverage and evokes considerable comment.

Poverty and unemployment currently are fairly well measured. The statistical series were initially constructed by highly competent social scientists on the staffs of federal agencies and have undergone improvement after improvement since they were established in the 1940s and 1960s. The actual data collection is undertaken by the Bureau of the Census, an agency that is widely respected for both its technical competence and the absence of political partisanship.

The unemployment rates are based on the Monthly Labor Force Survey, a quasi-longitudinal national household survey conducted by the Bureau of the Census. The survey charts the month-to-month movement of national unemployment rates and provides considerable detail on the distribution of unemployment by regions, for urban and rural areas, and by subgroups of the American population.

The annual March supplement to the Monthly Labor Force Survey (called the Current Population Survey) measures (among other things) how many American households fall at or below the "poverty level," a set of income boundary points established initially in 1968 (revised annually to reflect changes in basic commodity prices and in the value of the dollar)[29] that divides poor from nonpoor households and families. The "poverty line" was based on estimates of the income needed to maintain households of various sizes at a minimum standard of living.

Both the unemployment and the poverty indicators are oriented to households, not individuals, being based on data obtained from large samples of households living in conventional housing units.[30] Individuals living in such

29. The Monthly Labor Force Survey and the Current Population Survey are based on the same data. Income and occupation of a large sample of households (over 55,000) are gathered every March, and the households are queried monthly throughout the year on the employment status of each adult in them. One-quarter of the households are replaced every three months, each household remaining in the sample for a full year.

30. Households and individuals living in houses or apartments or other structures ordinarily used as dwellings are covered in the sample. Persons living in "temporary quarters" such as

conventional housing are covered, but the surveys pass over many of the people we are concerned with here, especially those living in hotels, boarding-houses, and emergency shelters. And of course homeless people living on the streets are also not included. To be technically precise, our national unemployment and poverty statistics pertain only to that portion of the domiciled population that lives in conventional housing.

The appropriateness of the definitions used in measuring unemployment and poverty have been questioned by many on other grounds as well. The unemployment rate is defined as the percentage of persons in the labor force who are unemployed.[31] Anyone not currently employed who is not looking for work is classified as "out of the labor force," a category initially set up to account for housewives, the disabled, and retired persons. One of the controversies over the unemployment rate concerns whether "discouraged workers" should be counted as unemployed. Discouraged workers have been unemployed for long periods and have become so disheartened in their futile job searches that they no longer look for work. Under current rules such persons are classified as out of the labor force along with persons who are "keeping house," retired, or disabled and therefore are not counted as unemployed.[32] Those questioning this classification rule claim it results in underestimations of the "true" number unemployed. In addition, the line between "looking for work" and "not looking for work" is not clear, especially when based on reports from third parties.[33]

From the viewpoint of the central interests of this book, there is considerable merit in this criticism of the current measurement of unemployment. As I will show in the next chapter, research has found that significant proportions of the domiciled extremely poor and of homeless persons were not looking for work and hence are not counted among the unemployed.

The measurement of poverty is even more controversial. Current measurement counts as income any earnings from employment, income transfers in monetary form (such as AFDC benefits and retirement pensions), and other sources (such as rent and interest). Omitted from current income are in-kind transfers such as food stamps, rent subsidies, and Medicare or Medicaid payments. Adding the cash value of the latter can shift the number of households below the poverty level by several million (GAO 1987). Also in controversy are the bases for assessing the minimum consumption needs of families; some

---

hotels, motels, boardinghouses, or emergency shelters, and persons in institutions such as hospitals or jails are excluded.

31. Keep in mind that the homeless are omitted from all measures of unemployment and poverty based on either the Monthly Labor Force Survey or the Current Population Survey.

32. Exceptions are provided for persons who are temporarily on vacation or "furloughed" from their regular employment.

33. The Current Population Survey data are obtained from some competent individual in each household who reports on the status of each adult member of the household. Hence, whether a member is looking for work may be measured poorly.

argue that since poor households pay a larger proportion of their income for housing than more prosperous families, corresponding upward adjustments ought to be made in the income-cutoff points.

Discussion of poverty in our country often centers on households below the poverty line. This emphasis tends to overlook the issue of extreme poverty as defined by the households that are a considerable distance below that cutoff point, subsuming them into a larger group that may be viewed as far better off. Furthermore, attention is paid primarily to measuring poverty as a household characteristic. Extremely low-income individuals living in households where other adults have adequate incomes are often not counted as poor, since presumably they share in the collective fortunes of the households in which they are located.

From the perspective of our concerns, the most serious problem in measuring either unemployment or poverty is that the surveys they are based on largely overlook the homeless and those housed in hotels and rooming houses. The samples used are of persons living in conventional dwellings: homeless people in shelters or on the streets or domiciled persons living in hotels, including SROs, or in rooming houses or boardinghouses are simply not counted.

Nor is the decennial census of population any better: although it does count people in shelters (and other temporary quarters), until recently the census has not made any serious attempt to enumerate those living outside conventional dwellings.[34]

Estimates of the Conventionally Domiciled Extremely Poor

Despite these limitations, the Current Population Survey can be used as the basis for estimating at least that portion of the extremely poor who are living in conventional homes. Bear in mind that these are estimates only of the conventionally domiciled extremely poor and do not include the homeless, especially those who are out on the streets. Nor do they include, as indicated above, persons living in hotels, motels, or rooming houses.

There are three critical assumptions in these estimates. First, parents' responsibility for full support ends at some point in their children's early adulthood. Second, married persons residing together have mutual support responsibilities. Third, people's responsibility for their own support is modified downward when they become senior citizens. Hence the income received by an adult in the productive middle years who is unmarried or not living with a spouse is a reasonable indicator of that person's poverty (or nonpoverty) status.

There are two critical ambiguities in these assumptions: At what age does adulthood begin? And when does someone become a senior citizen? The esti-

---

34. Current plans for the 1990 census promise to remedy this deficiency by undertaking a special census of persons in public places (such as bus stations).

mates given below employ two definitions of the beginning of responsible adulthood, at age twenty-two and at age thirty. The estimates also exclude students and persons living on farms, on the grounds that students are temporarily exempt from the rule that adults must support themselves and that farm families often act as collective economic units, pooling their labor without parceling out family income to individual members. We also set the onset of senior citizenship at age sixty.[35] Two income definitions of extreme poverty will be used, yearly incomes under $4,000 and under $2,000, amounts that are about 76% and 38% of the poverty-level cutoffs for single persons in 1986.

Table 3.4 presents the resulting estimates of extremely poor domiciled persons aged twenty-two to fifty-nine as tabulated from the 1987 Current Population Survey.[36] Keep in mind that these data are estimates of the *unattached, conventionally domiciled extremely poor,* since homeless persons either in shelters or on the streets are omitted in the Current Population Survey, as are those living in hotels or boardinghouses. Restricting the estimates in this table to unattached persons (not currently married) makes them pertain to that portion of the American population most subject to the risk of becoming literally homeless. Restricting the estimates to the nonfarm population avoids the problem of how to treat unpaid family farm workers.

The only income measures available from the 1987 Current Population Survey pertained to total cash income (before taxes) received in 1986.[37] The data on marital status, student status, and living arrangements are as of March 1987. The temporal disjunction means that for some the income measures do not fairly represent current 1987 income positions; some may have become employed in the last few months of 1986 or the first three months of 1987 and may have been currently receiving income that would place them for 1987 above the extreme poverty thresholds we used. Also, some who earned enough in 1986 were below those income thresholds in 1987. Unless these two forms of misclassification balance out to zero, the estimates presented may be either inflated or deflated.

The two columns on the right in table 3.4 pertain to the numbers and proportions of such persons whose 1986 income (before taxes) was below

35. This age cutoff was chosen to focus more clearly on persons comparable in age to the homeless and the extremely poor persons considered in earlier chapters. An estimated half-million unmarried persons sixty-one and over who were counted in the 1987 Current Population Survey had a 1986 income under $2,000. About half lived with relatives, most likely their adult children.

36. The Current Population Survey is a national household sample of approximately 55,000 households conducted during March of every year. Each of the sampled households is queried concerning a number of topics, including household composition, employment status, and income of each household member. The survey results can be weighted to project to the adult, noninstitutionalized population of the United States residing in permanent dwellings.

37. All income from employment, pensions, unemployment benefits, and welfare programs is included. In-kind welfare benefits, such as food stamps, rent subsidies and Medicare or Medicaid, are not included in income, nor are subsidies from private sources such as relatives or friends.

Table 3.4   1987 Current Population Survey Data on Income

| | 1986 Income | | | |
| | Under $4,000 | | Under $2,000 | |
Living Arrangements	Number (thousands)	Percentage	Number (thousands)	Percentage
Single parents living with children				
Living alone	1,747	24.1	767	18.9
With parents	293	4.0	173	4.3
With other relatives	62	0.9	38	0.9
With nonrelatives	141	1.9	93	2.3
Subtotal	2,243	31.3	1,071	26.3
Unmarried without children				
Living alone	1,229	17.0	619	15.2
With parents	2,348	32.4	1,445	33.5
With other relatives	615	8.5	447	11.0
With nonrelatives	802	11.1	485	11.9
Subtotal	4,994	69.0	2,996	73.7
All single parents and childless				
Living alone	2,976	41.0	1,386	34.1
With parents	2,641	36.4	1,618	37.8
With other relatives	677	9.3	485	11.9
With nonrelatives	943	13.0	578	14.2
Total	7,237		4,067	

Note: 1986 incomes of unmarried persons aged twenty-two to fifty-nine who are not students or living on farms.

$2,000, about the level that qualifies for General Assistance in Illinois or comparable programs in other states. According to the projections, there were more than 4 million persons in 1987 whose 1986 incomes were less than $2,000. Three out of four (74%) were unmarried persons who were not living with their children. The remaining one-fourth were single parents who were living with one or more of their own children (under eighteen).

Almost two in five lived in their parents' households; the largest group (34%) consisted of unmarried persons without dependent children, and about 4% were single parents. About one in three (34%) had set up their own households; 19% were single parents in households with their children, and 15% were childless and living by themselves. The rest were in a variety of arrangements, living with relatives other than their parents (12%) or sharing a dwelling with nonrelatives (14%).

The two columns on the left in table 3.4 are based on a higher income cutoff, $4,000 in 1986. Using this more lenient definition of extreme poverty raises the number of extremely poor persons to 7.2 million, with slight shifts in their living arrangements. Under the more lenient income definition, more of the extremely poor are single parents, mainly women, and more are living in separate households.

Depending on whether we take the $2,000 or $4,000 income cutoff as defining the extremely poor, there were either 4.1 million or 7.2 million unattached extremely poor persons aged twenty-two to fifty-nine in the United States in 1987. A good case can be made for either cutoff point. Annual incomes under $4,000 are well below the official poverty level of $5,250 for a single person and are certainly far below the poverty level for single-parent families.[38] (There were more than 2 million single parents with less than $4,000 annual income and 1 million with 1986 incomes under $2,000.)

Table 3.4 gives a clear message. Extreme poverty affects millions of unattached adult Americans in their most productive period. The pool the literally homeless are recruited from is very large. Assuming there are 350,000 literally homeless people in the United States and using the extreme poverty definition of $2,000 or less, about 8% of the extremely poor are literally homeless. Using the income cutoff of $4,000, the proportion drops to 5%. Given the uncertainties concerning the national estimates of the numbers of homeless in the United States plus the lack of any information about extremely poor persons living in SROs and rooming houses, these percentages can only be regarded as estimates of magnitude. Indeed, it is reasonable to believe that the risk of becoming literally homeless among the extremely poor may be as high as one in ten.

Given the incomes involved and the current prices for housing, the wonder is that so small a proportion are homeless. With weekly incomes ranging downward from $77 or $39, it is clear that only the very bottom of the housing market is accessible to the extremely poor. It is also obvious that the main way these extremely poor unattached adults get by is to live with their parents or with other persons. At the $2,000 annual income cutoff, about a third live on their own, and the remaining two-thirds live with their parents (mostly) or others. At the $4,000 level two out of five can be in their own quarters, and the remaining three out of five live with others.[39] Unattached extremely poor people who are not living with their children are especially likely to live with others. Single-parent households, composed mostly of women and their children under eighteen, are more likely to live separately.

An argument can be made that the lower age limit in table 3.4 has been set too low. People in their twenties may still be finding their way into the labor

38. Although in many of the more generous states AFDC payments would bring single parents above the $4,000 income level, in less generous states, such as Texas, Alabama, and Mississippi, full benefits even for very large families amount to considerably less than $4,000.

39. In the Current Population Survey, nonrelatives are defined as persons who are not parents, children, siblings, or grandparents. Hence aunts, uncles, cousins, and other more removed kin are not included among relatives. There is no way to estimate the extent to which such more distant relatives figure in the housing arrangements of the very poor.

market, and their parents and friends may be quite willing to subsidize them through periods of experimentation, with corresponding low income. Indeed, if we raise the lower age limit, the number of extremely poor persons drops considerably. Restricting the age range to persons thirty-one to fifty-nine, the number of extremely poor persons drops to 3.8 million with 1986 incomes under $4,000 and 2.1 million with incomes under $2,000.

The range of estimates produced by varying the lower age boundary and the income cutoff points are shown below:

Highest estimate: Unmarried, under $4,000, 22–59   7.2
Unmarried, under $2,000, 22–59   4.1
Lowest estimate: Unmarried, under $4,000, 31–59   3.7
Unmarried, under $2,000, 31–59   2.1

Of the estimates shown above, my own preferences are for the two that restrict the age range to twenty-two to fifty-nine. This choice is based on the assumption that this age range covers the period of the life course when most unattached adults are expected to be earning enough to sustain themselves. There can hardly be any dissent whether either $4,000 or $2,000 is a very low annual income, incapable of sustaining a reasonable standard of living for any protracted period. Whatever the choice among the four, there are clearly at least 2 million extremely poor persons and likely as many as 7 million.

Of course, these are clearly also partial estimates. Since the Current Population Survey omits persons living in SROs and other "temporary" quarters, the estimates also do not refer to them. In addition, the estimates pertain only to currently unmarried persons, omitting those who are married and living with their spouses.

Trends in the Number of Extremely Poor Persons

Because the Current Population Survey has been taken annually, it is possible to estimate the size of the extremely poor population in earlier years and plot trends over time. Of course the estimates must take into account the heavy inflation of the past two decades. Table 3.5 contains estimates of the extremely poor population in 1970, using cutoff points that express 1969 income in 1987 dollar equivalents.

The most dramatic feature of table 3.5, in comparison with table 3.4, is how much smaller the 1970 extremely poor United States population was: the number of extremely poor people has more than doubled since 1970, an increase of 224% both in persons earning under $4,000 and in those earning under $2,000. This increase does not simply reflect general population growth since 1970, which was less than 20%.

The distribution of the extremely poor among various living arrangements in 1970 appears to be quite similar to that in 1987. In 1987 the extremely poor are more likely to be single parents—31% in 1987 versus 26% in 1970. There

Table 3.5   1970 Current Population Survey Data on Income

| Living Arrangements | 1969 Total Income in 1987 Dollars | | | |
| | Under $4,000 | | Under $2,000 | |
	Number (thousands)	Percentage	Number (thousands)	Percentage
Single parents living with children				
Living alone	667	21	309	18
With parents	93	3	56	3
With other relatives	21	1	14	1
With nonrelatives	24	1	15	1
Subtotal	805	26	394	22
Unmarried without children				
Living alone	593	19	251	14
With parents	1,010	32	632	36
With other relatives	453	14	319	18
With nonrelatives	281	9	165	9
Subtotal	2,337	74	1,367	77
All single parents and childless				
Living alone	1,260	40	560	32
With parents	1,103	35	688	39
With other relatives	474	15	333	19
With nonrelatives	305	10	180	10
Total	3,142		1,761	

Note: 1969 incomes (in 1987 dollars) of unmarried persons aged twenty-two to fifty-nine who are not students or living on farms.

was no appreciable change in the proportions living with parents and living alone, but there was an appreciable shift in living with other relatives and with nonrelatives. In 1970 more of the extremely poor lived with other relatives and fewer with nonrelatives.

The message of table 3.5 is clear. The pool of extremely poor persons that the literally homeless are drawn from has increased enormously since 1970. If we assume that the proportion of literally homeless among the extremely poor has remained fairly constant over that period, then we can account for a doubling of the literally homeless population just by the increase in the number of extremely poor persons in the United States. Of course there is no firm reason to make that assumption: if the stock of very inexpensive housing declined drastically in that period, that change alone could increase the risk of becoming homeless and also contribute to the growth of homelessness.

Although the increase in the number of extremely poor people is consistent with interpretations that I will advance throughout this book, the changes in the extremely poor population from 1970 to 1987 could also reflect shifts in their living arrangements that cannot be discerned from the Current Population Survey. Because the survey does not cover people living in hotels and rooming houses, a shift in the location of the extremely poor from such places to conventional dwellings would appear as an increase in that population. As I will show in chapter 7, there has been a drastic decline in such "unconventional" dwellings in the same period, a force that, on the one hand, has produced an increase in homelessness and, on the other, may have also increased the number of unattached persons living in conventional housing, especially doubled up with other households. There are a number of reasons to suspect that the increase from 1970 to 1987 is not due simply to shifts in living arrangements, the strongest being that conventional dwellings are much more expensive than the hotels and rooming houses that were demolished. In short, I believe that the 224% increase in the number of extremely poor people is a real increase in that group.

The Household Burdens of the Extremely Poor

The Current Population Survey data indicate that almost half of the extremely poor manage by sharing the households of others. Most who do so live with their parents, but not all can do so. Parents average twenty-eight years older than their children. High parental mortality rates start at age sixty-five, typically when a child reaches thirty-seven. With increasing age, there is a steady increase in the proportion of the extremely poor who live either alone or in nonparental households.

Whether the extremely poor are in dire need, as their personal incomes surely indicate, depends heavily on the total resources available to the households they live in and the extent to which those resources are shared with them. Table 3.6 displays the total 1986 incomes of the host households. (Of course this table does not contain the household incomes of those living alone, which are by definition equal to household income.)

Although the average household income for those living with their parents or with other relatives is somewhat above the median for the United States as a whole, those sharing with nonrelatives are living in very poor households, whose average income is about $18,000. Furthermore, as usual, averages can cover a great deal of variation. One in five (20%) of the parental household incomes was under $10,000 and another one in four (25%) was between $10,000 and $20,000. In other words, close to half of the parental households were below the United States median. The households of other relatives were somewhat poorer, with more than half (54%) having 1986 incomes below the United States median.

As I will argue in greater detail in later chapters, extremely poor people who share dwellings with other poor people or live in poor households have an especially precarious hold on housing. Perhaps one can expect that primary kin who are comparatively well off would willingly share with adult children

Table 3.6   1986 Incomes of Households Containing Unattached Persons with Incomes under $4,000

| | Living Arrangements | | | |
Household Income	In Parents' Household	With Other Relatives	With Other Persons	Total
Under $10,000	19.9%	26.1%	41.0%	25.4%
$10,000 to $19,999	24.8	27.4	22.9	24.8
$20,000 to $29,999	15.1	21.4	17.5	16.6
$30,000 to $39,999	14.9	11.2	9.2	13.1
$40,000 and over	25.4	13.9	9.5	20.1
Average	$29,851	$22,729	$18,269	$26,219
N	2,348	615	803	3,766

Note: Data from 1987 Current Population Survey.

or siblings who are in extreme poverty, but the capacity for generosity must be severely strained for those whose incomes are close to the poverty line or below it.

Overall Estimates of the Homeless and the Extremely Poor

Although the discussion in this chapter should leave no one with the impression that we know the sizes of the contemporary homeless and extreme poor populations with any precision, it should also be clear that we can determine their magnitudes with some confidence. Least well known is the size of the literally homeless population, for which our best estimate is 250,000 to 350,000 throughout the country. We have better information about the size of the extremely poor population, but that is somewhat clouded by ambiguity concerning the age at which self-sufficiency can be assumed and by an absence of good data on persons living in hotels and rooming houses. Nevertheless, assuming that self-sufficiency should begin at age twenty-two, there are 4 to 7 million extremely poor people, persons whose income is below two-thirds of the official poverty line and who are thus at high risk of becoming homeless.

FOUR

The Condition of the Homeless
and the Extremely Poor:
Location and Economic Circumstances

To understand homelessness and extreme poverty properly, we must know who the homeless and the extremely poor are. That information will give us good clues to the processes that placed them in such positions. Of course, knowing their special characteristics is not enough, although it is indispensable for such an understanding. Much of what we think we know about the extremely poor and the homeless comes from accounts in the popular media, known more for hyperbole than for precise assessment. The data to be presented will correct some of these misleading impressions about the homeless and the extremely poor.

This chapter and the next two will portray the homeless and extremely poor populations with as much precision as the available social science research will sustain. Using the findings of a fairly large number of studies, I will identify the salient social and demographic characteristics of the extremely poor and the homeless. This chapter will focus on their location and economic conditions; subsequent chapters will describe their demographic characteristics and the prevalence of certain disabilities among them.

Some of this information was used in a preliminary way in chapter 2, mainly in comparing these groups with their counterparts in the past; now I will present considerably more information, in finer detail. In chapter 2 we learned more about the differences between the homeless of the 1950s and the homeless of today than we learned about the extremely poor of either period. To some extent I will remedy this imbalance, although the emphasis will still necessarily be on homeless persons, since they have received a great deal more attention from social researchers.

Data Sources

Recent Studies of the Homeless

A fairly extensive collection of research has been undertaken on homeless persons and families. Since 1980 there have been almost 40[1] credible studies

---

1. Many more publications contain information about the homeless: my personal bibliography on the topic contains, as of January 1988, more than two hundred entries. These forty were chosen for special attention here because they are empirical studies based either on official records of agencies that serve the homeless or on direct data gathered, usually through interviewing,

that present data on the characteristics of homeless persons, the earliest undertaken in 1981 and the latest in 1987, with most done between 1984 and 1986.
Of course there are many more "studies" available, but many, if not most,
rely either on "samples" of unknown validity or on the opinions of experts,
presented without substantiating data. All the studies I used were based on
original field investigations in which homeless persons and families were
studied directly in a systematic way.[2]

All the studies were of specific urban places: there have been no credible
empirical studies of states, regions, or the country as a whole. As I said in
chapter 3, there have been attempts to estimate the size and composition of the
homeless population of the entire country, but none can be regarded as based
on solid data. Although taken as a set the studies cover a variety of urban
places, ranging from New York City to Nashville, they cannot be regarded as
representative of all urban areas, much less the United States as a whole. A
range of cities is included in the collection, but we cannot tell whether even
the extremes are covered.

The studies also vary widely in their coverage of topics. For example, all
but one reported gender distribution among the homeless, but only ten looked
at income. All but one reported on the homeless in shelters, but only thirteen
researchers interviewed homeless people who were not shelter users.

There is also considerable variation in technical quality. Two studies were
attempts to census the total homeless populations of the cities they dealt with.
Unfortunately they collected very little information on the characteristics of
the homeless. Only one study, our Chicago Homeless Study (Rossi, Fisher,
and Willis 1986), was based on a strategy for sampling both sheltered and
unsheltered homeless people in all areas of a major city. Most were based on
uncertain sampling procedures applied to some vaguely identified subgroup of
the homeless selected out of convenience and were conducted under severe
budgetary constraints.

Each of the studies used is described in the annotated bibliography presented in appendix A. Despite the heterogeneity both in quality and in coverage of topics, I will use the findings of these forty studies (referred to as the
combined homeless studies) as part of the data base for this chapter and the
two that follow. Each of the studies was read carefully by me and by an advanced graduate student.[3] We extracted the data they presented on close to

---

from homeless persons. Most of my two hundred entries constitute opinions or guesses by "experts" or "advocates" and will not be used here.

2. To qualify for inclusion here, a study had to be based on some sort of systematic sampling
of homeless persons. Data had to be obtained by direct observation or by questioning the homeless (or both). The number of homeless people directly observed had to be larger than twenty

3. I am indebted to Jeffry Will for reading reports from close to one hundred studies, many
constituting eyesight-taxing second-generation photocopies. His careful reading of the studies
and his judicious decisions on which to include contribute considerably to this chapter.

fifty descriptors of the homeless and entered the extracts into a data base. Summary statistics were calculated using that data base and are presented at appropriate points in this chapter.

The Chicago Homeless Study

The Chicago Homeless Study will be given a central place for two main reasons: it was designed as a probability sample of both the sheltered and unsheltered homeless of Chicago and hence is technically the best of the studies; and it collected very detailed information on each of the homeless persons interviewed. More complete information on the Chicago Homeless Study was given in chapter 3; technical details on how it was conducted are contained in appendix B.

Studies of the Extremely Poor

Another important reason for using the Chicago Homeless Study (CHS) as the centerpiece is the fortunate circumstance that there exist several studies of the extremely poor population of Chicago. These studies, all conducted in the middle 1980s, provide data that can round out my analysis of the two groups of central interest. All told, I will use five studies bearing on extreme poverty. More detailed descriptions of these studies will be presented in appendix A.

The Chicago General Assistance Study (GAS)

First, I will rely heavily on a study by Stagner and Richman (1985) of a sample of Chicago General Assistance clients of the Illinois Department of Public Aid. General Assistance is an entirely state-financed income-maintenance program available to persons earning less than $1,800 a year who have no assets and do not qualify for any of the major federally assisted income-maintenance programs. This is a program aimed at providing income—maximum benefits in 1985 and 1986 were $154 a month—primarily to those who do not qualify for AFDC or Social Security retirement benefits or disability payments.

General Assistance (GA) is the major income-maintenance program available to unattached persons in Illinois.[4] In 1985 approximately 110,000 Chicago residents were participating. Because eligibility for General Assistance was tied to income below $2,000 annually, recipients are clearly among the extremely poor as defined in chapter 1. In addition, benefits under the program are not generous enough to remove them from that category.

---

4. Similar programs, often called General Relief, exist in most states, primarily to provide support to persons not covered by federally authorized (and subsidized) income-maintenance programs. States that do not have such programs, such as Texas, Mississippi, and Alabama, are also states in which welfare programs generally are restricted and skimpy in levels of payment.

The Chicago Study of AFDC Clients (AFDC)

Second, I will use data from a parallel study of persons receiving AFDC benefits during 1984, also conducted by Stagner and Richman (1986). Although many of the AFDC recipients were not among the extremely poor by virtue of those payments, most came close to that condition—average 1985 AFDC payments were close to $4,000 a year for a household consisting of a parent and two children—and almost all had been in that state at one time or another. In addition, many of the AFDC households contained unemployed adults attempting to subsist on GA payments or on close to zero income.

The Chicago SRO Residents Study (SRO)

Third, I will draw upon data collected in a 1985 survey conducted by Hoch and Spicer (1985) of 185 persons living in single-room occupancy hotels. Although many of the SRO residents interviewed were not among the extremely poor, some were. A significant proportion had been homeless at one time or another in the past, and their precarious economic positions put them at high risk of becoming homeless in the future. But the most important characteristic of SRO residents is that they live in some of the least expensive housing available to single-person households, providing some information on why even this portion of the housing market cannot be reached by the homeless and most of the extremely poor.

The Chicago Urban Family Life Study (UFLS)

The fourth Chicago study I will draw on in a limited way is a survey conducted by Wilson (1987) of several thousand parents, aged eighteen to forty-seven, drawn from households living in Chicago census tracts containing the highest proportions of families whose 1980 incomes placed them below the poverty level. I will use the data from this survey to round out a portrait of the extremely poor who are not on the Illinois General Assistance or AFDC rolls. Because the study was limited to parents and to persons eighteen to forty-seven, it covers only a portion of the extremely poor, diminishing its utility for comparative purposes.

The 1987 Current Population Survey (CPS)

Finally, I will also use the 1987 Current Population Survey, which I introduced in chapter 3. In using this study I will be concerned only with unattached persons (those not living with spouses) aged twenty-two to fifty-nine whose 1986 income was less than $4,000. Only limited use can be made of the Current Population Survey because it collected minimal demographic data on such persons.

In the true spirit of scholarly openness and professionalism, the authors of these studies made their raw data available to me. I am deeply in their debt for their generosity.

Existential Meanings of Homelessness and Extreme Poverty

What is it like to be homeless or extremely poor? Although the full flavor of these conditions cannot be captured and communicated from survey data, it can provide considerably more than a hint. The Chicago Homeless Study data I present ordinarily distinguish between those interviewed in the shelters and those interviewed in the street surveys. Bear in mind that the designation "street homeless" includes persons who were interviewed in public places, abandoned buildings, and sleeping in cars and trucks, as well as those found literally on the streets. These data have been weighted to accurately represent the conditions found in the total Chicago homeless population.[5]

Where Are the Homeless?

To locate and interview all the homeless is not an easy task. To be sure, many can be found each night in the shelters provided for them, but a large proportion do not go to the shelters every night. Locating the homeless during the daytime would waste a lot of effort, since so many of the people out on the streets or in public places are not homeless. To conduct our study in Chicago, we took advantage of the commonplace fact that in every city the "dead of night," between 1:00 A.M. and 6:00 A.M., is when we would find most citizens home in bed. We chose this time during the twenty-four-hour cycle to search for and interview the street homeless, because that is when there is the greatest separation between the street homeless and those with homes. Of course there are people who work at night, others on their way from one place to another, and even insomniacs restlessly walking about the city whom we also encountered when we made our searches. Nevertheless, the dead of night is when we are most likely to find that a relatively high proportion of those out on the streets are homeless.[6]

We tried to arrange with the shelters to interview their residents in the evening, after they admitted people for the night and before most of them had bedded down. In most cases we were successful: in a few shelters we had to do our interviewing in the early morning after most clients had risen and before they left for the day's activities.

Both the shelter survey and the street survey are nighttime studies. Perhaps

5. Our two surveys sampled larger fractions of homeless persons in shelters than of homeless persons living "on the street." To represent properly the total Chicago homeless, we had to weight data from the street sample more heavily. See appendix B for the exact weights used.

6. In our two street surveys we encountered more than 600 persons outside dwellings in our searches of the 412 Chicago blocks chosen in our two samples. The vast majority, over 90%, had homes. See appendix B for further details.

Table 4.1   Place of Interview: Chicago Homeless Study

Interview Location	Survey Source		
	Fall	Winter	Combined
Shelters	39.4%	73.9%	55.0%
Public buildings (bus or train station, air-port, building lobby, bar, theater)	16.4	24.6	20.1
Sidewalks, streets, or alleys	13.9	0.8	8.0
Parks	0.8	0.0	0.4
Abandoned buildings	1.6	0.3	1.0
Under bridges or viaducts	0.8	0.0	0.4
Parked cars, vans, trucks	0.0	0.3	0.1
Unspecified nonshelter location[a]	27.0	0.0	14.8
N	372	350	722

[a]Most of the persons classified here were interviewed in the pretest for the fall survey, in which the location of the interview was not noted. Most of those in the pretest were interviewed on the streets.

the best introduction to what it is like to be homeless is to describe where we found the Chicago homeless when we interviewed them at night, as shown in table 4.1. Combining the fall and winter surveys, more than half (55%) were in shelters on the nights of our surveys; the rest were found in the various public locations shown.

However, comparing the two surveys brings to light very different patterns of location in fall and winter. In the fall survey, fewer than half (39%) were found in shelters, in contrast to 74% in the winter survey.[7] The seasonal patterning reflects both the harshness of Chicago's winters and the responsiveness of its shelter supply.[8] There were more shelter spaces available in the winter, and more of the homeless used the shelters.[9]

7. This locational patterning is not a function of the nonsample interviews included in these tabulations. (See appendix B for a thorough discussion of the distinction between sample and nonsample interviews.) If we consider only the street interviews derived from the probability sample of blocks, the locations of respondents were as follows:

Location	Fall 1985	Winter 1986
Streets	15	2
Public places	3	24
Other	4	2

8. The average maximum and minimum temperatures as well as the ranges during the time periods of each of the two surveys are shown below:

Survey	Average High	Average Low	Maximum High	Minimum Low
Fall 1985	67	47	76	34
Winter 1986	34	23	42	17

9. "Emergency" shelter bed capacity increased from about 1,500 at the time of the fall survey to about 2,000 at the time of the winter survey. This increase in capacity was accomplished by

Table 4.2   When Do the Homeless Sleep?

Usual Sleeping Time	Street	Shelter	Combined
Day	12.9%	3.2%	5.4%
Night	46.6	70.7	65.2
Day and night	39.3	26.1	29.1
No answer	1.2	0.0	0.3
N	372	350	722

Note that in both surveys only a small proportion of the homeless were found literally out on the streets or in other places where they were unprotected from the elements. About one in ten were found in such open-air places, with proportionately more in the fall survey. Homeless people who were not in shelters tended to be in buildings to which the public has access at night—train and bus stations, airports, lobbies, and arcades—especially in the dead of winter.

The advantages of such public places are obvious. They provide shelter from the elements, especially the bitter cold of Chicago winters, and they are well lit and relatively secure. They also have some disadvantages: it is not easy to sleep sitting up, nor are the seats, if any, comfortable for long periods. Thus only a minority (47%) of the street homeless have a nighttime sleeping pattern, as shown in table 4.2. Most sleep for short periods both at night and during the day or sleep entirely during the day.

Some of the homeless we interviewed in the shelters also have irregular sleeping patterns: almost one in three (35%) does not regularly sleep at night. Although using the emergency shelters should allow for "normal" nighttime sleeping patterns, there is a considerable interchange between the street and sheltered homeless. Many alternate between sleeping in shelters and sleeping in public places.

Table 4.1 shows that Chicago's social service agencies manage to provide heated quarters and beds for a bare majority of that city's homeless. However, the shelters are far below even the modest accommodations of an inexpensive apartment or rented room, let alone luxury quarters. Many shelters, particularly those catering to homeless men, provide dormitories with many beds in each room, spartan bath and toilet facilities, and modest eating arrangements if food is offered at all. Privacy and comfort are minimal. In some shelters personal security is an issue. Certainly, from most viewpoints sleeping in the

---

expanding existing shelters and opening more. In addition, the Chicago Park District established the practice of opening up "warming places," usually in Park District buildings, when the temperature sank to fourteen degrees or below. These were places where homeless persons could keep warm in heated buildings (no beds were supplied in "warming places").

shelters is usually better than sleeping out on the streets, but it is far short of what most Americans would find adequate.

For the 25% to 40% who were not in shelters when our interviewers found them, the amenities those with homes take for granted are simply unavailable. Sleeping on the steps of the Greyhound bus station has nothing to recommend it other than being out of the very cold February weather and being sheltered from rain or snow. Those we found out on the streets typically were not sleeping but were walking about or simply sitting.

The locational patterns found in the two surveys are not simply accidental arrangements typical only of the particular days when the surveys were conducted. We also asked where the respondents had "rested or slept" over the seven days before the survey.[10] Table 4.3 presents the results of this inquiry in two ways: panel A gives the percentage of the past seven days' sleeping or resting times spent in each of the several alternative locations; panel B shows the proportion of homeless persons who had spent at least one resting or sleeping period in each place over the previous seven days.

Overall, the findings in panel A are consistent with the patterning of locations where our interviewers reached the homeless: 55% were reached in the shelters (table 4.1), and 55% of the resting or sleeping times of the previous seven days were spent in shelters. But there are some important differences. Because we could not reach persons who had made temporary sleeping arrangements by renting rooms or were sleeping in the homes of their families or relatives or other persons, those places necessarily were omitted from table 4.1. In panel A of table 4.3, however, such places can be counted. It appears that almost 11% of the past seven days' sleeping or resting periods were spent either in rented rooms (4.4%), with family or relatives (3.0%), or in other persons' dwellings (3.3%); thus about 1.5% of the homeless on any given night are in homes (10.7% divided by 7). In other words, the approach used in the Chicago Homeless Study misses the 1.5% who are homeless most of the time but are temporarily housed on any one night.

This pattern of intermittent access to conventional housing also involves a fairly large proportion of the homeless, as panel B shows: almost one-third had spent at least one sleeping or resting period over the past seven days either in a rented room (11.9%), with family or relatives (9.5%), or with other persons (10.1%). It appears that the boundaries between having a home and being homeless were frequently crossed. A significant minority of the homeless made temporary arrangements for access to some conventional dwelling from time to time. However, most of the time they spent their sleeping and rest periods either on the streets or in shelters.

10. During the pretest for the fall survey, we encountered several homeless people who claimed they never slept but simply "rested" from time to time. In writing the item soliciting information on sleeping patterns we adopted this terminology, asking when respondents "slept or rested."

Table 4.3   Resting or Sleeping Places Used over Past Seven Days

Place	Fall[a]	Winter[a]	Combined[a]
A. Percentage of Time Spent Resting or Sleeping in Various Places			
Shelters	41.4	70.7	54.8
Streets or parks	24.2	4.0	15.0
Public places	14.7	12.9	13.9
Rented rooms	5.4	3.3	4.4
With family or relatives	3.0	3.1	3.0
Other persons' places	3.9	2.6	3.3
N	372	350	722
B. Percentage of Persons Spending at Least One Night in Various Places over the Past Seven Days			
Shelters	64.2	82.3	72.5
Streets or parks	44.7	9.4	28.5
Public places	32.4	23.4	28.3
Rented rooms	13.8	9.7	11.9
With family or relatives	9.6	9.5	9.5
Other persons' places	10.3	9.8	10.1

[a]Column does not add up to 100%. Omitted because they are rare are proportions of the past seven days spent in abandoned buildings, vehicles, and "other" places not covered in the classification categories used.

Most of the homeless in both the fall (64%) and winter (82%) surveys spent some time in a shelter over the seven-day period. Indeed, in either season the single most likely place to sleep or rest was a shelter. The major difference between the seasons was the significantly greater use of shelters in the winter. Collectively, the emergency shelters for the homeless in Chicago provide beds for most of the homeless at least some of the time.

Thus the boundaries between those with homes and the homeless are easily crossed. Many of the homeless sleep at least part of the time in conventional dwellings. Almost all make use of the emergency shelters, some quite consistently, and a few spend almost all their nights out on the streets.

In contrast, the domiciled extremely poor are by definition mainly living in conventional dwellings—apartments, houses, and rented rooms. A few can set up living arrangements on their own, but most are "forced" by their poverty to live with others. To throw some light on this issue, let us turn to data from the Chicago General Assistance Study. As I will show in the next chapter, General Assistance clients are very similar to the homeless in demographic composition. When the GA clients were interviewed in March 1984, one in three lived alone, most in apartments and rooms.[11] The plurality—two in three—lived with other adults, slightly less than half with adult relatives, and the rest (17%) lived with other adults to whom they were not related.

11. One of the interviewees lived in a shelter for homeless persons.

Table 3.4 showed much the same pattern for the childless unattached persons identified in the 1987 Current Population Survey: 17% of those with incomes under $4,000 and 15% of the under $2,000 group lived by themselves, and the rest lived with other persons. Like the GA clients, most lived in their parents' households. On the national level, even fewer of the extremely poor could live by themselves.

Since most of the GA sample were not currently married, the relatives they lived with were parents and siblings. Indeed, as I will repeat over and over, the extremely poor remain domiciled mainly by being subsidized by family members. How the one in three of the extremely poor who lives alone in an apartment or room manages to get by on the monthly $154 GA benefits will be taken up later in this chapter.

What Do the Homeless Look Like?

It is easy to maintain a reasonably respectable personal appearance if one has more than one set of clothes, easy access to bathing facilities, and a place to store extra clothes and grooming equipment. Staying out of the dirtier parts of the community also helps: not all of Chicago's streets and public places are grimy, but many of the places where we found the homeless are in poor condition. It is therefore no wonder that the homeless have an image of poor personal hygiene and shabby appearance. For many of them the stereotype is not far off the mark, yet the shabby and the unclean are far from a strong majority.

To assess the personal appearance of the homeless, the CHS interviewers were asked to rate each person interviewed on a number of criteria.[12] Of course the NORC interviewers are neither fashion arbiters nor advocates of unconventional personal habits: they are hired because their appearances are not too far from the conventional on the side of either conservative or avant-garde dress and personal habits. As judges of the appearance of the homeless they are as good (or as bad) as most of us. These are commonsense judgments that can be relied on as representing a "conventional" view.

The ratings obtained that are relevant to appearance are shown in table 4.4, separately for persons interviewed in the shelters and on the streets. As can be seen in "combined" column that shows the overall patterns for both the shelter and the street samples, most (55%) of the homeless were found to be "neat and clean," but significant minorities were considered "dirty and unkempt" (21%) or "shabbily dressed" (32%) or were "carrying their personal belongings in packages or bags" (11%).

Most overall characterizations of the homeless are somewhat misleading because the shelter and street samples are often different in many respects. Differences in appearance between the two groups are striking: more than half

---

12. The ratings were binary and independent of each other. The items asked whether an interviewee was "neat and clean," requiring a yes or no answer.

Table 4.4   Interviewers' Ratings of Homeless Respondents' Appearance

Rating[a]	Street Sample	Shelter Sample	Combined
Dirty and/or unkempt	42.9%	9.7%	21.4%
Shabbily dressed	55.0	19.2	31.9
Carrying personal belongings	24.2	3.5	10.9
Neat and clean	27.5	70.5	55.0

[a]Ratings made by interviewers at end of interview.

(55%) of the street homeless were rated as shabbily dressed, and 43% were considered dirty and unkempt; correspondingly, only 28% of the street homeless were considered to be overall neat and clean. The corresponding ratings for persons interviewed in the shelters showed them to be significantly neater, less often shabby, and cleaner. Indeed, more than two out of three of the shelter homeless were judged to be neat and clean.

It is clear that using a shelter made it easier to maintain personal hygiene and a presentable wardrobe.[13] Bathing facilities are usually available in the shelters, and some have washing machines for the use of residents. The shelters provide enough amenities to enable many of the homeless to appear neat and clean, at least to the NORC interviewers.

We have no comparable data on the extremely poor. The social researchers who collected data on AFDC and GA recipients and SRO residents clearly did not think personal appearance was important in studying these populations. Indeed, as discussed above, the predominant pattern of living with others undoubtedly provided them with access to those amenities that make neatness and cleanliness easy and hence not an issue to the researchers.

The Fuzzy Line between the Homeless and Those with Homes

The line between being homeless and living in a conventional dwelling is frequently crossed for shorter periods, as table 4.3 indicated. These findings also suggest there may be longer periods of being housed, with episodes of homelessness interspersed between them.

Although we did not obtain a full residential history from each of the homeless persons interviewed in the CHS, we did obtain information on the length of the respondent's current episode of homelessness and whether there had been any additional episodes over the previous five years. To obtain the necessary data, both surveys asked about the last time (month and year) the respondent lived in an apartment, room, or house. *These duration measures*

13. There is also some evidence, to be presented later, that being neat and clean made it easier to get admitted to a shelter. The Chicago shelters exercise considerable discretion in their admissions policies, usually barring people who are drunk, visibly on drugs, or behaving in an aggressive or bizarre way. Although none of the shelter managers we interviewed claimed that dress and physical appearance per se were admissions criteria, there are strong clues that these characteristics were taken into account.

underestimate the total amount of time our respondents will remain homeless:
their current episode of homelessness obviously continued beyond the date of
interview. As a rule of thumb, the total duration of homelessness is likely at
least twice that shown in table 4.5.[14]

Panel A of table 4.5 gives the durations measured in the Chicago Homeless
Study: they vary widely. Large proportions of the homeless had been in that
state for relatively short periods—46% for six months or less, and 13% for a
month or less.[15] Were almost any other condition under consideration, these
statistics would be heartening. But homelessness even for short periods is a
serious condition that poses a significant threat to safety, health, and self-
esteem. Three months of homelessness is not just a transient episode to be
lightly passed over, but a string of close to a hundred nights and days of uncer-
tainty about bed and board.

The second salient feature of table 4.5 is that so many have been homeless
for very long periods: 13% have been homeless for four years or more, and
among these unfortunates are 6% who have been homeless for ten years or
more. Several claimed to have been homeless for two decades or more. For
this significant minority, homelessness appeared to be permanent.

Clearly the distribution of the length of current homelessness is dispersed,
as the bottom three lines of panel A indicate: the average time homeless is
21.9 months, a little less than two years. The median time homeless is much
lower, 7.6 months. And the modal time, 2 months, is lower still. The great
differences among these measures of central tendency mean that time homeless does not cluster around some typical value: many persons are homeless
for a short time, but there are also many who have been homeless for years.

Since the duration distribution is so dispersed, averages and other measures
of central tendency are not very useful. For many purposes it may be helpful
to distinguish among the following types of homeless people, classified according to length of time homeless: (1) short termers (32%), the one in three
persons homeless for up to three months; (2) medium termers (43%), the two
in five who have been homeless for four months up to two years; and (3) long
termers (25%), the one in four persons homeless for two years or more. Although all homeless persons should be the concern of those involved with social policy, interest is likely to be especially strong in short termers, where
there may seem to be a better chance of helping. However, one should keep in
mind that both the medium and long termers were short termers earlier in their

14. Assuming that the average total duration of homelessness is not increasing over time, the
average duration measured at any one point is about half of the total period.

15. In retrospect, it would have been better to have used a finer time scale in measuring duration. From interviewer comments penciled in the margins of questionnaires, there is considerable
evidence that many of those counted as being homeless less than a month had actually been homeless less than a week. Homelessness of a few days' duration appears to be common among those
who are precariously housed in SRO hotels or doubled up with friends or relatives.

Table 4.5   Length of Time Currently Homeless

A. Chicago Homeless Study	
Months	Percentage
0–1	12.7
2–3	18.9
4–6	14.7
7–12	14.3
13–24	14.3
25–48	12.1
49–119	7.0
120+	5.9
Mode (months)	2.0
Median (months)	7.6
Mean (months)	21.9

B. Combined Homeless Studies		
Measure	Average	Number of Studies
Months homeless	25.6	5
Percentage homeless for six months or more	44.6	13
Percentage homeless for one year or more	26.6	13

current episodes. This last group is likely to be very heterogeneous, consisting of some who will move out of the homeless state in a short time and some who will remain homeless, shifting first into the medium- and then into the long-term group.

Panel B of table 4.5 summarizes data from other empirical studies of home-lessness that contained information on duration of homelessness. Only five of the studies gave average duration, yet the average months homeless is 25.6, of the same general magnitude as shown in the CHS.

Thirteen more studies contained data on the proportion who were homeless for six months or more and for a year or more. The percentages are all lower than recorded in the CHS, suggesting that most cities have more short-term homeless than Chicago.

Perhaps the major message carried by the data reported in all the studies of the homeless is that the duration of homeless episodes varies greatly. Entering and leaving the homeless state are frequent transitions. At the same time, it is clear that there are large proportions of long-term, "chronic" homeless persons in all the cities studied.

So far I have focused primarily on the duration of the current episode of homelessness. The very permeable boundary between homelessness and having a home can be crossed in either direction, sometimes more than once. To measure the extent to which homelessness is repeated, we asked all those who had become homeless within five years of the interview date whether they had

Table 4.6   Prevalence of Episodic Homelessness, 1980–85

Pattern of Homelessness	Street	Shelter	Combined
Homeless continuously	13.5%	9.4%	11.2%
Homeless once, less than a year	29.2	43.6	37.2
Homeless once, more than a year	17.6	21.8	19.9
Homeless more than once	39.7	25.3	31.7
N	322	397	719

also been homeless at any time in each of the years 1980 through 1985.[16] The resulting data are summarized in table 4.6.

A small proportion, 11%, had been homeless continuously through 1980–85. More than half, 57%, had started their current homeless episode in that period but had not been homeless previously. Close to one-third (32%) had been homeless more than once during 1980–85. Typically those in the last group had had one additional episode, and a few had been homeless one or more times in each year during the five-year period. Apparently a large group of the Chicago poor moved back and forth across the line between having a home and being homeless.

The data presented so far have been drawn from studies of the homeless. To fully understand the extent to which the boundary is crossed, ideally we should supplement these findings with information gathered from the domiciled extremely poor. Unfortunately, data of that sort are neither very rich nor easy to come by. For example, among the respondents of the General Assistance Study, only one of the four hundred was identifiably homeless and living in a shelter, suggesting that the boundary is not often crossed from the side of that group.[17] We suspect the GAS underestimates episodes of homelessness by not asking about them directly.

Somewhat richer data can be obtained from the 1985 Chicago SRO study, in which a sample of SRO residents were asked whether they had ever been forced to "sleep outside." Taken literally, this question appears to ask about being homeless on the streets, excluding nights spent in shelters. (Unfortunately the SRO study did not ask about spending time in shelters.) One in four (25%) said they had spent time on the streets, with about 10% of the episodes occurring in either 1984 or 1985, for periods that averaged twenty-six days. If we assume that the SRO residents who spent some nights in a shelter were at least as numerous, then about half of them had at some time been among the homeless, with about one in ten experiencing homelessness over a year's time. In addition, 5% of the SRO residents said their previous place of residence,

16. Because a person could be homeless several times during a year, this measure undoubtedly underestimates the number of homelessness episodes.
17. That individual was living in a conventional dwelling when approached for another interview nine months later. None of the GA clients were homeless at the time of the second interview.

before moving into their SRO rooms, was either a shelter for the homeless or "living on the streets."

Those who try to make it on their own without subsidies from their relatives and friends live in SROs on a very precarious basis. Their incomes, though considerably greater than those of either the homeless or GA recipients, are easily disrupted, catapulting them from time to time into the homeless state.

Chicago's Shelter "Industry"

The shelters provided for homeless persons play such critical roles in the lives of that group that it is important to consider what they are like. Without the shelters, many of the homeless would be decidedly worse off, however minimal their facilities may be.

Providing shelter for homeless persons is an old custom in American cities. Many cities have had municipal "lodging houses" since the time they were large enough to have a significant number of homeless people. Religious and charitable organizations also have long provided a variety of accommodations for the poor generally and the homeless in particular. Perhaps best known are the shelters supported by such well-established religious groups as the Salvation Army, the Volunteers of America, and the Society of St. Vincent de Paul, whose mission shelters have been downtown fixtures in many American cities since the nineteenth century.

According to HUD's 1984 report, nonprofit groups operate 90% of the nation's urban shelters; among the nonprofit shelter groups, religious organizations run about 40%. Fewer than 10% were run directly by municipal governments. Only in New York City is a municipality the major supplier of shelter accommodations.

As discussed in chapter 2, up to a few decades ago, in most cities private enterprise provided lodging at very nominal rents in the form of cubicles in inexpensive "hotels" or "flophouses." Spurred by downtown urban renewal, most of the urban flophouses have been condemned and razed. Commercial sleeping arrangements renting for up to $5 a night, the equivalent of 1968's 50¢ to $1, were virtually nonexistent in Chicago in 1985 or 1986.

For unattached persons, housing a bit better in quality than the flophouse cubicles has traditionally been provided by inexpensive SRO (single room occupancy) hotels providing modest one-room accommodations, usually with shared bathrooms. In most of our cities a large portion of the stock of SRO hotels has been demolished or converted to other uses over the past two decades. The consequence is a shortage in city after city of inexpensive housing for unattached persons.

The growth in beds available in "emergency" shelters for the homeless is partially a response to this shortage. For someone with less than $80 a week income, the only "affordable" housing is the emergency shelters.

Most cities now have shelters run under a mixture of auspices, including the municipality, religious and secular charitable organizations, and private enterprise. The long-established missionary shelters have expanded and new ones have been opened. Only a few shelters have been constructed specifically for that purpose; most of the buildings have been converted from other uses. For example, one of the major New York City shelters for men, the Keener Men's Shelter, is an abandoned mental hospital, rehabilitated and put to a new use. Its large ward rooms now hold twenty to thirty beds. A major Chicago mission shelter is lodged in a converted loft factory building. Smaller shelters have been built by modifying apartment houses or small stores.

The Chicago shelters may well be unusual in several respects.[18] First, although there are substantial financial subsidies from the city and state, the Chicago shelters are virtually all run by private-sector groups. Only one shelter is entirely financed by the city, and it is managed by a private-sector group, Catholic Charities. Most of the shelters are run and largely financed by religious organizations. All receive grants from the municipality and the state.

Some are primarily missions, aimed at reaching the souls of the homeless at the same time as they feed and house them. Others are run by establishment churches out of an impulse that is more charitable than missionary, and a few are run by secular groups. The mission shelters tend to be among the larger ones and have been established longer.

The shelters vary widely in kinds of accommodations. The largest have several hundred beds, usually in dormitory arrangements. Family shelters provide small apartments. Small shelters with space for up to ten may house each homeless person in a separate room. Of course the large places house most of the sheltered homeless, so shelter accommodations ordinarily mean the use of a bed in a room that may hold fifty.

Second, the shelters collectively are very flexible. In planning the fall 1985 survey, we found twenty-eight that were eligible to be selected in the shelter sample.[19] In the harsher winter season the number had expanded to forty-five, with the total bed capacity correspondingly enlarged. Most of the added shelters were smaller ones with fewer than twenty-five beds each. From fall 1985 to winter 1986, the bed capacity had increased by 27%, involving 428 additional beds to provide a total of about 2,000 beds in February 1986.

Third, the shelters, whatever their sponsorship, were open to all comers of

18. The information presented in the next few paragraphs on the characteristics of Chicago shelters was obtained from telephone and personal interviews with shelter operators undertaken to determine whether each shelter was eligible for selection in the shelter surveys. (See appendix B for a description of shelter survey procedures.) For an excellent discussion of Chicago's "shelter industry" see Sosin, Colson, and Grossman (1988).

19. Eligible shelters were ones whose major function was to provide sleeping places for the homeless. Excluded were "special purpose" shelters such as detoxification centers and those exclusively for "battered women." See appendix B for a fuller description of the excluded shelters and their capacities.

all creeds and ethnic or racial origins. Among the twenty-nine that fell into our shelter samples in either survey, none were segregated de facto by race or ethnicity. Depending on their location, some had a majority of blacks and others a majority of whites among their residents, but the proportion of any ethnic or racial group rarely exceeded 70% in any one shelter, and then only in smaller ones. Indeed, the shelters were less racially segregated than most Chicago neighborhoods.

However, almost all shelters restricted admission in one way or another. Perhaps the most common restriction is by gender. About half take either only men or only women. The rest have gender quotas on admission, reflecting the capacities of their gender-segregated accommodations. Equally common were restrictions on age: few shelters will admit those under eighteen unless they are part of a family group and accompanied by a parent. Half are completely restricted to persons eighteen and over; unattached juveniles are referred to specialized juvenile shelters.

Most of the Chicago shelters have regular admitting hours. Very few restrict the number of consecutive nights a homeless person may stay. Indeed, only a handful (fewer than one in five) have length-of-residence restrictions of up to one month, and in more than half restrictions extend beyond a year. For all practical purposes, a person can return to most shelters night after night, using the shelter as a "regular" abode for extended periods.[20]

Many shelters have rules concerning when residents can be present; they usually ask everyone to leave during stated daytime hours, presumably so housekeeping activities can be undertaken more easily. Some require their clients to contribute labor, helping out in food service or housekeeping. Work requirements are waived when disabilities make working difficult.

Many shelters formally or informally bar the intoxicated or those acting bizarrely. Many have rules concerning conduct while in the shelters, prohibiting drinking, drug use, disruptive behavior, and smoking. Many said they would not admit clients who had violated these rules in the past. Several explicitly barred persons with chronic mental illness.

Although shelter rules do not completely determine the differences between the shelter and street samples that I have noted throughout this chapter, the compositions of the two groups are undoubtedly conditioned by such rules. For all shelters the ideal client appears to be a sober, well mannered, not obviously mentally ill man or woman whose personal appearance tends toward the neat and clean as opposed to the dirty and disheveled. Not all clients who present themselves fulfill this ideal, but to the extent that a client approximates it, the probability of admission is undoubtedly enhanced.

---

20. Indeed, many of the homeless do return night after night to the same shelter. For example, when it was not possible to interview a shelter resident, in most cases the interviewer could return to the shelter a few nights later and interview those missed on the first attempt.

Why Some Homeless Are Not in Shelters

Few would question that living and sleeping on the streets, in public places, or in abandoned buildings is uncomfortable, unhealthy, and unsafe, including most of the homeless. Seen in this context, shelters were better than being out on the streets. True, their accommodations were far from luxurious and in some instances were close to the minimum of decency and only marginally safer than the streets. Nonetheless, a night in any typical Chicago shelter appears clearly preferable to a night on the streets, especially during Chicago's winters.

Hence it is only natural to ask why more of the homeless were not in the shelters. Although the total shelter capacity fell short of the total persons homeless on any night, lack of space was clearly not the only reason. In both fall and winter surveys we found that the shelters were not used to capacity. Occupancy rates in fall 1985 were about 60%, and in winter 1986 they were 70%.[21] Although in fall 1985 the total shelter capacity (1,573) would not have accommodated all the homeless, by winter 1986 it had increased enough (2,001) to house almost all; but in fact only 75% of the homeless used the shelters on any one night (see table 4.1). Similar occupancy rates were found in HUD's January 1984 national shelter survey, in which the overall occupancy rate was 70%.

Of course, part of the answer is that where we found persons on a particular night is not necessarily where we would find them on another night. There is some interchange between the two subgroups of the homeless, as shown in table 4.3. Persons in the street sample did not spend all their nights homeless on the street or in public access buildings. Correspondingly, shelter persons spent some of their nights on the street. Nevertheless, there was a strong tendency for the two groups to be largely separate. Hence it makes sense to probe why the street homeless largely avoided the shelters.

To provide some information, we added a series of questions to the winter 1986 interview schedule to be asked only of persons in our street sample. The first issue is to what extent the street homeless knew about the shelters. We found that about one in four (23%) of the street homeless claimed to have no knowledge about the location of shelters in Chicago. This is a surprisingly high proportion, especially given that most street homeless were interviewed in public places where other homeless persons congregated.[22] It is difficult to imagine that in such circumstances knowledge about shelters and their locations would not be almost universal.

---

21. Defined as the proportion of occupied beds in shelters up to the total capacity of shelters.
22. We tried to find out the correlates of lack of knowledge about the shelters. However, the small number of cases involved—eighty-two—stymied any attempt to find strong patterns. A set of weak relationships existed between indicators of mental illness and lack of knowledge. No other relationships appeared, including such variables as length of time homeless, education, and so on.

Among those who knew about shelters, the overwhelming majority (79%) had tried to get into a shelter over the past year. But one in five had not tried. Among those who did try, 40% reported being turned down.[23] Asked why they had been turned down, they gave answers that cite, about equally, lack of space in the shelters and their rules and requirements. How much credence to give the answers of the fourteen persons who gave these reasons is hard to assess.

This probing into why there was not full use of shelters by the homeless people interviewed on the street has not been very fruitful, mainly because so few persons were involved. Apparently, most street homeless who knew about the shelters had tried to get in. A sizable minority had been turned down at least once. And there is some hint that at least some had been turned down because they did not fit some of the shelter requirements.

Homeless People's Assessments of the Shelters

In the winter 1986 survey we also added a battery of questions designed to get at homeless people's attitudes toward the shelters. These eight questions were statements about shelters, and respondents were asked to agree or disagree. Some of the statements were laudatory and some were derogatory. The statements are given in table 4.7, along with the proportions agreeing with each among the street and shelter components of our winter sample.

Looking over the results shown in table 4.7, it is abundantly clear that most of the homeless made positive assessments of the shelters. Majorities of between three in five and four in five endorsed the positive statements, and the same proportions rejected (or disagreed with) the negative statements. The only negative statement about shelters that close to half (47%) of the homeless agreed with concerned the lack of physical safety and the presence of theft. By and large, however, the shelters were seen as the only places providing a decent place to sleep, and as being relatively safe, evenhanded in their admissions policies, clean, helpful to those who want to get back "on their feet," not too religious in tone, and not too restrictive of personal freedom. Consensus is strong that the shelters are clean and are willing to take in all comers whether or not they look respectable.

The other side of this general tone of approval and endorsement consisted of the one-fourth to one-third who endorsed the negative side of the eight statements about the shelters. As mentioned above, close to half of the homeless agreed that the shelters are dangerous. Two in five (40%) complained that there is not enough freedom to do what one wants there. More than one in four

23. Unfortunately, we cannot tell whether the turndown was an isolated incident or a pattern of repeated refusals. Nor were there enough cases to sustain an analysis of who was refused admission, although there was a statistically insignificant tendency for homeless with indicators of mental illness to be turned down.

Table 4.7 Opinions about Shelters among the Homeless (Winter 1986 Survey Only)

	Proportion Agreeing		
Opinion Statement	Street	Shelter	Total
A. The shelters are the only places a person like me can get a decent place to sleep.	62.5%	77.4%	73.4%
B. The shelters are dangerous because you can easily get robbed or beaten up there.	55.7	44.1	46.6
C. The shelters take in everyone who needs a place to sleep.	69.0	72.8	71.9
D. The shelters are so dirty I would rather sleep on the streets or in a public place.	27.3	11.4	15.1
E. The shelters only take in persons who look respectable, so the homeless who really need help are refused.	28.7	16.0	19.1
F. There is too much emphasis on religion in the shelters.	28.7	21.5	23.3
G. The shelters can really help homeless persons to get back on their feet.	68.2	79.7	76.8
H. There is not enough freedom to do what you want in the shelters.	47.7	37.5	40.3

Note: Statistically significant differences exist between shelter and street homeless on all opinion statements except C.

(26%) denied that the shelters are the "only places" where the homeless can get a decent night's sleep. About the same proportion (28%) denied that the shelters take in everyone who needs a place to sleep. Similar proportions claimed that the shelters overemphasize religion (23%) and denied that they can help homeless people get back on their feet (23%). Smaller proportions endorsed the statement that the shelters are dirtier than sleeping on the streets (15%) and that the shelters select persons based on their appearance of respectability (19%).

On seven of the eight statements shown in table 4.7, homeless persons interviewed in the street sample were more negative in their opinions of shelters than those interviewed as part of the shelter sample, differences that were statistically significant. The minority of the homeless who did not think highly of the shelters were concentrated among those who were not using them.

Any set of attitudes usually has a complex set of connections with previous experiences, exposure to various influences, and other potential causes in the past. The Chicago Homeless Study did not collect such information about what had happened in the past, so we cannot proceed in any definitive way to investigate the antecedents of homeless people's attitudes toward the shelters. It is clear that those who use shelters have a more favorable attitude toward them, but the traditional cart and horse problem plagues any interpretation of this finding. Our attempts to go beyond it brought to light only two weak correlates of negative attitudes toward shelters: persons who scored high on our measures of depression and demoralization and whom interviewers regarded as incoherent, confused, and lacking in lucidity held negative attitudes toward the shelters. It appears that the more psychologically vulnerable homeless were more likely to have negative attitudes toward shelters and perhaps were also less likely to use them.

Overall, Chicago's homeless have a favorable opinion of the shelters. In contrast, shelters in other cities may not enjoy as much approval. For example, researchers asked residents of a New York men's shelter (Crystal and Goldstein 1982) to compare that shelter with their experiences in prison. The prisons were rated as superior in several respects—personal safety, privacy, cleanliness, and food quality—and were inferior mainly in freedom. Apparently the shelter in question, a renovated psychiatric hospital, resembled in many respects a poorly run minimum-security prison whose doors were open every morning. Clearly, shelters vary widely in quality.

Who Uses the Streets?

A useful index of behavioral preference concerning being on the streets is the proportion of nights over the week before the interview that respondents spent there (as opposed to shelters or rented rooms). These proportions are used as the dependent variable in the regression analysis presented in table 4.8, with various characteristics of the homeless interviewed in the winter survey as independent variables. The regression coefficients shown in each of the rows indicate the extent to which each dependent variable responds to changes in the characteristic in question. The column of numbers displayed in table 4.8 includes the regression coefficients associated with the percentage of the past seven nights spent on the streets. For example, the coefficient for being female is $-.100$, meaning that females spent 10% fewer nights on the streets than males, holding everything else in the equation constant. This estimate is independent of the effects of the other characteristics included in the analysis. The asterisks accompanying the regression coefficients indicate the level of statistical significance; no asterisks indicates that the coefficient is not statistically different from zero.

Five characteristics had regression coefficients that were statistically significant. First of all, if interviewers rated a homeless respondent's appearance as shabby, dirty, and unkempt, the person was more likely to have spent a larger proportion (about 8% more) of the past seven nights on the streets and in public places.

Second, if interviewers regarded someone as incoherent, drunk, confused, or lacking in lucidity, that person was likely to have spent more time on the streets and in public places. Third, a complementary finding was that those who scored high on a scale measuring depression were also more likely to use the streets and public places. The fourth finding, somewhat contradictory to the first two, is that homeless persons who had spent time either in detoxification units or in mental hospitals were less likely to use the streets and public

103

Table 4.8   Percentage of Nights Spent on Streets Regressed on Characteristics of the Homeless (Winter 1986 Only)

Characteristics	b
"Shabby and unkempt" interviewer rating[a]	.077***
"Incoherent and confused" interviewer rating	.071**
Detoxification, mental hospital, or both[b]	.075*
Depression scale	.014**
Psychotic symptoms scale	.000
Criminal justice experiences scale	−.029
Age (years)	.001
Female	−.100*
White	.045
Log of time homeless	.008
Worked sometime last month	−.006
Intercept	.021
R^2	.18***
N	335

Note: Dependent variable is percentage of past seven days spent on streets or in public places.
[a] Number of negative ratings made by interviewer of respondent's appearance, neatness, dress, and cleanliness.
[b] Count of mental hospitalization and having been in a detoxification center.
*$p < .05$; **$p < .01$; ***$p < .001$.

places. Perhaps those who had sought such help in the past were more accepting of the help offered by the shelters.

It is also important to note what things did not relate to the proportion of time spent on the streets. A measure of psychotic thinking symptoms did not relate to spending more time on the streets. This finding, taken in conjunction with the interviewers' ratings of coherence and lucidity, implies that what is obvious to interviewers, and by implication to shelter managers and operators, is what is critical: those who act out are noticed more. Age, criminal record, employment status and length of time homeless also did not significantly affect the proportion of time spent on the streets.

Overall, the analyses presented in table 4.8 support the interpretation that those who consistently use the streets and public places are most likely to fit one of the stereotypes of the homeless as disreputable in appearance, incoherent in speech, and demoralized and depressed. Why they also tend to hold negative views of the shelters is less clear: perhaps these views resulted from enforcement of the rules concerning behavior that many of the shelters claim to have. Certainly, as discussed earlier, a large minority (40%) claimed to have been turned down for admission at least once during the previous year.

Cash Income

It goes without saying that the homeless are extremely poor. As shown in panel A of table 4.9, among the Chicago homeless monthly cash income averaged $168, and half had incomes under $100. At the bottom of the homeless income distribution are the close to one in five who reported no income at all. The few whose incomes in the previous month ranged above $500 were reporting wages on jobs they had lost or one-time catch-up payments from benefit programs.

The Chicago homeless are far from atypical, as panel B shows. The combined information from ten homeless studies yielded income measures very similar to the Chicago findings: the average monthly income across the ten studies was $164.61 and the median was $94.55.

There are simply no humane standards by which most of the income levels reported can be considered adequate, especially for unattached persons. There are also no standards by which the modal, median, or mean income levels can be considered adequate to sustain any reasonable standard of living in Chicago (or almost any urban place in the United States in the middle 1980s). The *modal* income was zero, clearly impossible to live on. The *median* income amounted to less than $3.33 a day, hardly enough to buy one adequate meal. The *mean* income amounted to $5.61 a day, clearly insufficient for either adequate daily food or adequate shelter, and obviously inadequate to cover both food and housing.

Even the use of public transportation is a severe financial drain at these income levels. A round-trip fare on Chicago's public transportation system cost

Table 4.9   Cash Income Received in the Previous Month

A. Chicago Homeless Study			
Income Received Last Month	Fall	Winter	Combined
None	16.9%	19.1%	18.1%
$1 to $50	19.7	25.0	22.5
$51 to $99	9.6	7.9	8.7
$100 to $149	4.1	8.8	6.6
$150 to $199	12.6	15.0	13.9
$200 to $299	12.6	7.7	10.0
$300 to $399	11.4	7.7	9.4
$400 to $499	6.2	2.3	4.2
$500 and over	6.8	6.5	6.6
N	372	350	722
Mode	$0.00	$0.00	$0.00
Median	$130.61	$79.90	$99.85
Mean	$181.25	$156.90	168.39

B. Combined Homeless Studies		
Income Measures	Average	Number of Studies
Average monthly income	$164.61	10
Median monthly income	$94.55	10

$1.80, more than half the median income and about one-third of the mean daily income.

Median and mean daily incomes are useful abstractions but should not be considered at all representative of the cash on hand at the start of each day. What may be available each day is highly variable, and even those who are relatively well-off often find themselves without any money at all on specific days. Not only do the homeless have little income, that income is also received intermittently, and there are many periods over a week or month when a homeless person may have no funds at all.

To complicate matters further, cash income levels were higher in the fall survey than in winter, when more income is needed for shelter and clothing. In the fall survey, fewer homeless had zero income, and both median and average incomes were appreciably higher. Some of these differences reflect the chances for obtaining income in fall and in winter. Casual labor opportunities may be more plentiful in the fall. Begging and peddling also may be easier in warmer weather, when more pedestrians are out on the streets and there is less physical strain on the homeless. Indeed, there is some evidence that fewer homeless people received cash from such sources in winter.[24] One of the consequences: almost one in three (31%) of the Chicago homeless reported going without food for two or more days during the month before the survey.

The Chicago homeless managed to get by largely through in-kind donations of food, clothing, and shelter. As shown in table 4.3, more than half (55%) of the previous seven days' sleeping was done in the shelters, and 6% of the times temporary housing was provided by relatives and friends (6%). The rest of the time the homeless either made use of the inadequate shelter provided by places with public access (29%) or rented rooms (4%).

In-kind donations of meals and clothing and participation in the food stamp program supplemented the inadequate income of the homeless—72% had received at least one free meal during the previous month. One wonders why this proportion is not closer to 100%. One in four (24%) participated in the federal food stamp program.[25] And four in ten received free clothing, most likely from the shelters. In short, the Chicago homeless had to rely on social service organizations to satisfy their most basic needs.

From their meager incomes the homeless had to pay for their daily necessities, such as food and clothing, and for whatever luxuries and pleasures, such as cigarettes and movies, they could afford. Getting money for everyday needs and amenities was clearly a central task that the homeless had to work at each day.

24. Data not presented here.

25. An interesting issue is how food stamps helped out the homeless, most of whom did not have a place to prepare food or cooking utensils. Of course some food products can be purchased that need little or no preparation, such as bread, cookies and crackers, fruit, cheese, and milk. Furthermore, food stamps can be converted into cash, though not legally. Finally, some of the shelters that serve families do have cooking facilities.

Table 4.10   Income Levels among the Extremely Poor

A. Monthly Income Reported by SRO Residents (1985)	
Reported Monthly Income	Percentage
Under $150	2.2
$150 to $299	23.5
$300 to $399	21.3
$400 to $499	13.7
$500 to $599	7.7
$600 and over	31.7
N	183
Average monthly income	$580.48
Median monthly income	$426.23

B. Average Annual Income Levels of the CPS Extremely Poor [a]	
Living Arrangements	1986 Income
Single parents	$478.34
Living with parents	$880.97
Living alone or with nonrelatives	$692.94
Total	$687.47

[a] Unmarried persons aged twenty-two to fifty-nine who are not students or living on farms. Income includes public welfare and other cash benefits.

Unfortunately, the Chicago General Assistance Study did not collect any income data, presumably on the grounds that eligibility for benefits indicated income levels below the eligibility cutoff of $1,800 per year. We do know that GA recipients' benefits were $154 a month; how much more they received through part-time employment, odd jobs, or other sources is simply unknown.

Because their incomes were at least sufficient to cover rent, we know that the SRO residents must have had income levels considerably above those of the homeless. The SRO monthly income distribution shown in table 4.10, based on SRO residents' reports of the incomes received the month before the interview, bears out that expectation, with income levels far above those of the homeless. Only a small percentage (2.2%) had monthly incomes below $150, a level that could not cover the rents charged and hence was likely to be a transitory state. Almost half (45%) claimed incomes between $150 and $399, and the rest had incomes of $400 and above. This distribution resulted in an average income of $580 and a median income of $426. This average income puts the typical SRO resident above the official poverty level for unattached persons ($5,250 a year) with those at the median income level just below that line.

The SRO income levels show the extent to which the homeless fall short of the income levels necessary to connect with the bottom level of the housing market in Chicago of the middle 1980s. With average SRO rentals of $195 per month, unattached persons whose income hovered around the poverty level

($440 per month) could find accommodations they could afford without too much distortion of consumption patterns. Clearly the homeless with average incomes far below that were unable to deal effectively with that market.

The incomes of the extremely poor identified in the 1987 Current Population Survey are also of interest. Because we chose to define extremely poor persons as those whose 1968 income was below $4,000, these income figures are at least in part a function of the process of classification itself. As shown in panel B of table 4.10, the average 1986 income of the CPS extremely poor was $687.47, or about $58 a month.[26] Almost half had no income at all during 1986. Although there is some variation among the extremely poor according to their living arrangements, all groups received less cash income in 1986 than the homeless.

Sources of Income

From what sources do the homeless get their incomes? The CHS questionnaire used a checklist asking whether the homeless received any income from each of a variety of sources, ranging from paid employment to handouts. The resulting data are shown in panel A of table 4.11.

Although the largest proportion acknowledged only one source, almost a third reported two or more ways they received income. Surprisingly, the source most frequently cited was employment: one in three (32%) reported receiving some income from employment the previous month. Given the low levels of income reported earlier, the employment in question must have been intermittent casual labor at very low pay.

Slightly more than one in five (22%) received some income from General Assistance, a surprisingly low level, since a very high proportion (about 80%) of the homeless were eligible for this welfare program. This low level of participation, however, is consistent with the findings from the Chicago General Assistance Study, which showed that only a very small proportion of the GA recipients were homeless.[27]

Another one in five received cash in the form of handouts, mainly from public begging. It is likely that the gifts reported as an income source by 9% of the homeless may also have been handouts. Adding these two sources together, handouts and gifts were sources of income for about one in three of the

26. Recall that CPS income includes cash benefits such as welfare or Social Security payments.

27. Extrapolating from these proportions, about 600 homeless persons were receiving General Assistance payments. Given that there were approximately 100,000 persons on GA at the time of our survey, our best bet is that 0.6% of GA clients were homeless. The expected number of homeless in the GA sample should then have been 2.4: although only one homeless person was found in the GA survey, this outcome is consistent. Illinois General Assistance regulations do not require that recipients have a residential address, although they must have a place where benefit checks can be mailed. When asked whether they had a mailing address, almost three in four (72%) claimed to have one, and more than half were shelters.

Table 4.11   Sources of Homeless People's Cash Income in Past Month

A. Chicago Homeless Study

Source	Fall	Winter	Combined
Employment	32.2%	30.7%	31.6%
General Assistance	21.8	22.5	22.1
Handouts	22.7	18.1	20.6
Friends	18.9	10.0	14.9
Family/relatives	10.0	11.2	10.2
Swaps and trades	12.7	6.9	9.6
Gifts	11.4	6.9	9.4
Other sources	10.4	7.3	9.0
Supplemental Security Income	8.6	4.6	6.8
Social Security	8.3	4.9	6.8
Disability	5.6	2.6	4.2
AFDC	5.3	7.5	6.3
Unemployment insurance	2.2	0.9	1.6
N	372	350	722
Number of income sources reported			
Mode	1.00	1.00	1.00
Median	1.32	1.11	1.22
Mean	1.65	1.33	1.51

B. Combined Homeless Studies

Measure	Average	Number of Studies
Percentage on General Relief	18.3	20
Percentage on AFDC	5.0	8
Percentage employed	17.0	24

C. Chicago SRO Residents Study

Sources of Income	Percentage
Wages	42.6
Social Security benefits	14.8
Supplemental Security Income	14.2
Veterans pensions	4.9
Other pension benefits	2.2
General Assistance	22.4
AFDC	1.6
Food stamps	33.3
Unemployment insurance	2.2
Spouse or friend	5.9
N	183

D. The CPS Extremely Poor

Benefit Program	Percentage Participating
AFDC	13
Food stamps	30
Other public assistance[a]	6
Other benefit programs[b]	13

[a] "Other public assistance" covers General Relief or emergency welfare.
[b] "Other benefit programs" include Social Security payments, unemployment insurance, veterans pensions, and so forth.

homeless. Again, despite the prevalence of these sources, the generosity of donors was not enough to provide an adequate income flow.

The remaining income sources are cited by small minorities of the homeless. Friends and relatives provided gifts (respectively to 15% and 10% of the homeless). Perhaps most telling of all are the low levels of income from pensions, disability payments, unemployment benefits, and AFDC. These findings have two somewhat contradictory implications: on the one hand, the findings indicate the extent to which the homeless were overlooked by these major income-maintenance programs. The homeless caught in our survey may not have known about the programs, may have been discouraged from applying by the administering agencies, or may have been judged ineligible. On the other hand, benefits received under these programs may have provided sufficient income to take many recipients out of the homeless group. Hence the homeless in our survey may simply have been those who were unable to qualify for income support programs or to maintain their eligibility for long periods.

Panel B of table 4.11 contains information from the combined forty studies of homelessness on the average percentage of the homeless who were employed, receiving AFDC payments, and on General Assistance. Across the twenty studies that contained information on General Assistance (or equivalent programs) 18.3% received such payments, not substantially different from the Chicago findings. The average proportion who received AFDC payments, 5%, is also quite similar to the Chicago findings. In contrast, the average percentage employed across the twenty-four studies reporting is 17%, almost half that reported in the Chicago study, but this may be due to the different reporting periods.[28]

I was unable to find any detailed information on income and sources of income among the extremely poor. Of course we know that the Chicago General Assistance clients officially had incomes below the eligibility cutoff of about $1,800, but we have no information on how far they were below that point. The GAS asked whether any of the GA clients had received money from family or friends since their last full-time job: 54% said they had. Considerably more had received such help than is shown for the homeless in panel A of table 4.11, but the periods involved are hardly comparable. In addition, 43% stated that they moved in with family or friends because they lost their last full-time job.[29] Reporting periods aside, it is clear that the GA clients received considerably more help from relatives and friends and, considering their living arrangements, continue to do so.

28. The CHS asked whether the homeless had received any income from employment over the month before the interviews. Many of the studies report on the proportion currently employed. Given the intermittent employment of the homeless, at any one point in time far fewer are employed than over periods as long as a month.

29. This is consistent with the much larger proportion who are currently living with family or friends. The percentage reported who moved in as a consequence of losing jobs applies primarily to those who had not been living with others while they were working full time.

The General Assistance sample also earned income from part-time jobs: 14% had held a part-time job of some sort for a month or more after losing their last full-time job, 19% had held a part-time job for less than a month, and 17% had worked at odd jobs at least once a week.[30] It is difficult to compare the GAS and CHS results because the reporting periods are so different. Nevertheless, the GAS sample resembles the CHS sample in showing a pattern of intermittent, unsteady, and low-paying employment.

The income sources reported by SRO residents, as shown in panel C of table 4.11, do not present strong contrasts to those of the homeless, but there are consistent and important differences. Two out of five SRO residents (43%) have income from wages, about 10% more than among the homeless. Of course their employment was better paying and more consistent: 60% of those employed worked full time. Proportionately more of the SRO residents were on the relatively generous Social Security and veterans benefit programs (34% versus 18%). About the same proportion were on General Assistance (22%), but the SRO General Assistance clients supplemented those benefits with other sources of income. Unfortunately the SRO study did not ask about assistance from relatives or friends, or about money obtained from gifts or from street trading.

The only information on income sources available for the extremely poor persons identified in the 1987 Current Population Survey concerns participation in public benefit programs, as shown in panel D of table 4.11. Perhaps the most striking feature of these data is that participation levels in all of the programs were so low. Overall, 13% receive AFDC payments—not surprisingly, since only those supporting minor children are eligible. But among single parents, only 39% received AFDC payments in 1986.[31] General Assistance (or equivalent) payments are tallied under "other public assistance," which were received by only 6% overall and by 10% of the extremely poor who were living alone.

The food stamp plan has the highest participation of all the benefit programs: almost one in three (30%) received food stamps, and among single parents more than half (54%) received this form of aid.

Average Value of Income Sources

Although we did not ask directly in the CHS how much income was received from each of the sources listed in table 4.11, we are able to estimate the average amounts using multiple regression techniques.[32] The results of this

---

30. Wages reported for these part-time positions were predominantly at the legal minimum, $3.35 an hour. Most of the part-time jobs had been terminated a year or more before the interview.

31. Single parents were concentrated in southeastern and south-central states (47% were in those regions). AFDC payment levels in many of those states are among the lowest in the country.

32. The cash income reported for the previous month was regressed on a set of binary variables (dummies) noting the presence or absence of income from each of the sources shown. The

111

Table 4.12   Distribution of Homeless People's Income by Source

A. Chicago Homeless Study				
Source	Estimated Average Income[a] (1)	Standard Error of the Estimate (2)	Percentage of Homeless Reporting Source (3)	Percentage of Total Reported Income (4)
Steady job	366.35	34.03	3.0	7.5
Temporary job(s)	72.60	11.44	31.5	15.6
Unemployment insurance	25.33	39.16	2.3	0.4
Pensions (without disability)	278.51	32.92	3.0	5.7
Supplemental Security Income	251.47	24.22	5.8	10.0
Disability payments (except SSI)	345.54	39.65	2.2	5.3
AFDC	247.39	23.08	6.3	10.7
General Assistance	130.55	12.91	21.8	19.5
Family/relatives	16.51	19.94	10.7	1.2
Friends	15.09	18.32	15.7	1.7
Gifts	56.07	20.23	10.3	4.0
Handouts	6.92	15.35	24.2	1.1
Swaps and trades	74.26	21.76	10.9	5.5
Other sources	117.01	16.53	14.7	1.8

B. Chicago SRO Residents Study	
Source	Amount Received[b] (dollars)
Wages	742.13
Social Security benefits	331.70
Supplemental Security Income	273.77
Veterans pensions	356.89
Other pension benefits	394.75
General Assistance	145.74
AFDC	280.33
Food stamps	68.74
Unemployment insurance	576.00
Spouse or friend[c]	697.09

[a]Estimates were obtained from a multiple regression analysis of 639 cases with each source coded 1 if reported and 0 otherwise. Regression coefficients are estimates of the average income from each source.

[b]Average amounts received by those who received any funds from each source.

[c]In the context, "friend" implied a live-in partner.

analysis are presented in table 4.12. Listed in the table are the estimated average net incomes from each source (column 1) and the standard error of that estimate (column 2). Also shown are the percentages of the homeless report-

------

regression coefficients shown in table 4.12 represent the net average income received by the Chicago homeless from each source.

Table 4.13   Proportion of Total Income of the Chicago Homeless from Each Source

Source	Percentage of Total Income
Economic activity	29.0
Pensions and disability	21.0
Welfare	30.2
Family and friends	2.9
Charity	5.1
Other	11.8

ing each source of income (column 3) and the income in each source as a percentage of all income received by the homeless (column 4). The sources have been reclassified in this analysis to clarify the findings. For example, I distinguish between income from steady jobs and income from intermittent employment. In addition, I have combined some of the benefit programs that are often easily confused, such as the various Social Security benefit programs.[33]

There are several important findings in panel A. First, although employment is clearly a major source of income, the wage rates involved are low. Even those employed at steady jobs are clearly working at minimum wage and even then less than full time. Second, a major source of income comprises various benefit programs, among which General Assistance clearly predominates. As discussed earlier, General Assistance payments are far from generous. Few of the homeless are on the more generous benefit plans, such as disability or retirement payments, suggesting that those qualified for these plans may thereby maintain homes. Finally, the remaining sources of income on the average produce only very small amounts and cover very small portions of the homeless population.

Panel B of table 4.12 presents comparable income data from the Chicago SRO study. Consistent with the higher average incomes of SRO residents reported earlier, each of the sources brought more income than comparable sources produced for the homeless. For example, average SRO monthly wages were $742.13, almost twice the amount estimated for the homeless. Larger monthly amounts are also reported by the SRO residents for each of the sources. In short, not only do more of the SRO residents have these sources of income, but the amounts derived from each are greater.

To summarize the findings of panel A in table 4.12, I have reclassified the sources of income into broader categories—economic activity (including employment, trading, and unemployment payments), pensions and disability payments, welfare, gifts from family and friends, charity, and "other." The proportion of the total income received by the homeless from each of these

33. Reclassification was as follows: those reporting employment as a source of income were divided into two groups, depending on how much time had passed since they last held a steady job. Those who reported being on a steady job within the past month were considered as still on steady jobs. Those whose steady jobs had terminated one or more months ago were classified as having temporary jobs.

broader sources is shown in table 4.13. Welfare was the largest source of income for the homeless, followed closely by economic activity. Pensions and disability payments formed their third major source of income. These three sources accounted for 80% of the income received by the homeless of Chicago.

Employment

Although jobs are a frequent source of income for the homeless, their employment histories show that they had not held any but intermittent jobs for long periods. Asked when they last held down a "steady job" for more than three months, most of the homeless said it was several years ago. Panel A of table 4.14 shows that the average time elapsing since the homeless last held such jobs is 55 months, or about 4.5 years. The median number of months elapsed (40) is quite different, indicating that half have been without steady employment for up to 3.3 years and half for longer. Finally, close to one-fourth (22%) have been without full-time employment for a decade or more. Indeed, there are a few who have never held full-time jobs. These "never employed" tended to be under thirty.

The extremely poor on General Assistance show job history patterns that in some respects are quite different from those of the homeless (see panel B of table 4.14). First, the median time without steady work is twenty-six weeks, almost a year less than the comparable measure for the homeless. Similarly, the average months unemployed is less than for the homeless. These two measures indicate that the General Assistance clients have left employment more recently than the homeless. But there are also counterindications. About one in four of the GA clients has been jobless for a decade or more, a slightly larger percentage than found among the homeless. I believe this reflects the younger age composition of the GA clients, many of whom are less than twenty-five years old and have never been employed full time. The overall picture that emerges is that the General Assistance clients have experienced severe unemployment that typically has lasted more than a year and that the homeless have suffered even longer stretches of unemployment.

The employment patterns of the CPS extremely poor are shown in panel C of table 4.14. About half overall did not work at all during 1986, rising to two out of three among single parents. Few (about one in five) had worked half or more of the year. Current employment patterns were somewhat higher: nearly two out of five (37%) reported being employed during the week before the interview. Most striking are the proportion who currently are either disabled or have taken themselves out of the labor force: one in four of the extremely poor who are not single parents fall into this category, with an overall prevalence of one in five. Although some of those who were extremely poor in 1986 may have managed to find employment that was steady enough to enable them to leave that category in 1987, these upwardly mobile persons probably are not a majority.

Table 4.14 Employment Patterns among the Homeless and the Extremely Poor

A. Chicago Homeless Study

Number of Months Since Last Job[a]	Fall	Winter	Total
Under 2	6.3%	5.3%	5.9%
2–3	3.0	4.4	3.7
4–6	4.5	8.5	6.4
7–12	8.3	7.7	8.0
13–24	11.7	13.9	12.7
25–48	15.9	15.9	15.9
49–119	28.3	21.8	25.3
120+	21.9	22.4	22.2
Median (months)	49.4	35.3	40.0
Mean (months)	56.4	53.1	54.9

B. Chicago General Assistance Study

Median months since last full-time[b] job	26.0
Mean months since last full-time job	42.2
Percentage whose last job was over a decade ago or who never held a full-time job	25

C. The CPS Extremely Poor

Pattern	Single Parents	Other	Total
Did not work at all in 1986	66%	49%	54%
Worked 26 weeks or more in 1986	14	21	19
Employed[c] in 1987	25	40	37
Disabled or not in labor force[d]	12	25	21

[a]Defined as a full-time job held for at least three months.
[b]Defined as a job held for at least one month and involving at least thirty hours of work each week.
[c]Employed or temporarily unemployed during the week before March 1987 interview.
[d]Persons who reported themselves as disabled or were neither keeping house, looking for work, nor employed.

An extremely important feature of the employment pattern of the homeless is worth special attention. The time elapsed since last being employed is much longer than the time homeless (as reported in table 4.5). The median time homeless was 7.6 months, in contrast to the median of 40 months since their last steady employment. In short, the homeless have lived on inadequate personal incomes literally for years before becoming homeless. Apparently a bout of unemployment can be sustained for months and sometimes years without reducing a person to the homeless state. Few of the homeless were precipitated abruptly into homelessness by the loss of a job.

Although we did not gather any information on how they managed to maintain homes for the years of unemployment before becoming homeless, the

General Assistance data provide some important clues. Before becoming homeless, it appears that, like the current General Assistance clients, these people managed to stay in homes mainly through the generosity of family and perhaps friends, supplemented by casual employment that did not qualify as a "steady job." But apparently such generosity has limits, and the long-term unemployed eventually found themselves without access to a dwelling.

Fortunately, the CHS asked about the living arrangements of the Chicago homeless immediately before they became homeless. Nearly half (47.8%) had been living alone, one in four (26.3%) had been living with primary kin—parents, spouses, children, and siblings, one in five (20.2%) had been living with nonrelatives, and the remaining one in twenty (6.2%) had been living with other relatives. It is instructive to compare these prior living arrangements of the homeless with the current arrangements of the GA clients: more of the homeless had been living alone and fewer had been living with relatives, suggesting that the GA clients were more closely tied to active support systems and that, even before becoming homeless, the Chicago homeless had less of such support.

On the national level the extremely poor who are not single parents, as identified in the 1987 Current Population Survey (see table 3.4), resemble the General Assistance clients in their living arrangements. About one in five live alone, nearly half live with relatives, and the rest are living with others to whom they are not related.

Summary

This chapter has centered on the living arrangements and economic circumstances of the extremely poor and the homeless. It is abundantly clear that in the locations where we found them for interview and in their appearance the homeless are at the bottom levels of our society's distribution of basic necessities. It is also clear that their incomes afford little else. No one can get by on close to zero income without some help: the homeless are helped largely by the welfare organizations, public and private, that provide shelter, food, and clothing.

The extremely poor resemble the homeless only with respect to cash income. Both the homeless and the extremely poor work intermittently at best and have low-paying jobs. But the domiciled extremely poor are being helped, mainly by their relatives and friends. This pattern holds not only for the General Assistance clients in Chicago but also for the extremely poor identified in the 1987 Current Population Survey.

FIVE

The Demography of Homelessness and Extreme Poverty

This chapter examines the demographic composition of the homeless and the extremely poor. It will become abundantly clear that both groups are markedly different from the general adult population in demographic terms, although the proper interpretation of those differences may not be obvious. The demographic characteristics of any subpopulation are the outcome of many processes that operate over time, selecting persons with certain characteristics from the larger population. The demographic composition of the homeless and the extremely poor results from socioeconomic forces that make it more likely that those with certain characteristics will end up among their ranks.

Demographic Characteristics

Gender

At least in the twentieth century, homelessness has largely involved males. The gender distribution shown in table 5.1 indicates that males still outnumber females among the homeless, constituting slightly more than three out of four of Chicago's homeless compared with less than half of the city's general adult population. But there were differences among the homeless: four out of five (82%) encountered in our street sample were male, in contrast to two out of three (70%) of the shelter sample, a statistically significant difference. In part this difference between the shelter and street homeless gender distributions was a function of the kinds of accommodations offered by shelters, in which the sexes were segregated and special accommodations were offered to women accompanied by young children. In a later section of this chapter we will find that almost all the homeless families were headed by women. We found no family groups among the street homeless: all the family groups, mostly female-headed households, were found in special shelters established to house families.[1]

Panel B shows the average proportion male found in all thirty-seven studies of homelessness in the 1980s. Almost four out of five (79.7%) homeless per-

---

1. This does not mean there were no families among the street homeless; but their numbers were so small that our sample of blocks was not large enough to detect that number reliably.

Table 5.1 Gender Distribution among the Homeless and the Extremely Poor

A. Chicago Homeless Study

Gender	Street Sample	Shelter Sample	Weighted Total	1980 Chicago Census[a]
Male	81.8%	70.4%	75.5%	46%
Female	18.2	29.6	24.5	54
Unweighted *N*	165	557	722	

B. Combined Homeless Studies

Average percentage male	79.7
Number of studies	37

C. Chicago's Domiciled Extremely Poor

Population	Percentage Male
General Assistance	68.4
AFDC recipients	8.1
AFDC recipients plus spouses or partners[b]	11.7
SRO residents	78.9

D. The CPS Extremely Poor

Living Arrangements	Percentage Male
Single parents	9
Living with parents	69
Living alone or with nonrelatives	51
Total	44

Note: Differences are significant at $p < .05$
[a] As reported in the 1980 census for the city of Chicago for persons aged eighteen and over.
[b] Computed by adding spouses or partners to AFDC recipients when the latter are living with a spouse or partner.

sons were male. In individual studies, the proportion male ranged from 50% to 99%, with most of the studies clustered around 80%.

Based on the early studies of Skid Row populations, this heavily male gender distribution has been characteristic of the homeless over the past fifty years. Indeed, it appears that the proportion of women in the homeless population has increased: observers in the 1950s and 1960s uniformly remarked on the almost complete absence of women among the homeless groups they studied. The change from close to zero female to the 20% to 25% of today is a remarkable increase.

Panel C shows the proportion male among the domiciled extremely poor. Males predominate in the GA population, though not to the extent found among the homeless: a little more than two out of three of the GA clients were male. None of the female GA recipients had minor children of their own living with them: most women with minor children are taken care of by the AFDC portion of the income maintenance system. As a matter of agency policy, anyone applying to the Illinois Department of Public Aid for welfare assistance is placed on AFDC if eligible, because GA is a state-funded program whereas AFDC is partially supported by federal funds. Although AFDC recipients can in no way be regarded as living in luxury, they receive enough to lift them above the level of extreme poverty: the average annual Illinois AFDC payment in 1985 for a household with two children was about $4,000 plus additional benefits in the form of Medicaid and food stamps.

The overwhelming majority of AFDC recipients are female, as shown in panel C of table 5.1. Very few (8.1%) of this group are males. Even when we make the somewhat shaky assumption that spouses and "live-ins" in the same household as the AFDC recipients are being supported by the AFDC grant, the proportion male among AFDC recipients rises only to 11.7%.

The last line of panel C presents the proportion male found in the SRO resident study. Almost four out of five (79%) of the SRO residents were male, a proportion that is very similar to both the homeless population and the extremely poor GA recipients.

Homelessness may afflict males more often than females, but that is not true of extreme poverty. If we combine the GA and AFDC populations of Chicago as an approximation to the extremely poor of that city,[2] the proportion female among the combined group is very high. In 1986 there were about 400,000 AFDC recipients in Chicago and about 100,000 GA clients. Given the gender ratios within each group, it appears that the domiciled extremely poor are predominantly female, constituting about 75% of the combined GA and AFDC populations.

Among the extremely poor throughout the nation, as identified in the Current Population Survey, women also predominate, though not to the same extent, constituting 56% of unattached adults earning $4,000 or less (see panel D of table 5.1).

Extreme poverty apparently affects more women than men, especially those who are single parents. Given the responsibility single mothers take on for feeding, clothing, and housing their children, their poverty must be judged even more extreme than is the case for men, few of whom take on such responsibility. The greater poverty of single parents is mitigated only by greater access to AFDC benefits, a relatively generous benefit program compared with General Assistance.

Why more men than women become homeless when afflicted by extreme poverty is an issue I will address later in conjunction with other characteristics that may be associated with gender. But only part of the explanation can come from that direction: men and women are regarded differently by society in

2. Combining the AFDC and GA populations leads to an underestimation of the extremely poor. As shown in the Current Population Survey data, participation in AFDC and other public assistance programs comes nowhere near covering the entire eligible population. Without fuller knowledge of the extent to which AFDC and GA cover the eligible Chicago population, it is difficult to gauge the extent to which these figures underestimate the situation in Chicago.

general, and considerably more sympathy and support is extended to women, especially when they are rearing children. Not only is more help offered to women by society, but families are more protective of their female members. Intrakin support is more easily extended to females than to males.[3]

Age Distribution

In both mean age and median age, the Chicago homeless were very similar to the 1980 census adult population of Chicago (see panel A of table 5.2). Nor were the shelter and street homeless very different from each other. With median and mean ages about thirty-nine to forty, the typical homeless person was a young adult in the middle years. But means and medians can be misleading, as an examination of the age distributions in panel A of table 5.2 shows: the Chicago 1980 census contained proportionately more old and very young persons than either the shelter or the homeless sample. In contrast, the homeless were concentrated more heavily in the middle years, between thirty and forty-five. In short, the homeless were not drawn exclusively or largely from the archetypal dependent groups of the very young or the old, but were of all ages, with a propensity toward overrepresentation of those in the middle "productive years."

The preponderance of people in their thirties and early forties places the homeless squarely among the products of the post–World War II "baby boom." This position in demographic history explains some of their economic fate. The large numbers of this cohort adversely affected their competitive position in the labor market, an interpretation I will return to in the last chapter.

The virtual absence of people over sixty-five among the homeless deserves some comment, primarily because that low incidence is in stark contrast to the findings in the 1950s and 1960s. In 1958, 20% of the homeless of Chicago were over sixty-five, more than ten times the current 1.7% (Bogue 1963). Even higher percentages (45%) of people over sixty-five were found on New York's Bowery in that period (Bahr and Caplow 1974). An especially critical difference between the past and the present is the drastic improvement in Social Security old age pensions that occurred in the early 1970s: average Social Security retirement payments in Illinois in 1986 were over $500 per month, more than enough to allow pensioners to connect with the housing market. In addition, subsidized housing was made available to senior citizens, further enhancing their ability to obtain "affordable" housing. These changes have dramatically improved the housing conditions of the elderly to the point that very few are among the homeless.

Panel A of table 5.2 also shows strong age differences between male and

3. See especially the analysis of kinship obligation norms in Alice S. Rossi and Peter H. Rossi, *Of Human Bonding: A Life Course Perspective on Parent-Child Relations* (Hawthorne, N.Y.: Aldine-DeGruyter, 1989). We found that, among all kin, respondents acknowledged the strongest obligations to provide financial aid to unattached daughters and mothers.

Table 5.2 Age Composition of the Homeless and the Extremely Poor

A. Chicago Homeless Study (Street and Shelter Samples)

Age of Respondent	Street Sample	Shelter Sample	Weighted Total	1980 Chicago Census[a]	Males	Females
Under 25	8.9%	13.4%	11.4%	18.7%		
25–29	16.5	11.9	14.0	12.8		
30–34	10.9	14.7	13.0	10.3		
35–39	13.5	11.4	12.4	7.8		
40–44	15.7	12.8	14.1	6.8		
45–54	13.8	17.4	15.8	13.8		
55 and over	20.6	18.4	19.4[b]	29.6		
Unweighted *N*	165	557	722			
Mean age	41.5	40.0	40.3	39.4	41.6	36.6
Median age	40.2	38.4	39.0	40.3	40.4	34.4

B. Combined Homeless Studies

Measure	Years	Number of Studies
Mean age	36.1	23
Median age	36.1	21

C. GA and AFDC Clients and SRO Residents

Age	GA	AFDC	SRO
Under 25	43.4%	28.7%	5.9%
25–29	18.5	22.9	9.8
30–34	11.5	17.4	9.2
35–39	5.0	11.2	8.6
40–44	5.6	9.0	13.0
45–54	9.0	7.6	20.5
55+[c]	7.5	3.1	33.0
N	400	737	185
Average age	30.5	31.3	46.2
Median age	25.9	29.2	46.5

D. The CPS Extremely Poor

Living Arrangements	Average Age
Single parents	36.4
Living with parents	38.9
Living alone or with nonrelatives	38.4
Total	37.4

Note: Differences between shelter and street samples are not significant; gender differences are significant at $p < .05$.

[a] Adult persons eighteen and older.

[b] Only 1.7% of the Chicago homeless were over sixty-five.

[c] None of the GA or AFDC clients were over sixty-five. In contrast, 10.3% of the SRO residents were over sixty-five.

female homeless persons, women having mean and median ages some five to six years younger than men. This strong age difference by gender foreshadows several other differences that will build to a case that these groups had quite different reasons for being homeless. I will return to these important gender differences later in this chapter.

Chicago's homeless were older than the typical homeless person studied throughout the country, as panel B indicates. Calculated over twenty-three studies, the average age of the homeless was thirty-six and the median (based on twenty-one studies) also thirty-six, some four years younger than was typical for Chicago. No explanation comes to mind.

Panel C shows the age distributions found in the Chicago GA, AFDC, and SRO studies. General Assistance is dominated by the very young: half are under twenty-six, with an average age of 30.5. Although not quite as young as the GA clients, AFDC recipients are also much younger than the average homeless person: median and average ages were 31.3 and 29.2, with about one in four under 25 (28.7%).

It is easy to understand why AFDC recipients are so young because they must have dependent minor children. It is not immediately obvious why the GA recipients are so young. Clearly, families are willing to subsidize their relatively young adult dependents, say up to the age of thirty, as is true for most GA recipients, but they are not as willing to take care of their older adult dependents in their middle thirties and early forties.

The SRO age distribution stands out as very different from either the homeless, the GA clients, or the AFDC clients. Average and median ages are much higher, forty-six, with a large proportion, 10%, over sixty-five. Indeed, the SRO population comes closest in age to the residents of the Skid Rows of the 1950s and 1960s. Note that there are very few SRO residents under thirty. SRO residents over sixty-five subsisted on their old age pensions, which, as I mentioned above, are high enough to pay for SRO accommodations.[4]

The average age of the extremely poor of the nation, as shown in panel D of table 5.2, is slightly over thirty-seven years, closer to the average for the Chicago homeless than for any of the other groups discussed in this section. Of course, the age restriction (twenty-two to fifty-nine) placed on the definition of the extremely poor affects this average: many of the Chicago GA clients, as we saw earlier, are below the cutoff and would not qualify under the Current Population Survey definition.

Race and Ethnicity

The self-reported racial/ethnic composition of the Chicago homeless is shown in panel A of table 5.3, along with the 1980 census racial distributions

---

4. An element in the decline of SRO accommodations, according to SRO hotel owners and managers, is the availability of subsidized senior citizens' housing (Chicago Department of Planning 1985).

Table 5.3 Race and Ethnicity (Percentages)

A. Chicago Homeless Study

Race or Ethnicity	Street Sample	Shelter Sample	Weighted Total	1980 Chicago Census
Hispanic white	3.0	7.5	5.5	—[a]
Hispanic black	1.0	1.8	1.4	—[a]
Black American	55.6	50.8	53.0	35.5
American Indian	7.1	3.5	5.1	0.1
Asian or Pacific	1.0	0.4	0.7	2.3
White	28.9	32.1	30.7	55.1
Other	3.3	3.4	3.3	7.0
Don't know	0.0	0.5	0.3	—
Unweighted N	165	557	722	

B. Combined Homeless Studies

Race or Ethnicity	Average Percentage	Number of Studies
Black	45.8	31
Hispanic	11.8	19
American Indian	4.9	13

C. Chicago GA and AFDC Clients and SRO Residents

Race or Ethnicity	GA	AFDC	SRO
Black	71.2	76.4	54.1
White	12.0	9.7	40.5
Hispanic	13.2	12.1	3.2
American Indian	1.0	0.6	0.5
Other	2.4	1.5	1.6
N	400	737	185

D. Johnson-Pew Clinic Populations

City	White	Black	Hispanic
Albuquerque	58.2	4.6	24.9
Baltimore	35.7	64.5	1.7
Birmingham	53.9	46.1	0.0
Boston	75.2	20.6	2.0
Chicago	31.7	62.7	4.1
Detroit	27.5	71.1	1.4
Milwaukee	37.3	62.7	0.0
Nashville	79.5	16.0	3.4
New York	25.3	52.2	22.0
Philadelphia	35.8	57.2	4.4
San Antonio	55.8	6.9	34.1
San Francisco	72.4	22.3	5.3
Washington, D.C.	17.6	80.8	0.8

continued

Table 5.3 *continued*

E. The CPS Extremely Poor	
Living Arrangements	Percentage Nonwhite
Single parents	43
Living with parents	27
Living alone or with nonrelatives	33
Total	30

[a]The 1980 United States census does not provide counts of white and black Hispanics.

in Chicago.[5] It appears that all racial and ethnic groups are represented among the homeless, but some are overrepresented compared with their presence in the general Chicago population. Blacks constitute about one-third of the 1980 Chicago census adult population, but slightly more than half (53%) of both the shelter and street populations. (If we add those who consider themselves black Hispanics,[6] the proportion black goes up slightly, to 54%).

Perhaps the racial/ethnic group most overrepresented among the Chicago homeless is American Indians, who constitute 7.1% of the street sample, 3.5% of the shelter sample, and 5.1% of the total homeless, but only 0.1% of the Chicago census population.[7]

About one in three of the homeless is white (29% of the street and 32% of the shelter samples), indicating that whites are underrepresented among the homeless compared with their proportion (55%) in the general Chicago adult population. Note that there are no significant differences in ethnicity between the shelter sample and the street sample, although it does appear that American Indians are particularly numerous in the street sample.

Panel B of table 5.3 shows the average racial/ethnic distributions across the homeless studies that reported such information. Because ethnic composition varies between cities, these overall percentages reflect both the overrepresentation of minority ethnic groups among the homeless and the ethnic mixes of particular cities. Nevertheless blacks, averaging close to half (46%) of the homeless, are clearly overrepresented, especially in the largest urban centers—New York, Los Angeles, and Chicago—all of which reported that blacks constituted 53% to 70% of the homeless.

Panel C of table 5.3 shows the ethnic compositions of the Chicago AFDC,

5. Respondents were read a list of ethnic/racial categories and asked which group they considered themselves to be in. The list corresponds to the categories in panel A of table 5.3.

6. The two major components of Chicago's Hispanic population, those of Mexican origins and those of Puerto Rican origins, cannot be distinguished in the Chicago Homeless Study. The strength of the traditional family system varies considerably between these two groups with Mexican Americans showing much stronger family ties than Puerto Ricans.

7. Overrepresentation of American Indians among the homeless was found in both fall and winter surveys. Nevertheless, the small numbers clearly suggest caution in interpreting these findings.

SRO, and GA samples. Among the AFDC and GA groups the ethnic composition is even more distorted toward an extreme overrepresentation of blacks. More than three-fourths (76%) of the AFDC clients and 71% of the GA clients are black, compared with only 54% of the homeless. Similar distortions characterize Hispanics. Only whites and American Indians have lower representations in these two client groups, compared with their representation among the homeless. Apparently whites and American Indians are more likely to slip across the permeable boundary between the domiciled extremely poor and the homeless. In addition, that whites are so underrepresented in the GA and AFDC client groups suggests that black and Hispanic families are more likely to subsidize their dependent adult members. (I will return to this interpretation later in this chapter.)

In contrast, SRO residents are more comparable to the homeless in ethnic composition. A little more than 40% are white, and a little more than half (54%) are black. Compared with the other samples, Hispanics and American Indians are underrepresented.

The age composition of the several ethnic groups suggests that whites are not being recruited into the extremely poor segments of Chicago to the same degree as are blacks. In all the groups studied the average age of white members is higher than that of blacks. Among the homeless and among SRO residents, whites tend to be concentrated in the over-forty age bracket, whereas blacks constitute higher proportions of persons under forty. The young ages of AFDC and GA clients, who are heavily black, are also consistent with this interpretation that increasing numbers of young blacks and other minority groups are being recruited into Chicago's extremely poor population.

The ethnic composition of the homeless is heavily influenced by the ethnic composition of the community under study. Panel D of table 5.3 presents data on the ethnic composition of clients from the medical clinics for the homeless funded by the Robert Wood Johnson Foundation and the Pew Memorial Trust. The proportion who are white ranges widely, from a high of 79% in Nashville to a low of 18% in Washington, D.C., and these proportions strongly reflect the racial mix of the very poor in these cities. Note, however, that in almost every city shown, the proportion of either black or Hispanic clients is greater than those found in the general population.

On the national level there is also overrepresentation of blacks among the extremely poor as identified in the 1987 Current Population Survey, as shown in panel E. Overall, 30% of the extremely poor nationally are nonwhite,[8] the result of a considerable overrepresentation of blacks. Nonwhites are especially overrepresented among single parents, constituting 44%, and among those living alone or with nonrelatives, constituting 33%.

8. No finer ethnic breakdowns are possible in the CPS data. Nonwhites are mainly black. Hispanics are included in either white or nonwhite, depending on their race.

Table 5.4   Migration Status of the Homeless and the Extremely Poor

A. Chicago Homeless Study			
Residence and Migration	Street Sample	Shelter Sample	Weighted Total	1980 Chicago Census
Born in Illinois	40.5%	51.2%	45.8%	59.2%
Lived in Chicago				
10+ years	70.0	74.1	72.3	33.4[a]
5–9 years	6.0	5.9	5.9	
1–4 years	12.7	9.0	10.7	7.4[b]
Less than 1 year	11.2	11.0	11.1	
Unweighted N	165	557	722	

B. Chicago GA and AFDC Clients[c]		
	GA	AFDC
Born in Chicago	54%	56%

[a]Proportion not born in Illinois but living in Illinois more than five years.
[b]Proportion living in Chicago less than five years.
[c]No comparable information on migration exists in the SRO study.

Migration

Most homeless people are long-term residents of Illinois and of Chicago: 40% of the street sample and 51% of the shelter sample were born in Illinois. Other large minorities (30% and 23%) were born in some other state but have lived in Illinois for a decade or more (see panel A of table 5.4). The rest were born elsewhere and have lived in Chicago for less than a decade. Some are relative newcomers: 11% of both the street and shelter samples have lived in Chicago less than a year.[9] Compared with the shelter sample, the street sample contained a significantly greater proportion of migrants to Chicago, fewer having been born in Illinois.

Today's Chicago homeless are clearly not the migratory workers who inhabited the Skid Row of history. Most have been Chicagoans for some time and have a personal history in Chicago that reaches back a number of years. At the same time, the homeless were also more likely to be migrants than other Chicagoans: 11% have lived in Chicago less than one year, whereas only 7% of Chicagoans generally have lived there less than five years.[10]

Unfortunately we do not have access to entirely comparable data on either AFDC or GA clients. Panel B shows that more than half of both groups were born in Chicago, 56% and 54%, respectively. The most nearly comparable

9. Fewer than half of those who have been in Chicago less than a year are very recent migrants who arrived within the month before they were interviewed—4.1% of the street sample and 4.7% of the shelter sample.
10. Unfortunately the 1980 census does not provide data on migration over periods shorter than five years.

measure on the homeless, the proportion born in Illinois, is lower (45%), suggesting that the GA and AFDC clients were less likely to be migrants either from other states or from other places in Illinois.

Clearly there are more newcomers to Chicago among the homeless than among the extremely poor, but a common stereotype that sees the homeless as migratory is clearly contradicted by these data.

Educational Attainment

The average educational attainment of the homeless samples was not very different from that of the general Chicago population, as shown in panel A of table 5.5. The modal homeless person was a high-school dropout (37%), but

Table 5.5   Educational Attainment

A. Chicago Homeless Study			
Years of Education	Street Sample	Shelter Sample	Weighted Total	1980 Chicago Census[a]
0–7	7.9%	7.2%	7.6%	14.1%
8–11	35.1	8.9	37.2	29.7
12[b]	33.0	30.3	31.6	28.4
13–15	16.8	19.3	18.1	14.0
16[c]	4.6	2.8	3.6	6.8
17+	2.6	1.4	2.0	7.0
Unweighted N	165	557	722	

B. GA and AFDC Clients and SRO Residents			
Years of Education	GA	AFDC	SRO
0–7	2.0%	7.2%	9.2%
8–11	46.8	45.8	37.8
Subtotal	48.8	53.0	47.0
High-school graduate	28.9	23.2	32.5
Some college	20.3	22.5	15.1
College graduate	3.0	1.4	5.4
N	400	737	185

C. The CPS Extremely Poor	
Living Arrangements	Average Years of Education
Single parents	11.9
Living with parents	13.0
Living alone or with nonrelatives	12.2
Total	12.4

Note: Differences between street and shelter samples in panel A are *not* statistically significant.
[a]Census population consists of adults twenty-five and over.
[b]High-school graduate.
[c]College graduate.

so was the typical Chicagoan (30%). Almost as frequent among the homeless, however, were high-school graduates (32%), comparing favorably in that respect with Chicagoans generally (28%). The homeless have considerably less than their share of college graduates; the general population has almost twice as many college graduates and three times as many with postgraduate training. There appeared to be no substantial differences in educational attainment between the shelter and street samples.

Panel B of table 5.5 displays the educational attainment of Chicago AFDC and GA clients and SRO residents. If anything, the levels shown for the GA and AFDC groups are lower than those of the homeless. Almost half (49% of the GA group and 53% of the AFDC group) did not complete high school or earn a GED (general equivalency diploma). There are fewer who have completed college, but there are more who have taken some training beyond high school. These differences may be accounted for by the younger ages of the AFDC and GA clients: in a decade, more will have passed the GED examination and will then claim the equivalent of high-school graduation.[11]

The SRO residents and the homeless are quite similar in educational attainment. Considering the higher average age of the SRO residents, this similarity may mean that they are somewhat better educated than persons of comparable age among the homeless.

Of course, comparing the general Chicago adult population with SRO residents, homeless, GA, and AFDC samples does not take into account the differences in age distribution noted earlier. Older persons have significantly less education, and older persons were underrepresented among the homeless. If we were to correct for the age differences, it is very likely that the homeless population would show significantly lower educational attainment compared with the general population. The differences, however, would not be great.

By and large, Chicago's homeless population was not suffering from any serious relative deficit in years of education completed.[12] Of course this statement does not address the issues of educational quality or of the actual achievement of basic skills that formal education is supposed to impart. Unfortunately we have no measures of such skills except for self-reports from the GA clients: 16% said they had trouble reading instructions on job applications, and 25% had trouble doing arithmetic. Whatever the formal levels of education may have been, significant minorities among the GA applicants had problems in using basic skills.

Panel C of table 5.5 presents data from the Current Population Survey on the average educational attainment of the nation's extremely poor. On average, the extremely poor had gone a little beyond high-school graduation (12.4

11. Indeed, one in five of the AFDC and GA clients was enrolled in some kind of educational program when interviewed. Although for some this may have been employment training, for others it may have been aimed at improving their educational attainment level.

12. This pattern is radically different from those shown by homeless studies in the 1950s and 1960s, which all remarked on the severe educational deficiencies of the men studied.

years). Clearly, there appears to be no sign of gross educational deficiency among the extremely poor either.

Marital Status

One of the most dramatic contrasts between the homeless samples and the general Chicago population can be seen in current marital status, shown in panel A of table 5.6. In 1980 more than two out of five (43%) of all Chicagoans over age fifteen were currently married, compared with only 7% of the total homeless. Within the homeless group, only 5% of the street sample

Table 5.6 Current Marital Status

A. Chicago Homeless Study				
Marital Status	Street Sample	Shelter Sample	Weighted Sample	1980 Chicago Census[a]
Married	5.4%	8.2%	6.9%	43.3%
Not married	96.6	92.8	93.1	56.7
Divorced or separated	29.9	33.5	31.9	12.5
Widowed	3.6	4.8	4.3	9.4
Single, never married	61.1	53.3	56.8	34.8
Don't know	0.0	0.1	0.1	
Unweighted N	165	557	722	

B. Combined Homeless Studies		
Measure	Percentage	Number of Studies
Currently unmarried	88.5	26

C. Chicago GA and AFDC Clients and SRO Residents			
Current Marital Status	GA	AFDC	SRO
Married	7.7%	9.7%	6.5%
Not married	92.3	91.3	93.5
Divorced or separated	23.0	44.1	38.9
Widowed	3.3	1.7	10.3
Single, never married	66.0	54.2	44.3
Don't know and refused	0.0	0.2	0.0
N	400	737	185

D. The CPS Extremely Poor				
Marital Status	Single Parents	Living with Parents	Living Alone or with Nonrelatives	Total
Married	4%	2%	5%	4%
Widowed, separated, divorced	62	15	44	40
Never married	34	84	52	57

and 8% of the shelter sample were currently married. Furthermore, the homeless samples contained almost three times the all-Chicago proportion of persons divorced or separated (32% compared with 12%). Finally, a majority (57%) of the homeless have never been married (61% of the street and 53% of the shelter samples), a stark contrast to the all-Chicago proportion, 35%.

The contrast between the general Chicago population and the homeless would be even greater if we took age into account. The census tabulates marital status for all persons fifteen years old and older. Only a handful of the homeless are between fifteen and twenty-one, the age group in which many of the never-married persons in the census can be found. In addition, the homeless population contains relatively few aged persons, of whom many are widowed. Hence the contrasts in table 5.6 understate the extent to which the Chicago homeless were less likely to have been married than the general Chicago population. The homeless have failed in the marriage market about to the same extent as they have failed in the labor market, as a later section of this chapter documents.

In short, 92% to 95% of the homeless were currently not married. Homelessness is almost identical with "spouselessness." That so many have never been married has important implications. For example, many welfare programs are specifically reserved for married persons and families. Income-maintenance programs for those without families tend to be difficult to enter and are not generous in payments. In addition, homeless persons generally are not members of households and are therefore deprived of the financial and emotional buffering against life's vicissitudes that household membership provides.

Panel B contains the findings from twenty-six other homeless studies that reported on marital status. The average proportion currently unmarried was 88.5%, slightly lower than for the homeless of Chicago but certainly far from the typical marital status of the American adult population.

Panel C shows the marital status distributions from the Chicago GA, AFDC, and SRO studies. These three populations resemble the homeless more closely than they resemble the general Chicago adult population. More than nine out of ten are currently unmarried, with AFDC clients slightly more likely to be married. GA clients are more likely to have never been married (66%). The AFDC population is more heavily weighted with the formerly married. The SRO residents have a high proportion of widowed persons, which goes along with their high proportion of persons over sixty-five.

All the special Chicago samples show the same marital status characteristics, living outside marriage. For the homeless, GA clients, and SRO residents, this also means living outside primary family life altogether, while the AFDC women, by definition, are living with their children.

The extremely poor nationally, as identified in the 1987 Current Population Survey, were defined as "unattached" persons, living in households where no spouse was present. In part this definition exaggerates the proportion of the extremely poor who are not currently married, as shown in panel D. As in the

Table 5.7   Gender Differences in Current Marital Status

Current Marital Status	Males	Females
Married	6.1%	12.5%
Not married	93.9	87.5
Divorced or separated	33.2	31.8
Widowed	4.2	5.2
Single	56.3	50.5
Don't know	0.2	0.0
N .	527	194

Note: Gender differences are significant at $p < .05$.

case of the Chicago homeless and the extremely poor, very few (4%) of the nation's extremely poor are currently married. A majority (57%) have never been married, and two in five (40%) have had marriages broken by divorce, separation, or death. Note the strong variations among the living arrangements groups: 84% of those living with their parents had never married, and 62% of the single parents had broken marriages.

There were significant differences in marital status between men and women among the homeless, with women more than twice as likely to be currently married and correspondingly fewer women having never been married (see table 5.7). In part this gender difference reflects the fact that some of the shelters also served as "transitional" refuges for women trying to escape from marriages that had gone sour or from conflict-ridden households shared with parents or other relatives.

Parental Status

A majority (54%) of the homeless have had children, despite the low proportion who have ever been married (see table 5.8). A fair proportion (one in nine) have had four or more children, and one homeless man claimed to have fathered seventeen! Taking into account the marital status of the homeless, this pattern also means that few of the homeless have taken any responsibility for the children they brought into the world. Of course, given their incomes, as shown in chapter 4, they have little capacity to make any financial contribution.

Panel B of table 5.8 shows that GA clients have a profile very similar to that of the homeless. Almost half (47%) are parents, although almost two-thirds have never been married. As we saw in chapter 3, most are living with their parents and clearly do not provide homes for their own children.

By definition, all AFDC clients have children, and most are the heads of households containing their children: a few are taking responsibility for their grandchildren. Taking into account the gender patterning of the several subgroups, it is tempting to speculate that the mothers of the children fathered by homeless men and male GA clients constitute the bulk of the AFDC popula-

Table 5.8 Number of Children Ever Born

A. Chicago Homeless Study			
Number of Children	Males	Females	Total
None	49.5%	29.2%	46.2%
One	15.9	20.3	15.3
Two	14.0	20.3	16.2
Three	9.6	14.6	11.2
Four or more	11.0	15.6	11.1
N	527	194	722

B. Chicago General Assistance Study	
Number of Children	Percentage
None	53.2
One	17.2
Two	12.0
Three	6.3
Four or more	11.3
N	400

Note: Differences in panel A are significant at $p < .01$.

tion. Certainly it is likely that some of the mothers of the children so fathered are AFDC clients, but that can hardly be a predominant pattern. There are many more AFDC clients than there are homeless men or male GA recipients. In 1984 there were over 400,000 AFDC recipients in Chicago compared with 100,000 GA clients and about 2,000 homeless men, of whom fewer than half are fathers; this numerical asymmetry assures us that most of the fathers of AFDC children are not homeless men or male GA recipients.

As can be seen in table 5.8, homeless women were significantly more likely to have been parents; almost four in five have had at least one child. Males have apparently fathered children but never formed legal marriages and most likely never have formed households with their children and the women involved.

Homeless Families or Homeless Individuals?

Because the homeless people in our sample were relatively young, their children were likely not to be mature adults, but rather at most to be in late adolescence. This statement holds particularly for homeless women, who were younger than the men in our samples. The lower average age of the women means that many of their children were probably at most in early adolescence.

Nevertheless, whatever the ages of their children and whatever their current marital status, most (91%) of the homeless persons were currently alone in

Table 5.9   Homeless Alone or with Other Persons

	Street Sample	Shelter Sample	Weighted Total
Percentage alone[a]	97.9	86.1	91.4
Persons present with respondent[b]			
Children		80.3	
Spouse		27.9	
Other relatives		3.3	
Nonrelatives		6.6	
N		66	

[a]Differences are significant at $p < .001$.
[b]Computed only for the sixty-six persons who have others homeless with them. Proportions add to more than 100% because of multiple persons homeless with respondent. Proportions are based on weighted sample.

their homelessness, as table 5.9 indicates.[13] As might be expected, all the homeless in the street sample were totally alone, whereas about one in seven (14%) of the shelter sample had some of their family with them. Table 5.9 also considers the persons who accompanied respondents in homelessness. The predominant (80%) family members who shared homelessness with our respondents were children; only 28% had a spouse with them.

Again, this pattern strongly reflects the presence of women who brought their young children with them into the shelters when they left their previous living arrangements.[14] As shown in table 5.9, virtually all (91%) the homeless had no immediate family or other relatives with them in the homeless state. However, there are strong gender differences. Homeless men are almost all alone. In contrast, slightly more than one in four (29%) of the homeless women had someone with them, predominantly children. Needless to say, this gender difference was highly significant statistically.

Those who were homeless with their children were quite different from other homeless persons. Nine out of ten (88%) were women, and the few men were all accompanied by their wives as well as their children. All the homeless families were found in the shelters; none were among the street homeless. The heads of homeless families were much younger, their average age being twenty-eight, twelve years below the average for all the Chicago homeless. Finally, they had been homeless for relatively short periods, averaging 3.5 months, with half homeless for a month or less.

All told, these characteristics set homeless families apart from the other

13. The question that elicited these responses was, "Are you by yourself or do you have some family—husband/wife, children, or some other relatives—who are homeless with you?"
14. Several of the shelters had explicit policies of accepting only children under a certain age, usually sixteen, as part of family groups.

homeless. Certainly they share the same degree of poverty, but their prospects for moving out of the homeless condition are clearly much better, as their average time homeless indicates. Homeless families are households in transition: most consist of young women with very young children, many leaving their parents' households on the way to setting up separate establishments. The typical homeless family resembled the AFDC households, and I venture that most will join that group as soon as they can enroll in AFDC and find appropriate housing.

The Chicago homeless families apparently have better prospects than homeless families in other cities. In contrast, the more than 3,000 New York City homeless families currently being housed in welfare hotels have dismal prospects, reflecting the much more meager supply of low-rent housing in New York.

Employment and Occupation

In chapter 4 we saw that the homeless typically have not held steady jobs for several years. But intermittent and part-time employment that does not fit the category of "steady jobs" was not entirely absent. Minorities of the homeless managed to find occasional work during the period immediately before our surveys.

As panel A of table 5.10 indicates, three out of five homeless persons did not work at all during the month before the survey. But some did work: one in four had been employed during the previous week, and two in five had worked sometime during the previous month. Members of the shelter sample were more likely to have worked during the month before the interview.

Unfortunately, neither the GA nor the AFDC study collected any information on the current work status of those samples, presumably because to be eligible for benefits the GA and AFDC clients had to have zero or close to zero earnings. However, work status information was available from the SRO study and is shown in panel B. Although the average income level of the SRO residents was relatively high (as we saw in chap. 4), only two out of five were employed either full time or part time. About one in three was retired (8%) or too disabled to work (24%), receiving income from pensions or disability benefits. Almost one in four (24%) was unemployed and looking for work, presumably between jobs. Although this is a relatively high unemployment rate, it must reflect a pattern of intermittent full-time employment, perhaps working a few months full time, spending a short time unemployed, and then finding employment again. A very small proportion (3%) were discouraged workers, neither working nor looking for work. The Chicago SRO residents apparently got by by piecing together income from a variety of sources.

The contrast between the homeless and the SRO residents shows what employment patterns are necessary for unattached persons to connect successfully with the bottom of the housing market. Full-time employment is

Table 5.10   Proportions Who Worked for Pay Last Week or Last Month

A. Chicago Homeless Study			
Worked for Pay	Street Sample	Shelter Sample	Weighted Total
Last week	23.3	25.9	24.7
Not last week, but during last month	11.4	16.7	14.2
Anytime during last month	34.7	42.6	38.9
Not at all last month	65.3	57.4	61.1
Don't know	1.0	0.0	0.5
Unweighted N	165	553	718

B. Chicago SRO Residents Study	
Current Employment Status	Percentage
Full-time work	33.7
Part-time work	7.2
Unemployed, looking for work	23.8
Retired	8.3
Disabled	23.8
Discouraged worker	3.3
N	181

necessary or failing that, enrollment in one or another of the more generous benefit programs.

Mirroring findings in the general population, there were clear gender differences in the work experience of the homeless over the month before the survey: 31% of the homeless men and 16% of the homeless women had worked during the previous week. The gender differences were even stronger when we consider the previous month, with 51% of the men having worked then compared with 23% of the women.

Of course the jobs the homeless held mostly were part-time positions at very low wages, not employment that was steady and paid well. Nor did these jobs demand much previous experience or highly honed skills. Table 5.11 shows the types of work involved in the last month's employment. More than one in three (37%) was a job classified by the census as "laborer." One person in six sold newspapers,[15] and 10% worked in food-service occupations. The rest were scattered throughout the labor force with no concentration in particular jobs. Note, however, that the work was mostly at the bottom of the occupational hierarchy, with a concentration in service jobs.

The jobs held by the homeless in the previous month were similar to the last steady jobs they held (data on last steady jobs are not shown here). Although

15. The Chicago *Tribune* employed some of the homeless men to sell newspapers to motorists at stoplights in the Loop.

Table 5.11 Jobs Held by Chicago Homeless and General Assistance Clients

A. Job Held Last Month by Those in Chicago Homeless Study			
Type of Work	Males	Females	Total
Professional	1.0%	1.5%	1.0%
Clerical	3.5	14.2	5.1
Sales	3.9	6.8	4.3
Newspaper sales	18.7	0.0	15.9
Crafts	5.1	0.0	4.4
Operative	0.5	1.5	0.6
Transport	3.0	0.0	2.6
Taxicab driver	0.5	0.0	0.4
Laborer	39.4	25.4	37.3
Construction	0.3	0.0	0.2
Factory work	0.9	4.1	1.4
Cleaning service	7.3	8.3	7.5
Food service	11.5	1.5	10.1
Health service	0.0	5.6	0.8
Personal service	0.7	5.3	1.4
Protective service	1.0	1.5	1.0
Child care	0.0	2.6	0.4
Private household	0.0	1.5	0.2
Armed forces	0.3	0.0	0.2
Not codable and don't know	2.6	20.4	4.4

B. Last Full-Time Job Held by Chicago GA Clients	
Type of Work	Percentage
Manager or professional	3.4
Technician	5.9
Clerical worker	12.1
Protective service	3.1
Service worker	29.9
Construction worker	5.9
Skilled worker	1.9
Machine operator	10.6
Assembler	5.9
Transportation worker	18.7
Unskilled worker	2.4
N	421
Never employed full time	19.8

the occupational categories ranged more widely up and down the hierarchy, there was clearly a concentration on the lower levels, which demanded little skill and were correspondingly poorly paid. Almost three out of four of the steady jobs were in the semiskilled and unskilled sectors of the labor force. Chicago's homeless have held steady jobs, but that was more than four years before the time of interviewing, and those jobs were largely unskilled and semiskilled.

The last full-time jobs held by GA clients are shown in panel B of table 5.11. Since many of the GA clients are below age twenty-five, one in five (20%) has never held a full-time job. Those who had done so had positions quite similar to those held by the homeless. Almost one in three (30%) held a service job, and close to half held positions on the bottom levels of industrial production or in the construction and transportation industries.

The data presented in this section show clearly that neither the extremely poor nor the homeless have recently fallen into those conditions after losing even moderately skilled positions. Most held jobs at the bottom of the occupational hierarchy. If they had once held better jobs, they were further back in their job histories.

Gender and Age Differences among the Homeless

Although Chicago homeless persons vary in a number of ways, a consistent theme throughout the findings of our survey is that the major axes of differentiation were gender and age. Younger homeless persons differed consistently from older ones, and men differed consistently from women. To explore these lines of differentiation, we constructed four homeless subgroups, as follows: young males (under forty years of age); young females (under forty); older males (forty and over); older females (forty and over). Age forty was taken as the dividing line between young and old because it was approximately the median age of the Chicago homeless sample.

Shelter Use

Perhaps the most distinctive difference among the four gender/age types was in the use of shelters as sleeping or resting places. As panel A of table 5.12 shows, about four out of five of the young women were interviewed in shelters, in contrast to fewer than half of the young males. Compared with the young men, older males and older females were slightly more likely to be interviewed in the shelter sample than in the street sample (55% and 53%, respectively, compared with 48% for younger men).

Use of shelters over the seven days before the interview followed the same pattern (data are not shown). Young women spent about two nights out of three in shelters, the highest proportion among the four groups. Again, young homeless men were the contrasting group, with the lowest proportion of nights spent in shelters. Older men and women were very much alike in the proportions of nights they spent in shelters. The heavier use of shelters by the young homeless women undoubtedly reflected the fact that many were heading homeless families and therefore stayed in shelters with accommodations for families.

Young women also stood out with respect to their living arrangements immediately before becoming homeless, as shown in panel B of table 5.12. Although most of the homeless had been living alone in apartments or rented

Table 5.12 Gender and Age Differences among the Chicago Homeless

	Under Forty		Forty and Over	
Location	Males	Females	Males	Females
A. Sleeping Arrangements at Time of Interview				
Street	52.0%	18.8%	44.6%	46.9%
Shelter	48.0	81.2	55.4	53.1
B. Living Arrangement Immediately before Current Homelessness				
Living alone	44.9%	23.2%	59.9%	47.5%
With spouse and/or children	6.5	27.7	7.8	14.7
With parents, siblings, or other relatives	22.1	24.7	13.1	14.4
With other persons	26.5	24.4	19.2	23.4
C. Race				
Percentage white	20.4	15.3	40.9	45.1
D. Time Currently Homeless				
Percentage homeless three months or less	33.5	54.9	24.2	21.7
Average time homeless (months)	18.6	12.2	28.8	18.6
E. Work and Income				
Months since last steady job	46.3	63.0	58.7	63.0
Average income last month	$189	$236	$140	$121
F. Interviewers' Functional Ratings				
Appeared confused	13.4%	16.0%	6.8%	21.0%
Incoherent	2.8	2.4	• 3.3	10.8
Not lucid	27.5	20.9	31.2	34.5
G. Interviewers' Appearance Ratings				
Dirty	18.4%	4.5%	30.5%	19.8%
Shabbily dressed	23.7	18.8	42.3	36.3
Carrying belongings in packages	8.4	3.3	10.2	26.1
Not neat and clean	38.9	30.6	55.6	45.9

rooms before becoming homeless, young women were exceptional in having lived with their spouses and/or children or with their parents. Only a small minority had lived alone. In contrast, young homeless men only rarely left behind a spouse or children, coming from living either alone or with their parents.

Older homeless persons, both men and women, most frequently had lived alone. Especially likely to have lived alone were the older homeless men. Indeed, they were the most likely of all to have lived in rented rooms, possibly in SRO hotels. Given the age and gender distribution of the SRO population, the older homeless men appear very similar to the SRO population.

Some Critical Characteristics of Age/Gender Groups

The remaining panels of table 5.12 show some of the important characteristic differences among the four age/gender groups: First of all, older homeless persons were more likely to be white than younger ones—45% of the older women and 41% of the older men were white (see panel C). In contrast, 20% of the younger men and 15% of the younger women were white. Note that young homeless women were especially likely to be black. This strongly patterned racial distribution can have different meanings, which it is difficult to distinguish. The racial composition of the homeless population may be changing over time, with young nonwhites (mostly blacks) becoming a greater and greater proportion; or both young blacks and older whites may be more susceptible to becoming homeless than others in their racial groups. In the absence of longitudinal data in the Chicago Homeless Study, it is not possible to choose which possibility is more likely.

Since the older people are the longer they are likely to be in any particular condition, we can expect that the older persons, on the average, would have been homeless longer. Indeed, such is generally the case, as shown in panel D. On the average, men and women over forty had been homeless longer than those under forty—about one year longer for men and about six months longer for women. However, these are not very large differences, especially compared with the average gap in age between the two age groups. Indeed, it appears as if those over forty did not become homeless when they were very much younger; their current episode of homelessness typically began one to two years ago.

As we have come to expect, young women are conspicuously different. Among young women, having been homeless under four months predominated, being characteristic of more than half (55%) of that group. In short, young women generally were homeless for short periods, most likely in transition between leaving intolerable living arrangements and finding another home. It is likely that being eligible for AFDC made it possible for young homeless women to obtain their own housing within weeks.

The income data shown in panel E bear out this interpretation. The gender/age group with the highest average previous month's cash income was young women, and a large proportion of them were receiving AFDC payments. Clearly the worst off were older women, whose average cash income was $121.

All the age/gender groups were a long time away from their last "steady jobs," ranging from almost four years (forty-six months) for younger men to more than five years (sixty-three months) for both younger and older women.

Interviewers' Impressions

At the end of each interview, interviewers rated the functioning and appearance of the homeless person just interviewed. NORC interviewers were not clinicians, so their ratings of any of the functional issues cannot be regarded as more than laypersons' impressions, but on appearance issues their ratings are as good as anyone else's, since there are no clinical experts on, for example, whether people are neat and clean as opposed to shabby and dirty. However, interviewers' judgments of functioning can be used in comparisons among age/gender groups. That is, although an interviewer's rating that a person was incoherent cannot be taken as an expert judgment about that respondent's cognitive functioning, that men were more frequently judged to be incoherent than women may be viewed as indicating a relatively reliable difference.

Panels E and F of table 5.12 compare the interviewers' judgments about each of the four age/gender groups. Panel E shows ratings of how well respondents were functioning. Homeless women over forty appeared to be functioning least well; they were more likely to be rated as appearing confused, incoherent, and not lucid than any of the other age/gender groups. The other age/gender groups showed no particular uniform pattern. Young females were rated as confused slightly more frequently than young males and were seen as considerably more confused than older males. But older females achieved the highest rating in this respect, more than one in five being rated confused. No strong differences appeared in regard to incoherence; older women, as I mentioned above, were much higher in incoherence than any of the other groups.

Panel F shows the interviewers' ratings of appearance. Older women are most likely to have been carrying their belongings with them in packages. Apparently Chicago did have "bag ladies" amounting to about one in four of the homeless women over forty. In other respects homeless men over forty were rated most likely to be dirty, shabby, and not neat and clean. In these respects the opposite side was occupied by young women, with young men in an intermediate position and older women being closer to older men in appearance.

Summary

The Chicago homeless population displayed considerable heterogeneity, yet some patterns were discernible. The "typical" Chicago homeless person was a black male in his middle thirties with average educational attainment. Either he had never married or his marriage had failed. His last steady job was held more than four years ago. Although more than one in three worked for some period during the month before the survey, the jobs in question were temporary, involving low levels of skill and paying correspondingly low wages.

A significant minority among the homeless comprised young women in their early thirties, often married or recently living with someone but on their way to separation and divorce. These young women had young children, and many were with them in the shelters. This homeless group appeared to be escaping from intolerable marriages or other household arrangements.

Another minority group consisted of older white males in their early fifties who were steady shelter residents. These were unmarried or formerly married men of average educational attainment. They tended to be intermittently employed at marginal jobs.

The major axes of differentiation among the homeless were found to be age and gender. Homeless young men and women were both more likely to be nonwhite than their older counterparts. Homeless women over forty were most likely to fit one of the stereotypes of the homeless, the vague, incoherent "bag lady." Homeless men, whether young or old, were most likely to look like the stereotyped Skid Row inhabitant.

SIX

Vulnerability to Homelessness

Assuming that the estimates of the extremely poor derived from the 1987 Current Population Survey are reasonable, there are from ten to twenty times as many domiciled extremely poor people as there are homeless persons in the United States, assuming that the latter number about 300,000. If we assume that half of the extremely poor are only temporarily so, the ratio of the extremely poor to the "permanent" homeless rises to somewhere between twenty to one and forty to one. Either ratio raises the important question why some of the extremely poor become homeless and some do not. As shown in the last two chapters, the economic status of the domiciled extremely poor is not appreciably better than that of the homeless. Thrown on their own resources, neither group has the wherewithal to afford homes, but only a small minority are homeless. This chapter seeks to answer why some do become homeless by looking at those characteristics that make extremely poor people vulnerable to homelessness.

The living arrangements of the extremely poor offer an important clue to significant vulnerability factors. Most of them manage to remain domiciled by sharing homes with others. The Chicago General Assistance clients largely rely on their parents to provide shelter and probably food as well. The Current Population Survey extremely poor show the same pattern. Another guard against homelessness is welfare programs that provide relatively generous benefits. I have already remarked on how the expansion of old age retirement benefits in the 1960s and 1970s removed the aged from the pool of the vulnerable extremely poor. In states that have generous AFDC benefits, single parents are helped to maintain homes. These last two factors account for the low incidence of aged persons and single-parent families among the homeless.

For those who are neither aged nor eligible for AFDC, there remains the question why they are not like most of the extremely poor, being supported by their families and friends. The vulnerability-enhancing factors I will consider here are personal characteristics. Although they may help explain who becomes homeless, let me stress that fluctuations in homelessness as a social condition are likely to be explained better by conditions in the larger society. That is, the amount of homelessness is likely to be affected by the amount of inexpensive housing available: the less housing is available and the more expensive it is, the more people are homeless. But no matter what the availability of inexpensive housing, personal characteristics are likely to explain *who* becomes homeless.

In the preceding chapters there have been many clues that the homeless suffer from a variety of disabling conditions that hinder to varying degrees their full functioning in adult roles. Here we look at these disabling conditions in greater detail, with special attention to comparisons between the homeless and the domiciled extremely poor.

Almost all the data we will consider come from cross-sectional surveys. Hence it is always debatable whether a difference between the domiciled and the homeless led to homelessness or whether homelessness created the difference. Some conditions can interfere with a person's functioning so much that homelessness results. But being extremely poor and being homeless also carry penalties that can result in those conditions. For example, it will come as no surprise that many of the homeless are depressed and do not believe their futures are promising: the conditions of life in either the shelters or the streets are depressing, and their futures are not promising. Depression may be the precursor to homelessness, but it also may be its consequence.

Disabilities can take many forms. We will deal with the following kinds: physical health, mental health, social supports, and criminal convictions. Each can be regarded as a continuum ranging from no disability at all to serious functional problems. A person in poor mental and physical health with few social supports and an extensive criminal record is indeed in no position to function well in our society. Each of the conditions can disable an individual in different ways. People in poor mental or physical health may be limited in the kind of employment they can take. People without social supports may find it difficult to deal with the little setbacks in life. Those with no one to turn to for help can easily find themselves incapacitated by small accidents. For example, a sprained ankle is not too serious if a friend or relative can help out with shopping needs or other housekeeping tasks.

We are not accustomed to viewing criminal records as constituting a disability, as I will do in this chapter. Yet the postimprisonment experience of released felons clearly demonstrates the extent to which being in prison for a few years is a serious obstacle to employment (Rossi, Berk, and Lenihan 1980). Felony prisoners are usually young men, whose typical one to two years of imprisonment means they have that much less employment experience. In addition, many employers are loathe to hire convicted felons in any but the least skilled positions. An extensive criminal record consisting of several convictions and incarcerations may mean as much as a decade out of the labor force.

In the sections that follow I will take up each of these disabilities in turn, estimating the extent to which each is present among the homeless and among the extremely poor.

Mental Illness

Popular discussions of homelessness pay a great deal of attention to the impact that the deinstitutionalization of mental patients has had on homelessness. The emptying of our country's state mental hospitals in the 1960s is alleged to have increased the number of homeless persons. There can be little doubt that to the extent that those deinstitutionalized in the 1960s found their way into the shelters and onto the streets, deinstitutionalization must have contributed to the increase in homelessness experienced in the 1970s. But there already were mentally ill persons among the homeless, as the studies in the 1950s and 1960s found (Bahr and Caplow 1974; Bogue 1963). That there are mentally ill persons among the homeless today may simply reflect continuity with the past.

Bogue (1963) estimated that 9% of the Skid Row homeless were severely disturbed and another 11% showed milder signs of mental illness. He also commented that the cubicle and SRO hotels provided refuges for some mentally ill persons who wanted to avoid institutionalization and found the environment of Skid Row, with its tolerance for eccentricity, one where their behavior would not attract attention.

The presence of the mentally ill among the "old" homeless was also recognized by the courts: Bogue reported that the municipal courts serving the Skid Row districts in Chicago periodically screened arrestees for psychiatric problems. Those who did not pass the psychiatric examination were committed to state mental hospitals for treatment.

The major efforts to decant the mental hospital population took place in the 1960s and early 1970s, one to two decades ago. As that period recedes into the past, its effects on the composition and size of the current homeless population become weaker and weaker as more recent events and processes come to dominate. In particular, noninstitutionalization becomes more and more important: that is, in the past decade, it has become considerably more difficult to commit people to a mental hospital without their consent. Hence persons who might have been hospitalized before the 1960s are no longer sent to mental hospitals (Lamb 1984). All told, these changes in practice lead one to expect that the prevalence of chronic mental illness among the current homeless will be appreciably greater than that recorded in the 1950s and 1960s.

Indeed, a recent study by Lewis and his associates (Lewis et al. 1987) shows how strongly current institutionalization practices affect homelessness. Under current Illinois law it is difficult to commit anyone to a mental hospital involuntarily. Lewis and his colleagues found that only 1% of the patients going through the mental hospitals serving the Chicago area in 1985 were there involuntarily: almost all had committed themselves. Or so it would seem from the official records. In fact, the police and the courts had offered many the choice between self-commitment for a maximum of thirty days and involuntary commitment for a minimum of sixty days. Thus many people who would have been committed in the 1950s are no longer being admitted, or are admitted only because they come in contact with the police and courts—usually after performing some bizarre act—and then are "plea bargained" into accepting voluntary commitment. Under the pressure of heavy caseloads, the courts lower their work burdens by trading with the accused, offering the milder way of voluntary commitment as an inducement to avoid the more arduous (to the courts) procedure of involuntary commitment. Voluntary commitment is attractive because a patient can petition for release after seven days, a request the hospital must honor.

That there is still a heavy traffic back and forth between the mental hospitals and the homeless condition can be seen in the same study by Lewis and his colleagues. Not only did the 1985 mental hospital population resemble demographically both the homeless and the GA clients, being predominantly young, black, and male, but the researchers judged that about 18% were precariously domiciled: they claimed to have severe trouble in finding appropriate housing or to be tenuously housed, usually attached to a household as an "extra" adult. Two-thirds of those precariously housed (11%) were also likely to have been homeless at the time of admission.[1]

The heavy interchange between the mental hospital and homeless populations is also reflected in data from the Chicago Homeless Study. Table 6.1 presents findings on the mental hospitalization of the homeless. We find that about one in four of the Chicago homeless has had at least one episode of hospitalization in a psychiatric institution. Furthermore, the 23% who had any episodes of hospitalization tended to have several: 60% had been hospitalized more than once, and 30% had experienced four or more hospitalizations. Much of the hospitalization for psychiatric reasons is fairly recent: about two in three of the last episodes occurred within two years before the interview.

The prevalence of previous mental hospital stays found in other studies of the homeless is also shown. Averaged over the twenty-five homeless studies that contained such data, about one in four of the homeless had been in a mental hospital at least once.

Compared with the general adult population, in which the proportion ever hospitalized in a mental institution is less than 5%, these rates are extremely high. Clearly, a large proportion of the homeless have had episodes of mental

1. Given that more than 20,000 persons were admitted to Chicago-area mental hospitals over a year's time, that means that there were about 2,000 homeless or precariously housed persons among a year's admissions. This is about six times the estimated number of homeless persons in my projections who were discharged from mental hospitals over a year's time. I believe this discrepancy is due to the very loose definition of homelessness used in the Lewis (1987) study, which likely included precariously housed persons as well as the literally homeless.

The average patient load in the Chicago-area mental hospitals was considerably lower than the yearly number of admissions, 2,500 versus 20,000, indicating that most committed persons remained in the hospital for very short periods. Indeed, a person voluntarily committed can file a petition for release within days of admission and be released within a week.

Table 6.1   Psychiatric Hospitalizations

Chicago Homeless Study	
Been in mental hospital	23.1%
Combined Homeless Studies (25 studies)	
Average percentage with mental hospital experience	26.8%
Chicago General Assistance Study	
Spent over one month in mental hospital	3%[a]

[a] One person admitted to mental hospital between interview waves (March to December 1984).

illness severe enough to warrant hospitalization. In addition, the conditions warranting hospitalization are recent and likely are continuing ones.

Experience with the mental health system, however, does not fully measure the prevalence of mental illness. Given the "voluntary" nature of hospital admissions, it is likely that there are some mentally ill people who have never been hospitalized, especially if their illness is not manifest in bizarre or aggressive behavior. Others who were hospitalized some years ago may have gone into remission since that episode. In short, contemporary measures are needed to estimate more accurately the prevalence of severe or debilitating mental illness among the homeless.

The only evidence I could find concerning the mental hospitalization of the domiciled extremely poor comes from the Chicago General Assistance Study, also shown table 6.1. Only 3% of the GA clients reported having been in a mental hospital, a rate close to national adult experience and only about one-seventh the rate observed among the homeless.

Demoralization among the Chicago Homeless

An important form of chronic mental illness is clinical depression. Although a depressed person ordinarily is not a direct threat to anyone else, it is a painful condition that severely hinders functioning. Those who are severely depressed can sink into an apathy that affects cognitive and motor activity, reduces appetite, disrupts interpersonal relationships, and can make the simplest tasks difficult or impossible, such as those involved in self-care.

In an effort to measure the levels of depression among the Chicago homeless, the winter 1986 survey of our Chicago Homeless Study included six items drawn from the CES-D scale developed by the Center for Epidemiologic Studies at the National Institute of Mental Health. The scale was originally developed for use in the nationwide Health and Nutrition Examination Survey (HANES), conducted most recently by the National Center for Health Statistics between April 1971 and June 1974, making it possible to compare the Chicago homeless with national norms. The HANES survey was designed as a national sample of adults twenty-five to seventy-four years old.

The scale relies on respondents' self-reports (as opposed to ratings made by clinicians) to assess the extent to which feelings of depression are present in communities and in subpopulations of communities (Radloff 1977). The

CES-D scale accurately captures the presence of symptoms of depression, but it is not designed to discriminate among clinical subcategories such as major depression and minor depression; nor can it distinguish between primary depression (where depression is the diagnosis) and secondary depression (resulting from or accompanying some other mental illness).

It has been suggested that high scores on the CES-D and other depression scales indicate, besides depression, a sense of *demoralization* (Link and Dohrenwend 1980), that is, hopelessness and despair concerning one's prospects. The lack of institutional supports, especially if they are sorely needed, is thought to be sufficiently stressful to precipitate the physiological changes in brain function that constitute a depressive disorder. If the homeless condition can be said to engender mental illness, demoralization appears to be the most likely mechanism through which it has this effect, for the homeless clearly lack even the most common resources that others take for granted.

There are twenty items on the full CES-D scale as originally devised. They are designed to cover the following components of depressive symptoms identified in the clinical literature: depressed mood; feelings of guilt and worthlessness; feelings of helplessness and hopelessness; psychomotor retardation; loss of appetite; and disturbance of sleep. Because of survey length limitations, we could use only an abbreviated version of the CES-D scale. The six items used were chosen to cover the range of depressive symptoms,[2] and four of them seemed well suited to serve as indicators of the concept of demoralization described above.[3]

Table 6.2 compares average responses in the HANES survey to the average responses in the survey of the Chicago homeless on the six items taken from

2. The items chosen had been reworded slightly by Elmer Struening, of the State of New York Psychiatric Institute, for use in a study of the residents of shelters for the homeless in New York City. Because they had been used successfully with a similar population, we adopted Dr. Struening's modified wording.

3. The six items are listed below. Next to each is the wording that appears in the CES-D scale.

Homeless Questionnaire	*CES-D Scale*
1. Was your appetite so poor that you did not feel like eating?	I did not feel like eating; my appetite was poor.
2. Did you feel so tired and worn out that you could not enjoy anything?	I felt that everything I did was an effort.
3. Did you feel depressed?	I felt depressed.
4. Did you feel unhappy about the way your life is going?	I thought my life had been a failure.
5. Did you feel discouraged and worried about your future?	I felt hopeful about the future.
6. Did you feel lonely?	I felt lonely.

The wording on the homeless questionnaire simplifies the language and format of the questions. The interviewer asks the questions directly instead of asking the respondent to agree or disagree with each of a series of statements. In addition, we asked how frequently the respondents had experienced each of the six conditions during the week before the interview.

Table 6.2   Comparison of the Chicago Homeless Study and HANES Samples on Six CES-D Items

| | Mean Score[a] | | |
| | Chicago | | Difference |
Item	Homeless Study	National HANES	CHS − HANES
Poor appetite	0.56	0.30	0.26
Tired/worn out	0.78	0.60	0.18
Depressed	1.07	0.45	0.62
Unhappy	1.45	0.20	1.25
Worried about future	1.41	0.89	0.51
Lonely	1.11	0.38	0.73
Total	6.39	2.82	3.56
N	346	3,011	
Adjusted[b] CES-D scale score	19.20	8.50	10.70

Note: Winter 1986 survey only.

[a] Computed by giving numerical values to each of the response categories, corresponding to those used in HANES.

[b] Projected for differences in length and in the items used.

the CES-D. A high score represents responses indicating depression. In the last column of table 6.2 the HANES averages are subtracted from the Chicago Homeless Study averages, a positive difference indicating that the Chicago homeless score higher (are more depressed) than respondents in the national survey. Each difference is positive and statistically significant. Each comparison shows that the Chicago homeless gave much higher levels of depressed responses than the national sample.

The smallest differences are found for the first and second items. These items, "lack of appetite" and feeling "tired and worn out," tap the physiological changes associated with depression. High scores on these items suggest a depressive condition that merits professional treatment. In the national HANES sample 3% reported a poor appetite most of the time, compared with 10% in the Chicago homeless sample. In the national sample, 8% felt that most of the time everything they did was an effort, compared with the much higher 15% of the Chicago homeless who reported that most of the time they felt so tired and worn out they could not enjoy anything.

The strongest differences between the Chicago homeless and the HANES national sample were on the items most closely related to demoralization. Feeling unhappy about the way one's life is going showed the largest difference, 1.25 points on a 4-point scale. Of the respondents in the national sample 86%. said they never felt their life had been a failure, but only 25% of the Chicago homeless said they never felt unhappy with the way their life was going. It is clear that the homeless were generally very demoralized about their condition.

The demoralization of the homeless showed itself with special strength in the three items measuring depression, loneliness, and worry about the future. The differences from the national survey for each of these items were fairly large: 0.62, 0.73, and 0.51, respectively. About one-third of the national sample (33%) said they often felt depressed, but just under two-thirds (65%) of the homeless reported feeling depressed. Similarly, about one-fourth of the national sample reported feeling lonely, but the corresponding percentage of the homeless was 60%. Fewer than half (42%) of the national sample reported concern about the future, but three-fifths (61%) of the homeless were worried about what the future might bring.

In the HANES survey, the CES-D scores on each item of the full scale of twenty items were added together to form a summary total score for each individual surveyed. To compute a comparable score for the six items used in the Chicago Homeless Study, the average scores for the six items used were adjusted to account for the shortness of the scale.[4] The resulting adjusted score was 19.20, 10.70 points higher than the national estimate.

This adjusted score for the Chicago Homeless Study can be taken as an estimate of what the CES-D scale score would have been had all twenty items been given. This score is useful for comparison, since a score of 16 or higher on the full CES-D has been widely accepted as distinguishing cases requiring clinical attention from those that are less serious.[5]

Table 6.2 shows that the homeless in Chicago were, on average, considerably beyond the 16-point cutoff. Nearly one-half (47%) of the Chicago homeless had a total adjusted score that was equivalent to the CES-D score of 18. By contrast, only 16% of the respondents in the HANES survey had a CES-D scale score of 16 or more. Clearly the Chicago homeless showed far more clinical depression than the general adult population of the United States.[6]

---

4. The sum (over all twenty items) for the HANES survey is 8.5. Since only a subset of the twenty CES-D items is used in this study, the sum of the six items must be projected by a factor of 20/6 or 3.33 to estimate the CES-D scale score. For the HANES survey the projected sum is 9.42. The projection is 10.9% greater than the national estimated CES-D scale score based on all twenty items (mean = 8.5). To make the homeless estimates roughly comparable with the national data, the projected sum is multiplied by a factor of 0.90.

5. Weissman et al. (1977) found that the 16-point cutoff is very sensitive in that better than 90% of those who are clinically depressed score higher than 16 on the CES-D scale. But the scale is only moderately specific, because from 56% to 86% of those who are not clinically depressed still have scores higher than 16 on the CES-D scale. One should be cautious, therefore, in using this cutoff point to estimate the number of homeless who need professional treatment for depression.

6. One can ask whether the Chicago homeless are more depressed than other poor people. To answer that question we can point to a study that took poverty into account. In a study of residents of Kansas City (a large urban area, and in that respect more comparable to Chicago than the nation as a whole) conducted between 1971 and 1973, Comstock and Helsing (1976) found that 26% of all blacks and 20% of all whites had CES-D scale scores of 16 or greater. This study also found that 39% of blacks with incomes under $3,000 and 29% of whites with incomes under $3,000 had CES-D scale scores of 16 or greater. The percentages above the cutoff point dropped

Table 6.3 Self-Reported Attempted Suicides and Suicidal Feelings

Measure	Percentage
Has thought about suicide in past few weeks	10.7
Has actually attempted suicide	15.6
One suicide attempt	6.1
Two attempts	4.6
Three or more	4.9
N	401

Note: Chicago Homeless Study: winter 1986 survey only.

Note that what may be a pathological response in a normal, domiciled population may not be so for the homeless because of the striking differences in their circumstances. Surely there was little reason for many of the homeless to be sanguine about the future. Nevertheless, whether warranted or not, demoralization is just as real to those who feel it.

The high levels of depression and demoralization among the Chicago homeless have their behavioral manifestations in very high levels of reported attempts at suicide among this group. As shown in table 6.3, more than one in ten (11%) had had suicidal thoughts during the few weeks immediately preceding the interview, a striking incidence. Even more striking is the larger proportion, more than one in six (16%), who reported actual attempts to take their own lives and the one in ten (10%) who had made at least two suicide attempts. Although we do not have comparable incidences for the general population, suicide attempts appear to be much higher among the homeless than among the general population.

We were not able to find very comparable measures of the levels of depression and demoralization among the domiciled extremely poor. The closest approximations to such measures are shown in table 6.4 for the GA and AFDC samples. Only one relevant item could be found in the GA Study, namely how hopeful respondents were about the future. Among the homeless, about one in three (35%) was worried about the future most of the time. In contrast, about one in five of the GA clients (18%) saw very little hope that the situation would improve. If these responses are comparable, the GA clients are less depressed.

In contrast, AFDC clients appear to be more depressed than the GA sample and perhaps as much as the homeless. About one-third said they had been

---

sharply as income rose, reaching a low point of 7% for blacks with incomes over $16,000 and 16% for whites with incomes over $16,000. Income is the strongest predictor of high CES-D scores in the Kansas City study. If the effects of income on depression among blacks reported in Kansas City are extrapolated downward, they tend to reach at the very lowest income level the 47% highly depressed found for the Chicago homeless. Of course severe income deprivation is at the core of the condition of the homeless, so the findings of the Kansas City study are very much in line with our findings.

Table 6.4 Depression Indicators for the Extremely Poor

A. Chicago General Assistance Study (N = 400)			
Measure	A Lot of Hope	Some Hope	Very Little Hope
"Looking into future, do you see a lot of hope, some hope or very little hope for improving your situation?"	52.3%	30.0%	17.8%
B. Chicago AFDC Study (N = 737)			
Measure	Often	Sometimes	Never
"During the past month, were you bothered by feelings of depression or sadness—feeling blue?"	33.9%	49.9%	16.2%
"During the past month, did you feel so sad or have so many problems that you wondered if anything was worthwhile?"	20.4	43.3	35.9
"During the past month, did you feel confident?"	11.8	56.4	30.7

often bothered by feelings of depression over the past month, matching the one-third of the homeless who said they were often worried about the future or the one-third who said they were often discouraged about how their lives were going, and somewhat higher than the one-fifth of the homeless who said they were often depressed. Although there is sufficient evidence to claim that AFDC clients were more depressed than the GA clients and the general adult population, it is not very clear whether their depression levels equaled those of the homeless.

Psychotic Thought Patterns

The more severe conditions of mental illness are the various forms of psychosis, generally characterized by disturbances in thought and perception that impair one's contact with reality. Certain chronic mental illnesses, such as schizophrenia, are identified in part by the presence of psychotic symptoms in their acute phases. Specific forms of psychotic thought patterns include paranoid delusions, auditory and visual distortions, and extremely illogical reasoning.

In addition to depression, we attempted to measure those forms of psychosis that result in distorted views of the world by using five items taken from the Psychiatric Epidemiology Research Interview (PERI). Developed by Dohrenwend et al. (1980), the PERI consists of thirty scales measuring symptoms of mental illness. These scales showed "a superior ability to differentiate a sample of well respondents from the community from respondents in a sample of psychiatric patients" (Dohrenwend et al. 1983). The five items used in the CHS winter 1986 survey were taken from the eight-item PERI scale "False Beliefs and Perceptions." These items were modified slightly by Elmer Struening of the New York Psychiatric Institute to be used in a study of the mental health needs of homeless shelter residents in New York City. We retained Struening's wordings of the items.[7]

Respondents were asked to report how often they had experienced these symptoms over the past year. This time frame is longer than that used for the CES-D items (there the time frame was one week), because psychotic symptoms often occur in acute "episodes" of fairly short duration. Respondents were cautioned not to report symptoms that occurred while they were drinking alcohol or taking drugs.

All five items correlate rather well with each other, with correlations ranging between .39 and .69 and averaging .45, indicating that many homeless people tend to have multiple psychotic symptoms. This pattern, coupled with the higher average scores of the Chicago homeless on all five items, suggests that mental illness characterized by psychosis was both more prevalent *and more severe* among the homeless than in the settled community.

Table 6.5 shows how the responses of the Chicago homeless to these five measures compare with a sample of 267 (not homeless) residents of Washington Heights, a neighborhood in New York City. The comparison data, provided by Bruce Dohrenwend, were taken from the PERI methods study (Dohrenwend et al. 1980). Although Washington Heights is an ethnically diverse neighborhood of Manhattan that includes a wide range of incomes, poor households predominate. We can assume it is fairly representative of the population living in the inner city of a large metropolitan area.

On every measure the residents of Washington Heights had lower average scores than the Chicago homeless. The largest difference (0.44 points) is in the feeling that others want to harm or hurt the respondent, possibly reflecting the greater risks to personal safety that homeless persons experience.

The range of scores calculated for the Chicago homeless is shown in table 6.6. Unfortunately there is no widely agreed-upon standard establishing score

---

7. The five items are listed below:

1. Have you ever heard noises or voices that other people say they can't hear?
2. Have you ever felt that there were people who wanted to harm or hurt you?
3. Have you ever had visions or seen things that other people say they can't see?
4. Have you ever felt that you had special powers that other people don't have?
5. Have you ever felt that your mind was taken over by forces you couldn't control?

The first and third items test for auditory and visual hallucinations—the perception of objects that are not actually present. The second, fourth, and fifth items ask about delusions—beliefs that are persistently held even though they are patently false. The second item refers to paranoid delusions, a symptom often found in schizophrenia and certain forms of major depression. Grandiose delusions are tapped by item 4; these often occur in schizophrenia and manic-depressive illness. Item 5 probes for delusions of thought control; these occur far less frequently than the other forms of delusions, but they usually indicate severe impairment and high chronicity.

Table 6.5 Comparison of the Chicago Homeless Study Sample and Washington Heights, New York, Residents on Five Items from the PERI Scale

Item	Chicago Homeless Study	Washington Heights Residents	Difference Chicago– Washington Heights
Heard voices	0.470	0.363	0.107
Feared harm	0.980	0.543	0.437*
Visions	0.474	0.176	0.298*
Special powers	0.470	0.367	0.103
External forces	0.336	0.127	0.209*
Total	2.730	1.576	1.154*
N	345	267	

*Difference is significant at $p < .05$.

Table 6.6 PERI Score Distribution for Chicago Homeless

PERI Score	Percentage
5 (lowest)	51.5
6	17.4
7	7.0
8	6.7
9 (cutoff)	6.1
10	2.9
11	1.7
12	2.3
13	0.9
14	1.2
15 and higher	2.3
Cutoff at 9 or higher	17.2
Cutoff at 10 or higher	11.3

Table 6.7 Mental Health Measures on the Extremely Poor and Homeless from Other Studies

Measure[a]	Percentage
A. Chicago General Assistance Study	
Unable to work because of mental illness	3.8
Unable to work because of "nervous problems"	8.5
B. Chicago AFDC Study	
Experienced mental health problem last year	11.5
Has been hospitalized for that problem	5.0
C. Combined Homeless Studies (17 studies)	
Average percentage with chronic mental illness	34.3

[a] A comparable question on the fall 1985 Chicago Homeless Study yielded the following proportions: mental illness, 25%; "nervous problems," 9%.

ranges for the PERI that indicate definite signs of a clinically significant psychosis. A reasonable cutoff for the detection of serious problems might be at a score of 9, indicating that the respondent had at least four of the symptoms "sometime" over the past year and likely one of them "quite often." Accepting that cutoff, then 17% have some chronic mental illness. The next cutoff point at a score of 10 yields about 11% with chronic mental illness. Conservatively, between one in ten and one in five of the Chicago homeless shows definite signs of psychotic thinking.

Putting together the findings on depression and psychotic thinking, it appears that about 20% to 30% of the Chicago homeless either are deeply depressed or show definite signs of psychotic thinking.

The data from the GA and AFDC studies unfortunately do not yield comparable measures, as can be seen in table 6.7. No mental health measures were included in the SRO study. From the GAS the only measures available are from a question that asks whether respondents have any chronic physical or mental health conditions that impair their employability. In response, very small percentages state that they have been incapacitated by alcoholism, mental illness, or "nervous problems." In contrast, a comparable question on the fall 1985 survey (shown in note a to table 6.7) produced much higher proportions: 25% claimed mental illness as a disability, and 9% claimed problems with "nerves."

The measure used in the AFDC study asked what three major problems respondents had faced over the previous year. One in ten (12%) reported mental health problems, and half of those who did (5%) had been hospitalized for the problem. A handful said they had trouble with alcoholism but that the problem was drinking by someone else in the household.

Clearly, mental health problems are not encountered as frequently among the domiciled extremely poor as among the homeless. The differences appear to be great. Apparently fewer than one in ten of the domiciled extremely poor suffers from chronic mental illness, while the homeless show from two to three times that prevalence.

Comparable levels of mental illness have been found in most of the homeless studies that have measured those conditions (see table 6.7). The measures used vary widely, from simple impressions of interviewers to clinical judgments by trained psychiatrists. The average proportion calculated over the seventeen studies that included such measures was 34%: about one in three of the homeless was found to be chronically mentally ill.

Given the evidence displayed in the last few pages, there cannot be much doubt that the prevalence of chronic mental illness is very high among the homeless. Better measures might modify upward or downward the estimates presented here—that between one in four and one in three of the homeless suffers from chronic mental illness—but it is highly unlikely that improved measurements can lower these prevalence rates to the levels found either among other extremely poor persons or in the general adult population. In this respect the homeless show themselves to be a badly disabled population.

Alcoholism and Drug Abuse

Rivaling mental illness as a disability that receives attention in the literature on the homeless is alcoholism. The social scientists who studied the homeless of two decades ago found alcoholism so prevalent among the denizens of Skid Row as to be their distinguishing characteristic. Recent research on the homeless continues that tradition.

Unfortunately, the main measure of alcoholism used in the Chicago Homeless Study was self-reports on having ever been in a detoxification unit for alcohol or drug abuse (see panel A of table 6.8). One in three of the Chicago homeless reported being in a detoxification unit sometime in the past. Of course these self-reports measure the extent to which some kind of substance abuse—primarily alcoholism—had been serious enough to require detoxification. The only measure of current alcoholism stems from a question, used only in the fall 1985 survey, asking whether the respondents had some condition that prevented their working. In response, about one in ten reported being unable to work because of alcoholism. This last measure, of course, misses those persons with drinking problems they believe do not interfere with employment. In any case, self-reported alcoholism affects between one in ten and one in three of the homeless of Chicago.

Evidence from other recent homeless studies shown in panel B leads me to believe the current prevalence of alcoholism is closer to one-third. Averaging the prevalences found in the fifteen studies that measured alcohol abuse, it appears that alcoholism affects about one person in three (33%).

The contrast with the domiciled extremely poor is strong. Among the Chicago General Assistance clients, fewer than 2% claimed that alcoholism af-

Table 6.8   Prevalence of Alcoholism among the Homeless and the Extremely Poor

Measure	Percentage
A. Chicago Homeless Study	
Been in detoxification unit for alcohol or drug abuse	33.2
Unable to work because of alcoholism	10.1
B. Combined Homeless Studies (15 studies)	
Average percentage with alcohol problems	32.7
C. Chicago General Assistance Study	
Unable to work because of alcoholism	1.5
D. Chicago AFDC Study	
Problems with alcoholism either with self or in family over year before interview	1.5

fected their ability to work. The level among AFDC clients was even lower: in response to a question asking about serious problems faced over the previous year, fewer than 2% reported that alcoholism had been such a problem, with most naming it as a problem affecting family members rather than themselves.

Physical Health Problems

The presence of obvious health problems among the homeless can scarcely be overlooked. Seeing homeless persons on the streets with running sores or disfiguring skin blotches is enough to arouse public concern. In addition, the high incidence of communicable diseases among the homeless is clinical evidence that they may be a source of health problems for the general public.

Matching public policy concerns, there is undoubtedly a reciprocal relation between physical illness and becoming or being homeless. Severe illness and its aftermath may seriously impair earning capacity, pushing some people into the very low income classes and thus making them vulnerable to homelessness. Also, the conditions of homelessness are at best minimally healthful and more usually undermine good health. Those who live on the streets are subject to the vicissitudes of climate, substandard sanitation, uncertain nutrition, poor access to health care, and numerous other illness-producing conditions. Those using shelters may be better off in many respects, but dormitory conditions make transmission of disease easy, and facilities for self-medication or access to health care are far from optimal.

Whether they are on the streets or in the shelters, homeless people's access to health care is doubtful. The household amenities that make personal hygiene and self-administered health care easy are not available to them. On the simplest level of everyday self-medication for commonplace ailments, without a medicine cabinet, access to bandages, antiseptics, analgesics, and all the other household remedies becomes a problem. Without funds or medical insurance, certainly much of private-practice medicine is out of reach. Furthermore, although many of the homeless are eligible for Medicaid or for the use of low- or no-cost medical facilities, there are problems in establishing eligibility and getting to the places where medical care is dispensed.

These arguments apply with less force to the domiciled extremely poor, who may find access to medical care and medication difficult, but not to the same degree. Some of the extremely poor are in that state because of previous illness or trauma. Of course the living conditions of the extremely poor with homes are better, if not optimal. Even in a run-down SRO hotel, maintaining personal hygiene or a stock of home medication is easier than for the homeless, either in shelters or on the streets.

All these considerations lead one to expect that the medical problems of the homeless will be serious and extensive and that they will have difficulty obtaining medical care. The data presented in this section sustain those expectations.

The precise assessment of the health status of any population would require medical examinations. The periodic national Health and Nutrition Examination Survey (HANES) does give fairly intensive medical examinations to a carefully drawn national sample and provides the best information on the current health status of the American population. Such precision ordinarily is beyond the resources of social researchers. Hence all but one of the existing surveys of homeless and extremely poor populations rely on less precise measurements of health status. The only homeless study that used professional health assessments is based on clients of the Johnson-Pew medical clinics for the homeless (Wright and Weber 1987), whose data I rely on later in this section.

The best available approximations to medical examinations are self-reports, but they may overlook many conditions that do not produce painful symptoms or incapacity. In addition, the medical conditions may be inaccurately or vaguely reported. Nevertheless, symptoms that are painful or that hinder full functioning are likely to be reported.

I was fortunate to have access to very good information on the health condition of the homeless from the clinical records of the medical clinics financed by the Robert Wood Johnson Foundation and the Pew Memorial Trust.[8] Data on encounters with every person coming to the nineteen clinics for treatment has been entered into a data base maintained by the Social and Demographic Research Institute. Among the information entered into that data base are the medical complaints that led to the encounter, the diagnoses made by clinic personnel, and the treatments prescribed.

There are obvious limitations to the clinic data. First, they do not cover all homeless persons, but only those who came to the clinics for treatment. The clinic population consists of those who had medical conditions, as they saw it, and chose to come to the clinic rather than go elsewhere.[9] Second, the clinics did not screen patients for homelessness: hence the clinic population includes some unknown (but likely large) proportion of persons who have homes. Nevertheless, these data are valuable because they were generated by trained personnel whose diagnoses can be taken more seriously than self-reports.

The Chicago Homeless Study used two approaches in ascertaining the health status of individuals. In the fall 1985 survey, we asked whether respondents were subject to medical conditions that impaired their ability to work.[10]

---

8. Medical clinics for the homeless were established initially in eighteen cities by grants from these foundations, starting in 1985. The clinics set up medical stations in a variety of places easily accessible to homeless persons. In most cases they primarily dispense care for minor ailments and serve as referral points to hospitals and clinics for more serious cases.

9. Using data from the Chicago clinic and the Chicago Homeless Study, I estimate that the clinic population is about one-third the size of the homeless population of Chicago (see Wright and Weber 1987).

10. The question asked was "Do you have any serious illnesses or physical conditions that prevent you from working?" This was followed by "What are your serious illnesses or physical conditions?"

In winter 1986 we asked for a global health rating,[11] an approach that had been used in several health-status surveys of domiciled populations and hence provided a comparative framework for interpreting findings.

Panel A of table 6.9 presents the findings on self-reported health status, as measured in the winter 1986 survey. About one in five of the homeless (18%) reported "excellent" health, with an additional 46% reporting "good" health. If we take these two answer categories as reflecting at least the absence of serious impairment, about two out of three (63%) of the Chicago homeless said they were in that condition. Homeless persons reporting "fair" (25%) or "poor" health (11%) total more than one in three (37%).

When the homeless were asked in the fall 1985 survey whether they had any physical or mental condition that made them unable to work (see panel C), a surprisingly high proportion (28%) reported such conditions.

Because self-assessments of health status have been obtained from national surveys, we can compare the Chicago homeless with a national sample of American adults, as shown in note a to table 6.9. A 1982 national survey sponsored by the Robert Wood Johnson Foundation found that only 18% of American adults claimed "fair" or "poor" health, about half the level found in the Chicago homeless. Clearly, the Chicago homeless reported considerably worse health than the general population.

Table 6.9 also contains some data on the relative health of subgroups among the homeless. Although the homeless interviewed in shelters did not differ significantly from those interviewed "on the street," as shown in panel A, there were some strong differences by age (see panel B). Homeless men and women over forty reported high levels of either poor or fair health (46% for men and 36% for women) when compared with their under-forty counterparts (28% and 29%). Note, however, that all age groups reported worse health than the 1982 national sample.

Panel D presents the average proportion reported in poor health in the fourteen homeless studies that contained such measures. Slightly more than one in three (37%) were so reported, again a figure close to that reported for the Chicago Homeless Study. In addition, for the ten studies that asked about disabilities, the average proportion claiming to be too disabled to work was 33%.

All told, the data presented in this section substantiate a characterization of the homeless population as overall reporting a moderate level of health but containing a sizable minority with serious chronic conditions, some of which ordinarily require continuing medical care and attention. Based on the self-reports, it appeared that between a fourth and a third of the Chicago homeless have such conditions.

The lower panels of table 6.9 present information on the health of domiciled extremely poor persons. Although the data from domiciled extremely

---

11. The item used in the winter survey was "Would you say your health, in general, now is excellent, good, fair, or poor?"

Table 6.9   Self-Reported Health Status

A. Chicago Homeless Study

Health Status[a]	Street Sample	Shelter Sample	Weighted Total
Excellent	16.9%	18.2%	17.9%
Good	38.2	48.1	45.5
Fair	30.3	23.6	25.4
Poor	14.6	10.1	11.2

B. Chicago Homeless Health Status by Gender and Age

	Under Forty		Over Forty	
Health Status	Males	Females	Males	Females
Excellent	24.0%	24.4%	10.2%	19.9%
Good	47.9	46.7	43.1	44.5
Fair	20.7	26.6	29.9	22.3
Poor	7.4	2.2	16.8	13.3

C. Chicago Homeless Study, Fall 1985 Survey

Reporting illness prevents employment	28.3%

D. Combined Homeless Studies

Measure	Average Percentage	Number of Studies
Average reported in bad health	36.8	14
Average reported too disabled to work	32.5	10

E. Chicago General Assistance Study

Has "some physical, emotional or other problem that makes it hard to work"[b]	28.1%

F. Chicago SRO Residents Study

Rates health as fair or poor	38.1%
Reports a chronic medical problem	42.7
Handicapped or physically impaired	14.6

G. Chicago AFDC Study

Mentions physical health as one of three most serious problems of past year	11.5%

H. Chicago Urban Family Life Study

Measure	Males	Females
Reporting "fair" or "poor" health	18.7%	35.2%
Work limited because of health	14.7	24.1
N	251	665

Note: Shelter/street differences are not significant in panel A.

[a]Combining fair and poor produced a figure of 36.6% for the Chicago homeless, compared with 18% for a national sample, as reported for the adult United States population (1982) in the Robert Wood Johnson Foundation *Special Report* 1 (1983). The contrast would be even greater if standardized for age and gender distribution.

[b]The wording of the item was "Do you have any physical, emotional, or other problems that make it hard for you to work?"

poor are not strictly comparable, they are of some worth for comparison. Panel E shows that about one in four (28%) of the GA clients claimed to have some physical or emotional problem that made it "hard to work," about the same proportion of the Chicago homeless who claimed to have some condition that made working "hard." Whether this question is equivalent to the one used in the Chicago Homeless Study concerning being "unable to work" is hard to judge. Apparently there are some disabling physical conditions among the GA clients.

The few health measures available on the SRO residents suggest a level of physical disability as high as that among the homeless (see panel F). Of course, as was shown in chapter 5, many SRO residents are over sixty-five, and a good proportion are on disability pensions of one kind or another. More than one in three (38%) claims to have either fair or poor health, certainly far higher than in the general adult population (18%), but about the same as among the homeless (37%). More than two in five (43%) claim to have a chronic health problem, and 15% claim to be handicapped or physically impaired.

In contrast, AFDC clients appear to be relatively free of health problems. As shown in panel G, a little more than one in ten (12%) stated that physical illness was among the three most serious problems experienced in the previous year.

Panel H presents the self-report health status of the extremely poor unattached parents studied in the Chicago Urban Family Life Study. The young fathers show a fairly high level of subjective good health: about one in five (19%) reports either fair or poor health, and about 15% report that illness affects their ability to work. In contrast, the mothers, many of whom are heading their own households, show poor physical health and work impairment comparable to that in the homeless: more than one in three (35%) claims to be in fair or poor health, and almost one in four (24%) says that illness impairs her ability to work. Indeed, the domiciled mothers studied in the Chicago Urban Family Life Study appear to be in worse health than the under-thirty homeless women, the group most comparable to them in age.

I next present data on the clients seen in sixteen of the Health Care for the Homeless (HCH) clinics supported by the Robert Wood Johnson Foundation and as reported in Wright and Weber (1987). These are diagnoses of acute and chronic conditions found among persons asking for treatment in the clinics. The diagnoses are made by the medical personnel of those clinics, and ipso facto are more credible than the self-report data given above. However, clinic patients are by definition self-selected and hence underrepresent the healthy portion of the homeless population. For example, I estimate that at most the Chicago clinics could have seen and treated only about one in three (29%) of the Chicago homeless;[12] the rest either required no medical care or sought care

12. Reported in Wright and Weber (1987).

Table 6.10   Occurrence of Acute Physical Disorders: HCH Clients and NAMC Population

Acute Illness	HCH[a]	NAMC[b]
Infestational ailments (e.g., lice, scabies, worms)	4.9%	0.1%
Nutritional deficiencies	1.9	0.1
Obesity	2.3	2.7
Minor upper respiratory ailments	33.2	6.7
Serious upper respiratory disorders	3.2	1.0
Minor skin ailments	13.9	5.0
Serious skin disorders (abcesses, carbuncles, cellulitis)	4.2	0.9
Injuries		
Any injuries	23.4	NA
Fractures	4.5	2.2
Sprains and strains	7.1	3.1
Bruises, contusions	5.6	1.0
Lacerations, wounds	8.6	1.2
Superficial abrasions	2.2	0.4
Burns of all severities	1.1	0.2
N	11,886	28,878

[a] Adult clients seen more than once in one of sixteen of the Health Care for the Homeless clinics sponsored by the Robert Wood Johnson Foundation and the Pew Memorial Trust.
[b] Data from the National Ambulatory Medical Care study, consisting of a sample of patients seen in the offices of a national sample of primary-care physicians. Study conducted in 1974.

elsewhere. In addition, the clinics rightfully did not screen patients for homelessness: some proportion of the clients seen were domiciled.

Fortunately for our purposes, largely comparable data can be obtained on the general adult population and are reported by Wright and Weber (1987). The National Ambulatory Medical Care (NAMC) study, conducted in 1979, collected diagnoses on the patients seen by a national sample of primary-care physicians. Since these patients are self-selected in much the same way as the Health Care for the Homeless sample, they also overrepresent persons sick enough to seek out medical care.

Table 6.10 presents the distribution of diagnoses of acute illnesses from the HCH and NAMC studies.[13] Except for obesity, in every category shown the homeless patients had higher levels of each condition. For example, the impact homelessness has on health can be seen dramatically in minor respiratory ailments, mostly common colds: one in three (33%) of the HCH patients seen had upper respiratory complaints, compared with only 6.7% of primary-care patients. Much higher levels of infestation (lice, scabies, intestinal worms, etc.), skin ailments, serious respiratory problems, and injuries of all kinds are

13. The HCH patients shown in tables 6.10 and 6.11 include only persons seen more than once in the HCH clinics. Patients seen only once tend to have skimpy records, with entries focused primarily on the presenting complaint. As patients were seen again and again in the clinics, more complete medical assessments were usually made.

shown for the HCH patients, compared with the national sample of adult primary-care patients.

Table 6.11 compares the occurrence of chronic physical disorders among HCH and NAMC patients. Several comparisons stand out: first, two out of five (41%) of the HCH patients were diagnosed as having a chronic condition, compared with one in four (25%) of the NAMC patients. HCH patients showed especially high rates of gastrointestinal disorders, hypertension, peripheral vascular diseases, and female genitourinary problems. Also, one in ten was pregnant.

Finally, the HCH study contains some information on mortality among the homeless. Because there was no mechanism in place to ensure that all deaths among the homeless patients were brought to the attention of the clinics, the HCH data underrepresent, possibly seriously, their actual mortality. Wright and Weber (1987) estimate a death rate of 787 per 100,000, a morality three to four times as great as for others of comparable age and gender.

Summarizing our findings concerning physical health, there is no doubt

Table 6.11   Occurrence of Chronic Physical Disorders: HCH Clients and NAMC Population

Chronic Illness	HCH[a]	NAMC[b]
Any chronic physical disorder	41.0%	24.9%
Cancer	0.7	3.5
Endocrine disorders	2.2	1.6
Diabetes mellitus	2.4	2.7
Anemia	2.2	2.4
Neurological disorders	8.3	1.8
Seizures	3.6	0.1
Eye disorders	7.5	5.5
Ear disorders	5.1	1.6
Heart and circulatory disorders	6.6	6.2
Hypertension	14.2	8.0
Cerebrovascular accidents	0.3	0.7
Chronic obstructive pulmonary disease	4.7	3.2
Gastrointestinal disorders	13.9	5.6
Dental disorders	9.3	1.3
General genitourinary problems	6.6	2.9
Male specific genitourinary problems	1.9	3.2
Female-specific genitourinary problems	15.8	7.3
Pregnancy	11.4	0.5
Peripheral vascular disease	13.1	0.9
Arthritis	4.2	3.7
Other musculoskeletal disorders	6.0	5.8
N	11,886	2,887

[a] Adult clients seen more than once in one of sixteen of the Health Care for the Homeless clinics sponsored by the Robert Wood Johnson Foundation and the Pew Memorial Trust.
[b] Data from the National Ambulatory Medical Care study, consisting of a sample of patients seen in the offices of a national sample of primary-care physicians. Study conducted in 1974.

that physical ailments among the homeless and the extremely poor are far greater than in the general population. Among the subgroups studied, AFDC clients appear to be the healthiest, with SRO residents and the homeless having the highest level of illness.

Criminal Convictions

The homeless and the criminal justice system have always had frequent contact. In the 1960s Bahr and Caplow (1974) estimated that about one in four arrests in New York City was of a Bowery resident, typically on charges related to public inebriation, loitering, or creating a disturbance, polite ways of stating that the current police practice was to round up homeless men. Similar practices prevailed in Chicago, as reported by Bogue (1963), with several hundred Skid Row residents being brought to the courts nightly. Indeed, local jails were one source of shelter for the homeless, and several hundred were housed on any typical night.

With the decriminalization of public inebriation and lowered emphasis on enforcing other public behavior laws, police practices changed in the 1970s. No longer are there wholesale arrests of the homeless. Nevertheless, the contact of the homeless with the police and the courts remains frequent.

Table 6.12 summarizes the information available on the criminal records of the homeless, based on self-reports. Among the Chicago homeless (panel A) more than one in six (17%) have served time in a state or federal prison. Ordinarily, such sentences are given for felonies. Furthermore, current practice in the courts is usually to place a first-time offender on probation, so the homeless who have served prison sentences are likely to have multiple felony convictions. Indeed, as shown also in panel A, another one in three has been convicted and placed on probation. All told, about one in three of the homeless has a felony conviction, and about one in six has multiple convictions. Minor offenses are usually handled by short-term sentences, up to one year, in a local jail. More than two out of five (41%) of the Chicago homeless have served jail sentences.

Comparable levels of court convictions were found in other homeless studies. The average proportion (see panel B) with at least one prison term is 21%. Jail sentences were served by an average of 35%. Those studies that did not distinguish between jail and prison sentences recorded incarceration of more than two out of five (42%) of the homeless.

Comparable information about the criminal justice experiences of the extremely poor is meager. About 14% of the GA clients (panel C) have been convicted in an adult court, but only 8% have served prison or jail sentences since 1981. Given the lower median age of the GA clients (twenty-six, compared with thirty-nine for the homeless) and hence their shorter exposure to the risks of conviction and sentencing, these lower rates may simply reflect the difference in age.

Table 6.12   Convictions and Sentences among the Homeless and the Extremely Poor

Measure	Percentage
A. Chicago Homeless Study	
Served sentence in state or federal prison	16.5
Served sentence in city or county jail	40.6
Given probation by a court	28.3
B. Combined Homeless Studies	
Average with prison experience (12 studies)	21.3
Average with jail experience (9 studies)	34.7
Average with prison or jail or both (16 studies)	42.1
C. Chicago General Assistance Study	
Convicted in adult court (nontraffic only)	14.0
Served time in jail or prison since 1981	8.0
D. Chicago Urban Family Life Study	
Ever been in jail, prison, or detention	
Males	30.7%
Females	5.9%
Average time spent in jail, prison, or detention	
Males	5.6 months
Females	1.6 months

Some data are available from the Chicago Urban Family Life Study, as shown in panel D. Unfortunately the study did not distinguish among jail, prison, and juvenile detention institutions, so that the almost one in three (31%) of the fathers reporting imprisonment is including all three kinds of incarceration. Nevertheless, this is a rate of contact with the criminal justice system that is almost as high as for all the homeless, although not as high as the rate for homeless men (45% of homeless men have been in jail or prison).

Clearly the homeless have much higher conviction rates for felonies and minor crimes than the general adult population and perhaps higher rates than the domiciled extremely poor. Having a criminal record is clearly a disability in obtaining jobs that require the absence of a criminal record. Of course such jobs are not in the majority, nor are they frequently found in the occupations typically followed by the homeless or the extremely poor. But there are additional forms of disability that are indexed by a criminal record. Aggressive people are not easy to get along with, and someone with a history of convictions for crimes involving harm to others may find it difficult to find and keep friends or to have friendly relations with kin.

The Social Networks of the Homeless and the Extremely Poor

The social researchers who studied the "old homeless" of the 1950s and 1960s were struck by the lack of ties between the old men on Skid Row and their families or any nonkin in the larger society. Indeed, one of the monographs on homelessness was titled *Disaffiliated Man* (Bahr 1970); furthermore, the author defined homelessness as "a condition of detachment from society characterized by the absence or attenuation of the affiliative bonds that link settled persons to a network of interconnected social structures." This view of homelessness did not go unchallenged. Qualitative researchers using ethnographic approaches (Wiseman 1970; Spradley 1970; Wallace 1965) found that the old men on Skid Row were "connected" not with the world outside Skid Row but with each other. That is, at least some Skid Row inhabitants formed small friendship groups engaged in mutual sharing and help. A typical Skid Row grouping would involve a set of men who shared drink, looked out for each other's safety, and exchanged survival information.

In fact, the two views of affiliation among the old homeless were quite compatible. Ties to family members and persons who lived in the mainstream were attenuated, although there was strong evidence of informal groupings of homeless men on Skid Row. Of course the ties involved in kinship and friendship are not qualitatively the same. Kinship ties ordinarily involve much more lasting commitment and stronger obligations.

The extent to which the homeless and the extremely poor are tied into social networks, especially with kin, constitutes an important issue. For most people, the first-line buffer against any of the vicissitudes of life is a network of kin and friends. Especially important are families and households, which to some degree, ordinarily share their resources. Many working married couples pool their incomes, and most share at least some of the household's recurring expenses, such as food purchases, rent, utilities, or mortgage payments. In addition, a division of household maintenance tasks, child rearing, food preparation, and other home activities ties members into a miniature household economy. In one-earner households pooling income may not be possible, and the division of household labor may constitute the main knots in the net of relationships.

A primary family in a household is usually defined as a married couple and their dependent minor children. In our kinship system it is ambiguous when a child ceases to be a minor dependent who is "entitled" to support from parents. By all state laws a child under sixteen must be supported by the parents, but the age when their responsibility ends may be higher. Of course legal definitions do not necessarily coincide either with practice or with popular beliefs. A majority of children between eighteen and twenty-five are still in their parents' households. Large minorities of children over age twenty-five still live with their parents. Parents acknowledge strong obligations to provide financial help to their adult children.

Within a household, adults who are not dependent minor children have an ambiguous standing in the pooling of income and the sharing of household tasks. Almost all (90%) of the GA recipients who lived in households made financial contributions, averaging $85 per month, a little more than half the

GA stipend from the state. Though these payments probably do not fully reimburse the households for the GA clients' share of household benefits, they cannot be seen as inconsiderable. The GA study does not contain any information on the nonfinancial contributions GA clients made by doing household tasks.

Household members are thus to some degree cushioned against abrupt and drastic downward swings in fortune. If one wage earner loses a job, others in the household can help take up the burden of rent payments and food purchases. The impact of other adverse events such as illness or setbacks in interpersonal relations can also be softened by sharing. The division of labor among household members can also mean a higher level of comfort through more efficient household production.

As was shown in chapter 5, the outstanding characteristic of the homeless is their lack of ties to family units, especially their own but also their parents'. Most had never married or, if they had, were no longer married. As persons who had typically passed through early adulthood and were now in their early middle years or even later in the life cycle, they had also left their parents' homes. They lived alone and as single-person households faced life events without the buffering of family.

Although General Assistance clients also had not formed families of their own, more than two out of three were members of households, usually living with their parents. Even when they lived alone, they managed it by receiving help from parents and other relatives. Compared with the homeless, GA clients were closely tied to kin. To be sure, GA clients living with their parents are not a total drain on parental resources; although payments of $154 a month were not enough to maintain a single-person household, they made it possible to contribute to household costs, and most GA clients did so.

A majority (56%) of AFDC clients lived in a family unit consisting of the recipient and her children. A few lived with spouses or partners (11%), but the rest lived in households with their parents, their siblings, and their own adult children. AFDC clients were not as closely connected as the GA recipients, but then the AFDC payments, while hardly generous, are sufficient to sustain separate households.

Almost all of the extremely poor identified in the Chicago Urban Family Life Study lived in multiple-person households, reflecting the research design. The same characteristic holds for the extremely poor identified in the national Current Population Survey.

The main point of the last few paragraphs is that most of the extremely poor are members of multiperson households and can be regarded as in constant mutual helping and sharing relations with family and friends. In contrast, the immediate social world of the homeless is quite different. There may be some sharing and mutual aid, but it typically cannot reach the scope and frequency experienced by those in multiple-person households.

Sharing a household is a major way people stay in close contact with others,

167

but it is not the only way, though few substitutes can reach the same level. Visiting is an important kind of contact, and as was shown in chapter 4, the homeless, on the average, spent one night every four weeks in the home of a relative, a pattern that was especially prevalent among homeless men under forty. We do not know about other visits that did not involve sleeping over, but they probably were more frequent.

In addition, one may maintain contact by writing or telephoning, which is good for sociability but may not involve mutual help in material things. Friendships are maintained in much the same way—by visiting, writing, and telephoning. The data presented in chapter 4 indicated that the homeless spent, on the average, another night every four weeks in the homes of nonkin, most of whom were probably friends. Telephoning and visiting without staying over were probably more frequent.

Maintaining Ties with Kin

Maintaining kinship and friendship ties is easier if those involved live nearby. Most of the homeless are native Chicagoans, and most of their friends and relatives also live in that city. For the three in five (58%) whose parents are still alive, 57% of the parents live in Chicago, and 47% of the brothers and sisters are Chicagoans. Somewhat lower proportions—about two out of five (42%)—of "other relatives" are Chicagoans, possibly reflecting the migration to Chicago of their parents' generation. Similar high proportions of former spouses and children also live in Chicago (see tables 6.13 and 6.15).

In short, most of the homeless have a reservoir of kin living in Chicago. Only one in twenty (6%) has neither parents, siblings, spouse, former spouse, nor children who live in Chicago. The potential for membership in a vital kinship network exists among the homeless. Of course whether that potential is realized is problematic, an issue this section addresses.

Because the homeless are typically outside multiple-person households, kin relations must be realized through other types of contact. To measure such contact with kin and friends, the questionnaires contained a battery of questions on the extent to which the homeless maintained ties with kin and friends. The question sequence started with finding out whether homeless persons had anyone alive in a particular category, then whether anyone in that category lived in Chicago, and ended up asking whether they maintained contact with these persons. Our definition of "maintained contact" was not very stringent, at a minimum consisting of writing, telephoning, or visiting once every two or three months. Under this definition, for a relationship to qualify as being maintained, the minimum contact can be rather infrequent, and many of the maintained contacts I have enumerated may be very superficial. Consequently, relationships consisting of four telephone calls a year are counted as well as ones maintained by daily contact.

Table 6.13 contains the findings on contacts with parents, siblings, and

Table 6.13 Maintaining Ties with Kin: Chicago Homeless Study

Parents still alive	58%
Parents living in Chicago	57[a]
In contact with parents	70[a]
Overall proportion in contact with parents	25
Siblings still alive	75%
Siblings living in Chicago	47[a]
In contact with siblings	57[a]
Overall proportion in contact with siblings	43
Other relatives still alive	66%
Other relatives living in Chicago	42[a]
In contact with other relatives	42[a]
Overall proportion in contact with other relatives	28

[a] Of those with kin still alive.

"other relatives."[14] Most of the homeless have parents living in Chicago: almost three out of five (58%) had at least one living parent, most of whom (57%) lived in Chicago. Of those who had living parents, 70% were in contact with them. Overall, taking into account those whose parents were dead, one in four maintained contact with parents. The extent of contact with parents varied strongly with age. Reflecting the impact of mortality, a minority (39% and 34%) of homeless persons over forty had living parents, and the corresponding percentages for those under forty were 75% and 87%. The consequence is that about half of the younger homeless persons had contact with their parents as opposed to fewer than a tenth of the older ones.

Unfortunately we were not able to find highly comparable data on the contact patterns of either GA or AFDC clients. The measures that do exist are of household sharing, a much more intense level of contact than is shown in table 6.13. Given the residence patterns of GA clients, with most living with parents or siblings, we can infer that contact with parents is considerably greater than among the homeless. About one in eight (12%) of the AFDC households included one or both parents, and in one in ten (11%) a sibling was present, from which we can infer a higher level of contact with parents and siblings.

Since brothers and sisters are of the same generation, and because sibling sets are on the average larger than parent sets, mortality did not take as much of a toll on siblings. In table 6.13 we learn that three out of four homeless persons had living brothers or sisters, about half (47%) of whom lived in Chicago. The homeless were less often in touch with their brothers or sisters than with their parents: 57% were in touch, compared with 70% for parents. But because more of the homeless had live siblings, the overall contact with sib-

14. Defined in the questionnaire as "other relatives, such as grandparents, aunts, uncles, or cousins."

lings (43%) was higher than the comparable figure for parents (25%). Neither the GA study nor the AFDC study provides any comparable data on contact with siblings, except for shared residence, as discussed earlier.

The "other relatives" of the homeless constituted a miscellaneous category whose size depends on the fertility of previous and current generations and on respondents' possibly varying definitions of the boundaries of kindred. ("Other relatives" do not include spouses and children, discussed separately below.)

It is not surprising that two out of three (66%) had living "other relatives," of whom 42% lived in Chicago. The homeless had a fairly low level (42%) of contact with this group, leading to an overall level of 28%, slightly higher than the overall contact with parents.

Apparently "other relatives" tends to be defined as persons up the generational ladder, since, compared with those under forty, older persons were much more likely to claim they had no living representatives of that group.

Although fifteen of the forty studies of homeless populations throughout the country contained measures of contact between the homeless and their "families," the measures tended to be imprecise. Colloquial American kinship terminology does not clearly distinguish primary kin, such as spouses, parents, or children, from secondary or higher-order kin that can range from siblings to distant cousins or aunts and uncles some degrees removed. Typical measures consisted of asking respondents whether they were "in touch" with their "families." Be that as it may, the average proportion of the homeless who were in contact with their families so defined was 68%. In short, one in three of the homeless studied reported not being in contact with any "family" members.

Living with Relatives

How important were these ties with kin? Could the homeless call on them for help? Would they want to live with their relatives, assuming the relatives assented to such a move? To cast some light on these issues, we asked two questions. First, we set up the condition that one or another of the relatives[15] living in Chicago had room to accommodate the respondent and also wanted to do so; then we asked whether the respondent would favor or oppose going to live with the person in question. Second, in a separate question, we asked whether respondents believed their Chicago relatives would be opposed to or in favor of their moving in. These two questions were asked only of persons who acknowledged having relatives currently living in Chicago, defined as parents, siblings, and "other relatives." Spouses, former spouses, and children were explicitly omitted.

15. The full question was explicitly worded to cover parents, siblings, and other relatives, as follows: "You mentioned that you have (parents/brothers or sisters/other relatives) here in Chicago. Assuming that they would want to and have the room, would you be opposed to or in favor of going to live with them?"

Table 6.14   Homeless People's Views of Living with Relatives

	Under Forty		Forty and Over		
	Males	Females	Males	Females	Total
Wants to live with relatives	52.6%	18.7%	31.5%	39.9%	38.3%
Relatives want respondent to move in	40.8	18.2	42.9	40.0	35.9
Both relatives and respondent favor	23.7	3.1	14.3	20.0	16.3
Respondent opposes but relatives favor	17.0	15.6	28.6	20.1	19.9
Relatives oppose but respondent favors	20.8	12.5	11.4	19.9	19.8
Both relatives and respondent oppose	27.0	62.5	39.9	33.4	39.0

Source: Chicago Homeless Study: winter 1986 survey only.

The answers given to these two questions are shown in table 6.14. Because age and gender have strong effects on potential kin networks, the answers are shown separately for men and women and for those under and over forty. Overall, as shown in the last column, a little under two in five (38%) of the homeless would want to live with relatives if the latter would have them. And a slightly lower proportion (36%) believed their relatives would have them. In sum, most of the homeless (almost two-thirds) would not want to live with their relatives, and most believed their relatives would not want them.

Although we cannot know whether the Chicago homeless correctly assessed their relatives' views, it is clear that they themselves believe they are not wanted as housemates. It is also obvious that they would not want to live with their relatives. What biographical events lie behind this widespread state of alienation we do not know, although we do know that in most cases they did share the households of (mainly) their parents and siblings in the past.[16]

Homeless women under forty were the most alienated and believed that very few of their relatives would have them. Only one in five (19%) would live with relatives, and only 18% believed their relatives would favor such a move. In contrast, homeless men under forty were much more favorable to living with relatives (53% in favor), and many (41%) believed their relatives would have them. Older men and women fell between the other two groups, with older women showing more interest in living with relatives.

The bottom part of table 6.14 shows the joint distribution of the answers to the two questions. The trends discussed above are even clearer in these data. Young women clearly saw that they were not welcome in their relatives'

16. Piliavin and Sosin (1987–88), in their analysis of a sample of homeless persons in Minneapolis, found that as children a very large proportion had been placed in foster homes at one time or another. It may well be that alienation from parents is a long-standing feature of homeless people's biographies.

homes and certainly did not want to move in; only 3% both wanted to go to their relatives and also saw themselves as welcome.

In contrast, about one in four (24%) of the young men wanted to move in with relatives and believed relatives would have him. Another one in five wanted to go but believed relatives would not have him. Older men and women fell between these two groups. Note that these patterns are also reflected in the residential arrangements of the extremely poor. Compared with unattached women, more of the unattached men are living with their parents, and most unattached women who were single parents had established their own households. This patterning is shown both for the Chicago extremely poor and for those in the Current Population Survey.

Maintaining Social Ties with Spouses and Children

The next category of kin is ties with spouses, former spouses, and children, considered in table 6.15. As I noted in chapter 4, very few of the homeless, save younger women, are currently or formerly married, and most therefore do not have spouses or former spouses. That is why so few (31%) have living spouses or former spouses. Contacts were high for those who do, with nearly two out of three (62%) maintaining ties. Of course it is probably the enduring ties through children that kept the level so high even though most of the marriages in question had long since been broken. But the low level of current and former marital ties made spouses and former spouses the least frequent of all (19%) in overall contact.

Although very few of the Chicago homeless had ever married, a much larger proportion had children. Almost half (47%) had living children, of whom close to two out of three lived in Chicago. Among homeless people who were parents of living children, two out of three (64%) maintained ties with them, a level of exercised contact that was exceeded only by the category of living parents. Primary ties up or down the generational ladder were the ones that were maintained most often.

Homeless women under forty had the highest level of contact with their

Table 6.15 Maintaining Social Ties with Spouses or Former Spouses and with Children

Measure	Percentage
Spouse or former spouse still alive	31
Spouse or former spouse living in Chicago	35[a]
In contact with spouse or former spouse	62[a]
Overall proportion in contact with spouse or former spouse	19
Children still alive	47
Children living in Chicago	65[a]
In contact with children	64[a]
Overall proportion in contact with children	30

[a]Of those with spouse or children still alive.

children—scarcely surprising, since many had children with them in the shelters. At the other extreme, homeless men had the least contact with their children.

Maintaining Friendship Ties

The size and the complexity of one's kindred are largely out of one's control. By marrying and having children or not doing one or the other, one can enlarge or restrict one's kindred, but otherwise it results from others' marriage and fertility patterns. Not so with friends, however. Having a friend is purely volitional, often not even requiring that the other person fully reciprocate. Hence having friends and maintaining contact with them is a better index of sociability and interpersonal skills than is maintaining contact with relatives.

As might be expected, fewer than half (48%) of Chicago's homeless people had friends they could "count on" [17] (see panel A of table 6.16). Nine out of ten (90%) lived in Chicago. Contact was maintained with the overwhelming majority (92%). (It appears that the term "friends you can count on" implies regular contact.) Overall, slightly less than half (44%) were currently in contact with one or more good friends. Thirteen of the forty homeless studies asked about friendships (see panel B), some using definitions that were close to the implied trust and aid relationships used in the Chicago Homeless Study, but most leaving the issue largely undefined. The average of those who stated they had no friends was 36%; the majority (64%) claimed at least one friend. Using this criterion, most other studies found the homeless more closely tied into friendship networks. Of course we do not know how much these measures are affected by the explicit or implicit definition of friendship used.

Unfortunately, the Chicago GA and AFDC studies collected no data on friendships. The only information on the extremely poor comes from the Chicago SRO and Urban Family Life studies.

The Chicago SRO study asked about "friends and neighbors," and close to three out of four (74%) claimed to have friends or neighbors they felt close to. A follow-up question asked whether there were any patterns of aiding one another for each person the SRO respondents designated. As shown in panel C, in only one-third of the cases (31%) was any aid given or received. Most (69%) had no friends or neighbors they aided or received help from. The two definitions used in the Chicago SRO study straddle the one used in the Chicago Homeless Study. We asked for "friends you can count on," implying more than someone you feel close to but not as demanding a definition as mutual aid.

The Chicago Urban Family Life Study has some rather detailed data on people respondents can call on for help, as presented in table 6.17. Unfortunately, the two questions ask whether the respondents have anyone they can

17. The exact wording of the item was "Do you have any friends you can count on?" It was so worded to measure friendship relationships that involved more than superficial acquaintance.

Table 6.16   Maintaining Social Ties with Friends

Measure	Percentage
A. Chicago Homeless Study	
With good friends	48.0
With good friends in Chicago	90.0
In contact, among those with good friends	92.0
Overall proportion in contact with good friends	44.0
B. Combined Homeless Studies (13 studies)	
Average claiming no friends	36.0
C. Chicago SRO Residents Study	
With "friends and neighbors" they feel close to[a]	74.1
With friends or neighbors they aid or receive help from[a]	31.4

[a]$N = 185.$

Table 6.17   Social Supports among the Domiciled Extremely Poor

Measure	Males	Females
Knows persons who can be depended on for everyday favors		
No person cited	31.1%	20.9%
Persons cited		
Friends	32.9	40.3
Mother	29.3	22.0
Siblings	21.5	26.8
Father	10.4	9.3
Spouse	5.2	9.3
Other relatives	12.4	12.9
Children	0.0	4.8
Knows persons to provide help in major crises		
No person cited	29.9%	39.5%
Persons cited		
Friends	20.7	25.1
Mother	28.3	25.4
Siblings	20.7	11.1
Father	12.0	7.4
Spouse	4.8	4.5
Other relatives	13.5	16.5
Children	2.0	3.2

Source: Chicago Urban Family Life Study.

rely on, the one for "everyday favors" and the other for help in "major crises," not strictly comparable to those used in the Chicago Homeless Study. One of the major difficulties is that the Chicago Urban Family Life Study did not ask about relationships separately, allowing the respondents to cite close or distant relatives or nonrelatives. For example, the first question asked whether respondents had anyone they could depend on for everyday favors.[18] A respondent could cite a household member, a neighbor, or kin. The second question asking about people who could help in a major crisis has much the same format. Nevertheless, these are the best data we have on hand to look at how extremely poor persons are tied into social networks.

Table 6.17 first presents the persons respondents cited as ones they could depend on for everyday favors. About one in three male respondents (31%) could not name at least one such dependable person: on average, fewer than two persons (1.6) were cited, although there might be up to six. Women respondents reported more dependable persons, with more than three out of four (79%) reporting at least one, for an average of 1.9 friends.

Friends were cited as persons to depend on by about one-fifth of the males and one-fourth of the females. Indeed, friends turned out to be the most frequently cited. Among kin, mothers and siblings—in that order—dominate among dependable persons, mothers being cited more frequently by males and siblings by females. Considering that more than four out of five had mothers still living (84%) and that almost all (96%) had living brothers or sisters,[19] this high incidence of possible everyday helping behavior is likely matched by high levels of visiting, telephoning, and the like.

Fathers and spouses rank fairly low, the latter understandably, since the poorest respondents were selected because their spouses were not in the household. Note that fathers are less reliable than "other relatives," consisting of grandparents, grandchildren, parents' siblings, and cousins, in part because the latter are a much larger pool to draw from.

The Chicago Urban Family Life Study also asked about people the respondents could turn to for help in major crises, examples cited being serious illness or death or needing a place to stay.[20] Again, most respondents, both men and women (70% and 60%), could cite someone they could turn to in major crises. In this case the reporting levels were lower for women than for men. The relationships the respondents cited are similar in distribution to those given in answer to the first question except that friends appear to be slightly less important compared with mothers.

Clearly, most of the extremely poor in the Chicago Urban Family Life

18. The item used was "I will ask you about people you can depend on, such as friends, relatives and professionals like ministers and social workers. Many people help each other with everyday favors, such as getting rides, borrowing a little money, or going to the store. Please tell me the names of the people you most depend on for everyday favors."

19. This proportion of respondents' mothers still alive appears also to be much higher than the proportion of the homeless who claim to have living parents (58%), probably a function of both the lower age of the extremely poor (median age is thirty years) and the possibly higher mortality of the parents of the homeless. (The CHS study asked whether the respondent had one parent or both parents still alive.)

20. "Tell me the names of the people you could turn to for help in a major crisis, such as a serious illness or death, or if you needed a place to stay."

Study have some form of support in their social environment. If we take the answers to the second question seriously, slightly fewer than two in three have someone who would take them in if they had no place to go.

Overall Social Ties among the Homeless

Although it appears clear that the homeless had low levels of contact with relatives and friends, it is quite possible that few were completely isolated. Many may have had no friends but still had contact with relatives and possibly children. This raises the question how these contacts overlapped or compensated for each other.

Table 6.18 presents data on this question. First I have put together data indicating whether each person has some contact with parents or siblings or other relatives (family of orientation). Nearly nine out of ten (88%) had some relative alive in these categories. Three out of five had contact with some member of their family of orientation. Correspondingly, about two out of five of the homeless have no contact with their parents or siblings, even the quite superficial kind measured in the Chicago Homeless Study.

Next the table shows contact with spouses and children (family of procreation). More than half (55%) had living members of their family of procreation (primarily their children), but only 32% were in contact with any of them. Of course, two out of three of the homeless either never had children or spouses or, if they did, were no longer in contact with them.

The last section of table 6.18 combines the information on contacts with both family of orientation and family of procreation to measure isolation from kin—the proportion who had no contact with members of either group. Thus measured, one in three of the homeless was isolated. Adding contact with friends gives another measure of isolation, persons who had contact neither with friends nor with members of their families of procreation and orientation. Isolation in these terms characterized about one in four (24%) of the homeless. Contact with relatives thus does not compensate for isolation from friends or vice versa. Persons who were kin isolates also tended to be friendship isolates.

Note that there were consistent age and gender variations in both measures of isolation. Homeless persons over forty were more likely to be isolated than those under forty. Least isolated were young women, whose enduring ties with their children disqualified them as isolates. Most isolated were homeless women over forty; two out five had neither friends nor family with whom they maintained contact.

Overall, the strong impression left by the data presented in this chapter is of persons who have extensive ties to neither relatives nor friends. Of course it is not possible to state whether the relationship between low levels of social ties and homelessness is reciprocal or more directly causal. Surely it must be difficult to maintain social ties when one is so poor there can scarcely be any reci-

Table 6.18 Summary Contact Measures

Measure	Percentage
Family of orientation (parents, siblings and other relatives)	
Has living members	88.3
Is in contact with at least one member	59.6
Family of procreation (spouse and children)	
Has living members	54.8
Is in contact with at least one member	32.8
Isolation measures	
Not in contact with any relatives, spouse, or children	33.3
Not in contact with family and has no friends	23.7

Source: Chicago Homeless Study.

procity. Many of the homeless must also be persons with whom it is difficult and perhaps painful to maintain a pleasant relationship. Whatever the process, the outcome is that many of the homeless are completely isolated, and most have only very superficial ties to others.

The Accumulation of Troubles

Each successive section of this chapter has documented another set of problems experienced by the extremely poor and especially the homeless. In the previous chapter we also saw that unemployment and underemployment are endemic, and in this chapter we learned that so are signs of chronic mental illness, alcoholism, and poor health. The homeless have also frequently had run-ins with the criminal justice system, and their social supports are minimal. The accumulation of these conditions results in a profile of the homeless showing that only a handful do not suffer from one disability or another.

Table 6.19 presents the result of counting up each individual's problems, including unemployment, criminal records, indicators of mental illness, and self-reported fair or poor health. Adding them all together, fewer than 4% of respondents had no problems at all to report. Another one in three (35%) had only one or two such problems. The remaining three out of five (61%) had three or more problems, with 16% reporting five to seven. Obviously, virtually none of the homeless were completely without problems, and more than half have multiple problems.

When the various components of the overall problem count shown in table 6.19 are considered separately, as in tables 6.20 and 6.21, similar results appear. Table 6.20 shows that more than four in five (83%) had employment problems, and table 6.21 shows that more than four in five (82%) had mental health or crime problems or both.

The measuring devices used as the basis for tables 6.19 through 6.21 are hardly finely tuned instruments that could be used in clinical practice. Never-

Table 6.19   Accumulated Reported Problems of the Homeless

Number of Problems Reported[a]	Percentage
0	3.4
1	14.6
2	20.9
3	26.3
4	18.9
5	10.0
6	4.6
7	1.4

Source: Chicago Homeless Study: winter 1986 survey only.
[a] Problems consist of the following conditions: Not employed at all in last month; being without a steady job for one year or more; having higher than average scores on the demoralization scale; having higher than average scores on the psychotic thinking scale; being in jail, in prison, or on probation; having been in a mental hospital or detoxification unit; and reporting fair or poor health.

Table 6.20   Reported Employment Problems

Number of Employment Problems Reported[a]	Percentage
0	16.9
1	41.4
2	41.7

Source: Chicago Homeless Study: winter 1986 survey only.
[a] Problems consist of being totally unemployed during the previous month and having last held a steady job more than one year ago.

Table 6.21   Reported Mental Health and Crime Problems

Number of Problems Reported[a]	Percentage
0	18.3
1	29.7
2	25.4
3	16.0
4	8.3
5	2.3

Source: Chicago Homeless Study: winter 1986 survey only.
[a] Problems consist of having been institutionalized for mental illness, having been sentenced by a court, having been in a detoxification center for alcohol or drug abuse, scoring above average on CES-D, and scoring above average on psychotic thinking scale.

theless, those tables can be interpreted to mean that almost all the homeless had disabilities of one kind or another to some degree. These findings certainly are no surprise. All the literature on the homeless has described these conditions as afflicting sizable proportions of them. What may be unique about the findings in this chapter are two main themes: First, the homeless are different from most of the domiciled extremely poor in having much higher incidence of these problems. Second, I have presented evidence that the joint impact of the disabilities produces a situation in which the overwhelming majority of the homeless have at least one disabling condition, and most have more than one.

The Implications of High Disability Levels

Especially critical are the contrasts between the homeless and the domiciled extremely poor. Despite the demographic and economic resemblances between these two groups, the main difference lies in the higher prevalence of certain disabilities among the homeless. This constitutes the underpinning for one of the major interpretations advanced here: among the extremely poor, those with disabilities are the most vulnerable to homelessness. Especially critical are those disabilities that make it difficult for relatives, especially, but also friends, to generously provide shelter and support. In particular, those with chronic mental illness, severe alcoholism, and criminal records do not make good housemates and are eased out from under the protective wing of their relatives and friends.

SEVEN

Why We Have Homelessness and Extreme Poverty and What to Do about Them

In the preceding chapters, the descriptions of the extremely poor and the homeless were based on fairly good empirical data. Even so, many of the findings had to be qualified by doubts concerning data quality and relevance. In this chapter I will tread on even shakier ground, using them as the basis for interpretations. I will take these descriptions as background against which to discuss two main topics. First, what were the underlying social forces that produced the resurgence of homelessness in the 1980s, maintained its level, and influenced the aggregate characteristics of homeless persons? Second, what reasonable set of public policies would both alleviate the condition of the homeless and the extremely poor and reduce both populations?

Housing and Homelessness

In discussing the distinguishing characteristics of homeless Americans, it is easy to lose sight of the fact that the essential and defining symptom of homelessness is lack of access to conventional housing. Clearly, if conventional housing were both everywhere abundant and without cost, there would be no homelessness except for those who preferred to sleep in the streets and in public places.[1] That there are homeless people in fairly large numbers means that our housing market is not providing appropriate housing abundantly at prices the homeless can afford. Nor is it providing affordable housing for the extremely poor, who must double up with others.

To be sure, there is no way any housing market dominated by private providers can offer housing at an "affordable price" for those who have close to zero income. But market-offered housing is not the only option. Most of the extremely poor are domiciled, and their housing chances are affected by the supply of low-cost housing generally, a market factor that affects the households they live with. There is abundant evidence that homelessness is related both directly and indirectly to the shortage of inexpensive housing for poor

---

1. Many commentators and researchers on homelessness claim they have talked to homeless people who said they preferred homelessness to conventional housing. I have no doubt that such statements have been made. I also have little doubt that when offered an option under realistic conditions, few homeless people would make such a choice.

families and poor unattached persons that began in the 1970s and has accelerated in the 1980s.

The decline in the inexpensive segment of our housing stock has been precipitous in the largest cities, such as New York and Los Angeles, but it also has characterized cities of all sizes (Wright and Lam 1987). The Annual Housing Survey, conducted by the Census Bureau for the Department of Housing and Urban Development, has recorded in city after city declines in the proportion of housing renting for 40% or less of poverty-level incomes. These declines ranged from 12% in Baltimore between 1978 and 1983 to 40% in Washington D.C. for 1977 to 1981 and 58% in Anaheim, California, in the same period. In twelve large cities surveyed between 1978 and 1983, the amount of inexpensive rental housing available to poor families dropped precipitously, averaging 30%. At the same time, the number of households living at or below the poverty level in the same cities increased by 36%. The consequence of these two trends is that in the early 1980s a severe shortage occurred in housing that poor households could afford without bearing an excessive rent burden. Note that these calculations assume that such affordable housing rents for 40% or less of the poverty level, a larger proportion of income than the customary prudent 25% for rent.

Most of the housing I have discussed so far consists of multiroom units appropriate to families. If we restrict our attention to that portion of the housing stock that is ordinarily occupied by poor unattached single persons, then the decline is even more precipitous. Chicago's Planning Department estimated that between 1973 and 1984, 18,000 single-person dwelling units in SRO hotels and small apartment buildings—amounting to 19% of the stock existing in 1973—were demolished or transformed for other uses (Chicago Department of Planning 1985).[2] In Los Angeles a recent report (Hamilton, Rabinowitz and Alschuler, Inc. 1987) indicated that between 1970 and 1985 more than half of the SRO units in downtown Los Angeles had been demolished. Of course there is nothing wrong per se with the demolition of SROs; most were certainly not historical landmarks or examples of any notable architectural style. Nor can they be said to have been of high quality. The problem is that units comparable in function or price were not built or converted in sufficient volume to replace them.

In chapter 2 I noted the almost complete demolition of the cubicle flophouse hotels in the 1960s and 1970s. In 1958 about 8,000 homeless men were accommodated in such units in Chicago; by 1980 all the cubicle hotels had been removed.[3] In New York, by 1987 only one of the cheap hotels that domi-

---

2. At the same time, 11,000 subsidized senior citizens' units had been added to the stock, and 8,500 section 8 senior citizens' housing vouchers were issued. Provision was made for replacing housing stock, but only for a portion of the single-person housing, that used by persons sixty-five and over.

3. In 1980 the last two Chicago cubicle hotels, the Star and the Major, were demolished to be replaced by Presidential Towers, a 1,200-unit luxury apartment complex.

nated the Bowery in the 1960s remained (Jackson 1987).[4] Similar changes have occurred in other large cities. Of course it is difficult to mourn the passing of the often dirty and always inadequate cubicle hotels. Like the SROs, they had little or no symbolic or aesthetic value. But only the emergency dormitory shelters have replaced the housing stock they represented. There are virtually no rooms in Chicago today that can be rented for $1.80 to $2.70 a night, today's dollar equivalent of the 1958 rents. The emergency dormitory shelters are arguably cleaner than the cubicle hotels, but they are certainly not much closer to decent housing. Indeed, the old Skid Row residents regarded the mission dormitory shelters as considerably inferior to the cubicle hotels, lacking in privacy and personal safety (Bogue 1963).[5]

The decline in inexpensive housing influences homelessness both directly and indirectly. Indirectly, the effect can be felt through the increased financial housing burden placed on poor families, whose generosity toward their dependent adult members becomes more difficult to extend or maintain. Housing prices partially reflect the amount of housing involved, with larger units commanding higher prices. Faced with declining real income, poor families may have had to opt for smaller dwellings, restricting their ability to shelter adult children.

The direct effects are upon the homeless themselves, putting inexpensive housing, such as SRO accommodations, beyond the reach of most of the new homeless. For example, in a study of SROs in Chicago, Hoch (Jewish Council on Urban Affairs 1985) found that the average monthly rental for SRO hotels in Chicago in 1984 was $195 if rented by the month or $240 ($8 a day), if rented day to day. For most of the homeless, with median monthly incomes of $100, renting an SRO room steadily was out of the question.

Because rents were so high relative to income, the tenants of Chicago's SROs were forced to spend a very large proportion of their income on housing. When some out of the ordinary expense occurred, many had to resort to the shelters and the streets. According to Hoch, about one in ten of the SRO tenants had been homeless for some period during the previous year, apparently too short of funds to pay the rent. Hoch does not tell us whether these SRO tenants lived in shelters or on the streets when they became homeless. But in our survey of the Chicago homeless, both the shelter and the street samples claimed they spent about 10% of their nights in rented rooms, presumably in SRO hotels.

Some of the homeless people we interviewed on the streets or in the shelters ordinarily spent most nights in SRO hotels and were just temporarily home-

4. Jackson's essay on the history of the Bowery relates that by 1987 gentrification had begun to convert land to upscale condominiums.

5. The dormitory shelters in the old Skid Rows were those offered by the religious missions. At least part of the old Skid Row men's dislike for the shelters centered on the typical requirement that they attend religious services in return for access to the dormitory beds.

less.[6] Others occasionally spent a night or two in an SRO, perhaps when they received a windfall. Apparently there is a considerable interchange between the homeless and the SRO populations, the latter being a cut above the former in income. Similarly, Piliavin and Sosin (1987–88) found that homeless people in Minneapolis typically moved between having homes and being homeless several times a year.

High rents relative to income also forced some of the SRO tenants to overspend on housing and, accordingly, to skimp on other expenditures. Hoch reports that many SRO residents resorted to the food kitchens, to the medical clinics set up for homeless persons, and to the clothing depots. In a study of the homeless in downtown Los Angeles, one out of every three persons in the soup-kitchen lines was renting a room in an SRO (Farr, Koegel, and Burnham 1986). Further confirmation can be found in Sosin's 1986 study of persons using Chicago food kitchens and day centers (Sosin, Colson, and Grossman 1988), which found that about half were living in SROs and apartments.

The impact of the housing market on homelessness in the aggregate was shown dramatically in a recent analysis by Tucker (1987). There are several deficiencies in Tucker's procedures; nevertheless, some of his findings are both useful and relevant. Using the HUD estimates[7] of the number of homeless in each of fifty cities to compute a homelessness rate for each city,[8] Tucker was able to show a fairly strong negative correlation, $-.39$, between housing vacancy rates in 1980 and homelessness rates in 1984 across cities. In other words, the higher the vacancy rate in a city, the lower its homelessness rate. Tucker also showed that the vacancy rate is highly sensitive to the presence of rent control measures, but that need not concern us here. The point Tucker's analysis drives home is that the tighter the housing market from the buyer's (or renter's) point of view, the greater the housing burden on poor families and the more difficult it becomes for the extremely poor to obtain housing, and consequently the easier it is to become homeless.

In a perfect unrestricted housing market, the range of housing offered by sellers at equilibrium would supply all buyers who can enter bids. But this statement is more a matter of faith than of fact. The American housing market is neither unfettered nor perfect. Nor would we have it any other way. Our building codes are designed to ensure that the housing industry provides ac-

---

6. This information comes from interviewers' comments on the filled-out questionnaires. Unfortunately, we did not ask shelter residents for enough detailed information to estimate the prevalence of this pattern of intermittent homelessness.

7. These estimates are simply averages of what informed persons in the cities studied thought were the total number of homeless people there. Although no one can gauge their accuracy, it is likely that they reflect well the differences among cities in amount of homelessness. Note that these intercity differences in homelessness are the focus of Tucker's analysis.

8. HUD analysts related the number of homeless people in each city to the population for the Rand McNally metropolitan area in which the city was situated, a strategy that was heavily criticized. Tucker computed his rates by using only the populations for the central cities.

commodations that meet minimum standards of public health and safety. Zoning laws attempt to regulate the externalities surrounding existing structures. Occupancy laws discourage overcrowding of dwelling units. These regulations also accomplish other ends, some undesirable to many citizens: for example, zoning laws designed to ensure that structures occupy no more than some given proportion of urban land plots, a desirable aesthetic amenity, also make neighborhoods socioeconomically homogeneous. In some cities rent control is an additional restriction whose burden falls heavily on households entering the market and provides a bonus in the form of cheaper rents to long-term residents. These regulations are not the only factors restricting the amount of "affordable housing" available to the poor, but they certainly drive up the prices of even minimum standard housing.

However, there can be no market where there is no effective demand. The market cannot provide affordable housing for the homeless because their incomes are so low and variable that their demand is too weak to stimulate housing providers. The housing market was not always unresponsive to the demand of poor people. The Skid Rows of the nation were such responses, but the old cubicle hotels of the 1950s and 1960s were responding to a much stronger demand. Recall that the constant-dollar income of the Skid Row residents in 1958 was at least three times the income of the current homeless. Even so, as Bogue and the other social researchers observed in the 1950s and 1960s, the cubicle hotels were experiencing high vacancy rates.

The records are silent on whether the cubicle hotel owners and operators welcomed or fought the exercise of eminent domain in the urban renewal of Skid Row areas. Perhaps they welcomed the bulldozers as a way to recover some of the equity they had sunk into an increasingly unprofitable business.

In the past, when the housing industry was unable (or unwilling) to provide homes for the extremely poor they sometimes built their own. In the Great Depression of the 1930s, "shantytowns" consisting of shacks cobbled together out of scrap materials were built on New York's riverfronts and even in Central Park. Similar settlements were erected on Chicago's lakefront, in Washington's Anacostia Flats, and on vacant sites in other cities. In the 1980s no comparable settlements have appeared, unless one counts the cardboard and wooden packing cases used as living quarters by a few of the homeless. It may be that vacant land is not as available now or that law enforcement officials are quicker to respond.[9] Whatever has caused the difference, the self-help response of the homeless to market failure has not been as strong as in the past.

As the rents the homeless could afford declined with their incomes during the 1970s and 1980s, housing providers found them an increasingly unattractive set of customers, especially in contrast to others. There is no mystery

---

9. Indeed, in 1987 when homeless people in Los Angeles built a "tent city" on a vacant downtown parcel, the mayor ordered the police to tear it down. Temporary shacks and tents have been built in Washington's Lafayette Park, but they must be removed every evening.

about why no housing is offered on the unsubsidized market that is affordable to the homeless. If there is a question, it is why local, state, and federal government have not intervened in the market to ensure that such housing is supplied.

The Labor Market and Homelessness

In chapter 2 I gave some attention to the important labor market function the Skid Rows of the past played in providing unskilled labor to employers who needed temporary workers episodically. Some were seasonal workers: in Chicago, Skid Row residents provided crews for summertime railroad maintenance and in all seasons supplied day labor. In Philadelphia, Skid Row men were hired over the summer by the Pennsylvania and New Jersey summer resorts. In addition, in each of the cities a labor market existed year-round that provided temporary or spot employment by the day, unloading freight cars and trucks, washing dishes in restaurants and hotels, distributing advertising fliers, and doing similar unskilled tasks.

A major factor in the 1960s and 1970s decline of the Skid Rows was the shrinkage of the casual labor market in urban economies. This decline in labor demand is carefully documented in Barrett Lee's (1980) analysis of the trends in Skid Row populations in forty-one cities from 1950 to 1970, showing that as the proportion of each city's labor force employed in unskilled labor and unskilled service occupations declined in that period, so did the population of its Skid Row.

In earlier decades, urban employers needing muscle power to wrestle cargo apparently put up with the low productivity of the Skid Row inhabitants because they could hire them as needed for low pay. Apparently, materials-handling equipment such as forklifts put both the homeless and Skid Row out of business. Cause and effect are almost hopelessly muddled here. As Skid Row populations declined, employers may have been motivated to invest in equipment that lowered their need for casual labor, and at the same time the lowered need for such labor meant that Skid Rows were populated more and more by persons out of the labor force (e.g., pensioners either retired or disabled).

The lack of demand for unskilled labor contributes to contemporary homelessness and helps account for the poor employment and earnings records of the extremely poor and the homeless. Labor market factors are especially important in understanding the sharp decline in the average age of the extremely poor and the homeless over the past three decades. Between 1955 and 1985 there was a drastic increase in unemployment among young males in general and blacks in particular. Unemployment reached catastrophic proportions in 1985 with 40% rates among black males under twenty-five (Freeman and Holzer 1986). Freeman and Holzer showed that young black males were considerably more likely to be employed only for short periods and were more likely to be fired.

The demographic processes at work during the post–World War II period also help explain the declining average age of the homeless. Recent decades have seen a bulge in the proportion of persons in our population who are between twenty and thirty-five, an outcome of the postwar baby boom. This excess of young people, especially males, depressed the earnings level for young adults and elevated the unemployment rate. As Easterlin (1987) has shown, the earnings of workers under thirty-five declined between 1968 and 1984 to about 80% of the 1968 level, computed in constant dollars. In contrast, the real wages of workers forty-five to fifty-five rose in the same period to 125% of their 1968 levels. Easterlin showed similar trends in the unemployment rate. At the beginning of the period under study, unemployment rates for young men below thirty-five were under 5% and rose to a high of 15% in 1980, declining to 13% in 1984. Older workers did not show such fluctuations.

The point of this analysis of the labor market is to show that the employment opportunities for young men has been extremely poor over the same period when the homeless population has increased and its composition has changed, with a time lag of five to ten years. As usual, the burdens of a poor labor market fall disproportionately upon precisely those groups we find overrepresented among the homeless—the disabled and minorities.

The impact on females of labor market and demographic trends since 1965 is a little more subtle. Easterlin's analysis shows that young women did not suffer as much from increased unemployment and decreased earnings as young men, although their positions on the labor market certainly showed no improvement over time. In comparison with those of young men, their earnings did not show as radical a decline in real dollars, and unemployment rates did not rise as dramatically.

But there is also an indirect effect on household formation that did affect the proportion of women with children who are married and thus contributed to what has been called the feminization of poverty. As I noted in chapter 5, homeless women are younger than homeless men—on the average five to ten years younger. Almost all the homeless heads of households were female. The abrupt rise in female-headed households from 1968 to 1984 in part reflects the uncertain economic fate of young men, who thereby become less attractive as mates, less willing to become household heads, and less able to fulfill the economic role of husband and father when marriage does take place.[10] In this respect it is significant that almost all the families housed in New York's welfare hotels are black or Hispanic female-headed households. Likewise, almost all the young homeless women we studied in Chicago were black, and almost all the homeless families were headed by black females.

In short, the uncertain labor market and earnings fates of young black men

---

10. Although few of the homeless men had married and those that had were divorced or separated, a majority (60%) claimed to be fathers. It is tempting to speculate how many of the fathers of the children in the homeless female-headed households are to be found among the homeless men.

jeopardized family formation among young blacks. The consequence is that young black women became heads of extremely poor households with high risk of becoming periodically homeless. In his analysis of poverty among blacks in Chicago, Wilson (1987) attributes much of the rise in female-headed households to the lack of marriageable black males. Owing to their catastrophically high unemployment rates, few young black men were able to make economic contributions to the households formed by the mothers of their children, let alone be the major providers.

The Limits of Kinship Obligations

It is an easy wager that there are few if any readers of this book whose families and kin would allow them to sink into literal homelessness. It is another easy wager that few if any readers would allow a family member or a near relative to become homeless. At least that would be our initial reaction to someone close to us who had become destitute through disabling illness, severe alcoholism, or an episode of mental disturbance. We would certainly offer financial help and even make room in our homes. American norms concerning obligations owed to kin support strongly such actions.[11] But how long could we keep it up? One would not begrudge support over a few weeks or months or even a year, but imagine having to supply maintenance and food for several years and, in addition, to share crowded housing.

Sharing might not be too hard for those of us who have room to spare in our houses and apartments and who have some discretionary income left after we finance a reasonably good standard of living. The generous impulse would be harder to extinguish if the dependent family member or kin was well behaved and did nothing bizarre or in poor taste. Even so, it would be hard to put up with. Doubtless we all know, and admire, people in our circles of kin, friends, and acquaintances who have made such sacrifices for fairly long periods.

Indeed, that families often take on the burden of providing for adult kin was shown in chapter 3 (see table 3.4). Using data from the Current Population Survey, I showed that in 1987 2.6 million extremely poor adult children aged twenty-two to fifty-nine were living in their parents' homes, and an additional 677,000 were living with siblings or grandparents. Of course many, if not most, of their families could sustain the additional burden: the household incomes of the supportive families were slightly above average. In addition, some families subsidized their impoverished adult members without taking them into their homes. Unfortunately, the Current Population Survey does not provide enough information so we can estimate the extent of such cash subsidies: we do know that there are at least 3.5 million impoverished dependent

---

11. In a recent study of kinship norms, Alice Rossi and I found that almost all of a sample of metropolitan Boston adults acknowledged strong obligations to provide financial help to primary kin (parents, children, and siblings) who were suffering from the effects of illness, psychological difficulties, or unemployment.

adults who are being subsidized by their parents and possibly as many as 6.5 million.

But now imagine the situation of poor parents, living at the poverty level or below in cramped quarters, on whom the responsibility for supporting an impoverished unemployed adult family member has fallen. How long could they keep it up? Imagine, in addition, that this dependent adult child has a serious alcohol or drug problem or has been in prison or exhibits the bizarre thinking or behavior of the chronically mentally ill.

It appears from our Chicago data that the average life of tolerance and help under such conditions is about four years, the period that the homeless were without steady work before becoming homeless. For that length of time they were presumably supported by their families' and friends' sharing housing, food, and maintenance. In addition, keep in mind that the families and friends are also poor and all those necessities are in short supply. Indeed, it is also a euphemism to talk about families, since many of the homeless come from single-parent households: their mothers and siblings may have been all there was to the "family" they relied on for support.[12] Piliavin and Sosin (1987) and Sosin, Colson, and Grossman (1988) comment that many of the homeless grew up in foster homes and may have had no parents at all or ones who were unable to fulfill their parental responsibilities.

There is good evidence that many of the homeless have worn out their welcome as dependents of their parents or as recipients of aid and funds from their friends. Chapter 6 presented some important evidence in the striking differences between the extremely poor unattached persons in the General Assistance population and the homeless. Recall that the groups are almost equally destitute, but most of the GA recipients are not living in shelters or out on the streets.

There are other important differences between the two groups that go along with their living arrangements. First, the levels of disability among GA clients are much lower on every indicator we can find in the data. Chronic mental illness, alcoholism, serious criminal records, and physical illnesses are far less prevalent among the domiciled. Second, the GA recipients largely manage to get by because their family and friendship support networks subsidize them, either by providing housing and maintenance or by supplementing their income.

Recall also that the GA recipients are on the average six years younger than the homeless men, suggesting that they have not yet worn out their welcome in their parents' households. Their much lower levels of alcoholism and chronic mental illness may also mean it is more acceptable to share housing with them. At least some of the GA recipients may thus simply be younger versions

---

12. Many of the mothers may also have been on AFDC during much of the time the sons were growing up and in their late teens or early adulthood. The Chicago AFDC study showed that 10% of AFDC recipients had children over eighteen living in their households.

of the homeless and may wear out their acceptance if their dependence goes on too long. The demoralizing and debilitating effects of long-term unemployment undoubtedly also play a role: the longer a person goes unemployed, the more likely it is that the disabilities of depression, mental illness, and even alcoholism will take their toll.

I suggest that the poverty of the families the homeless come from and their levels of disability both contribute heavily to their being homeless. Generosity may come up against the constraints of poverty when disability makes it difficult to exercise that virtue.

The Erosion of Public Welfare Benefits

We have seen that at least part of the burden of supporting extremely poor unattached persons is borne by poverty-stricken households who stretch their meager resources to house and maintain dependent adult children and sometimes friends. We can see national trends in young people living with their parents, especially among the poor. Indeed, black young men are especially likely to live in their parents' households. According to the census, in 1970, 39% of both black and white young men aged eighteen to twenty-nine lived with their parents. By 1984, 54% of black young men lived with their parents while only 41% of white men of comparable age did so.

Evidence for the extent of the burden on poor families is difficult to come by, since we do not know much about the households the homeless come from. But we do know that those households are poor and that many are supported by welfare—in particular, AFDC payments. Strong indicators of the declining positions of poor families can be found in the downward trends of transfer payments from 1968 to 1985. The level of welfare benefits also directly affects the capacity of the extremely poor to take care of themselves without the help of their parents. It is obvious that at the heart of homelessness and extreme poverty are the extremely low incomes of those groups. Among those states that have programs of income support to unattached persons, none provides enough to reach $4,000 a year. In addition, there are many states— for example, Texas, Alabama, and Tennessee—that have no income support programs at all for this segment of the population.

The importance of income support in alleviating extreme poverty is obvious. What is not obvious is that income support programs that cover unattached people below retirement age have undergone a severe deterioration in value over the past decade and a half, exacerbating the erosion of the life chances of the poor caused by labor and housing market trends.

Table 7.1 presents the average dollar values of several income transfer programs (in constant 1985 dollars) over the period 1968 to 1985 for the state of Illinois and for the nation as a whole. Except for the Social Security old-age pensions, the constant-dollar value of benefits declined drastically. Indeed, Social Security old-age payments actually increased by 162% from 1968 to

Table 7.1   Constant-Dollar Average Monthly Transfer Payments, 1968–85

Transfer Program	1968	1975	1980	1985
A. National Monthly Average Payments				
Social Security old age retirement	$295	$414	$446	$479
Social Security Disability		452	485	484
Social Security widows/orphans		388	406	433
Supplemental Security Income for the aged	217	182	167	164
SSI for the blind	285	294	278	274
SSI for disability	257	282	259	261
AFDC	520	464	366	325
B. Illinois Monthly Average Payments				
Social Security old age retirement	$311	$434	$474	$511
Social Security Disability			506	505
Social Security widows/orphans		435	466	
Supplemental Security Income for the aged	204		159	100
SSI for the blind	263			108
SSI for disability	269		246	142
AFDC	644	568	362	342
General Assistance	322			154

Note: Shown in 1985 dollars; consumer price index used as a deflator.

1984, and most other benefit programs under Social Security remained fairly steady in value. In contrast, there were radical declines in the constant-dollar values of both AFDC and General Assistance payments over the same period.

On the national level, in 1985 AFDC payments declined to 63% of their 1968 value. Illinois AFDC payments declined to 53% of 1968 value in the same period. An even more drastic decline occurred in Illinois's General Assistance payments, the program most often available to homeless persons and to unattached persons generally: 1985 General Assistance payments in Illinois were only 48% of 1968 payments in constant dollars. The major drop in value of these two transfer programs occurred in the five years between 1975 and 1980, reflecting the ravages of inflationary trends that were not sufficiently compensated for by raising payment levels.[13] As the burden of supporting unemployed adults fell upon families who in turn were dependent on AFDC or GA payments, such poor families entered the 1980s with considerably diminished financial capability and hence reduced capacity to help.

In addition, the reduction in the real value of AFDC payments contributed directly to the appearance of female-headed households among the homeless.

13. Of course there were some compensatory increases in other programs for which unemployed persons became eligible. Food stamps in 1985 could provide an additional $70 in food purchases, a benefit of dubious value to the homeless. Medicaid coverage was also extended in some states (Illinois, for example) and provided for most medical needs. Although food stamps and housing subsidies compensate in a very direct way for low income, Medicare or Medicaid is more questionable: you cannot pay the rent or eat with Medicaid coverage.

Female-headed households dependent on AFDC surely must have had a hard time meeting housing and other expenses on payments that barely covered average rents for small apartments. Living so close to the edge of financial disaster and often slipping into crisis, households headed by young females understandably often become literally homeless. Indeed, it is difficult to understand how the typical Illinois AFDC household composed of a mother and her 1.5 children managed to get by on $4,014 a year in direct cash payments and $798 in food stamps. More than a third of the AFDC households received help from other persons (presumably relatives) over a year's time. The Chicago AFDC study provides considerable evidence that AFDC families had a tenuous hold on their housing, with close to one in four experiencing problems over the previous year.

Illinois's AFDC payment schedule in 1985 and 1986 was among the ten most generous state plans. AFDC households in Illinois fared much better than comparable households in, say, Alabama or Texas, where payments averaged under $2,000 a year. Indeed, a major reason the extremely poor female-headed households were concentrated in the southern regions was that even with AFDC payments total annual income rarely reached $2,000.

The similar drop in the dollar value of General Assistance payments also influenced homelessness. General Assistance payments in 1968 were generous enough to cover SRO rent, with a bit left over for other types of consumption. In addition, in 1968 unattached adults on General Assistance had enough income from their benefits to make significant contributions to the income of a household, possibly making their dependence more palatable to their hosts. By 1985, with General Assistance payments more than cut in half, GA clients could neither make large contributions to host households nor get by on their own.[14]

The low levels of GA benefits may help explain why so few homeless applied for and received them. Such benefits were not enough to allow recipients to leave the homeless state and were difficult to obtain. Applying for GA benefits in 1984, as described by Stagner and Richman (1986), involved at least three interviews with Illinois Department of Public Aid caseworkers, a determination of employability, and an assignment either to an unemployable

14. Contributions toward rent reported by the GA recipients were more than half of the benefit level received, as shown below:

Living Arrangements	Average Monthly Rent or Contribution
Living alone	$159
Living with nonrelatives	$122
Living with relatives	$ 97

Note that GA recipients living alone paid more in rent, on the average, than they received in GA payments. Most (84%) GA recipients living alone also received help from their relatives. (Unfortunately the survey did not ascertain either the kind or the amount of help received. It is a fair presumption, however, that financial help must have loomed large.)

class or to a "jobs" program in which a person had to sustain eligibility by applying for work to at least eight employers a month. A person assigned to the jobs program who did not find employment within sixty days was assigned either to the unemployable class or to a public service workfare task. Keeping to the complex schedule of interviews and reporting requirements must have been difficult for the homeless.

Table 7.1 also contains clues to why so few aged persons are found among the homeless and the extremely poor in the 1980s. Fewer than 2% of the Chicago homeless were sixty-five or over. Only 500,000 of the extremely poor persons in the 1987 Current Population Survey were sixty-one or older with incomes under $4,000. Old age Social Security retirement benefits increased by 162% from 1968 to 1985, thanks to favorable changes in the benefit levels in 1972 plus the indexing of such benefits by tying them to the consumer price index. The constant-dollar value of the average old age pension in Illinois in 1968 was slightly below the value of General Assistance payments, but by 1985 it had increased by 164% and was 3.3 times the value of General Assistance.

Note also that the absolute amount of Illinois average monthly old age pension payments in 1985, $511, was enough to rent accommodations at the bottom portion of the conventional housing market and certainly sufficient for the subsidized senior citizens' housing developments.

The sharply enhanced economic well-being of the elderly is one of the great program success stories of the twentieth century. Throughout the century, until the 1970s, the elderly were greatly overrepresented among the poor; today, for the first time in our history, the poverty rate for persons aged sixty-five and over is less than that for the rest of the population. How this was accomplished says a lot about how the problem of homelessness will have to be solved, if indeed it ever is. We virtually wiped out poverty among the aged by providing generous benefits. Public spending on the elderly, through Social Security pensions, Medicare, and housing subsidies, dwarfs every other item in the federal human services budget.[15]

There are two main lessons to be drawn from the past decade's decline in welfare. First, our policies have undermined the income positions of the extremely poor and the capacity of poor families to care for their dependent adult members. In every state, income support programs for unattached persons are not generous enough to support minimum standard housing and diet. In addition, by allowing welfare payments to be eaten away by inflation, we have reduced the capacity of families to care for their dependent adult members. Second, we have not sufficiently assimilated the lessons of the recent

15. In 1984 the total federal social welfare expenditure was $419 billion. Social Security pensions and Medicare expenditures alone amounted to $302 billion, 72% of the total social welfare expenditure. See *Statistical Abstract of the United States: 1987* (Washington, D.C.: U.S. Department of Commerce, 1986, table 574.

history of the Social Security retirement program. By providing decent payment levels, this program has virtually wiped out homelessness and extreme poverty among the aged.

An Interpretation of Homelessness

Throughout this book I have described the characteristics of the current homeless, highlighting those that mark off this population from that of the old Skid Rows and from the current domiciled poor. Drawing these various threads together, we can now begin to weave an explanation both of why some people are more likely to be found among the homeless and of why homelessness has apparently increased over the past decade.

First of all, it is important to distinguish between the short-term (episodic) homeless, and the long-term (chronic) homeless who appear likely to remain so. Most of what I have to say below concerns the latter group; the former consists primarily of people in the lower ranks of the income distribution who meet short-term reversals of fortune. This is not to deemphasize the problems of the short-term homeless but simply to say that their problems are different.

The "dynamics" of episodic homelessness are distressingly straightforward. So long as there is a poverty population whose incomes put them at the economic edge, there will always be people who fall over that edge into homelessness. Small setbacks that those above the poverty line can absorb may become major disruptions to the very poor. Several homely examples illustrate this point. The failure of an old refrigerator or stove and a subsequent repair bill of $50 can make the nonpoor grumble about bad luck, but for someone whose monthly income is under $500 and whose rent is $300, the bill represents one-fourth of the monthly resources used to buy food, clothing, and other necessities. For a poor person who depends on a car to travel to work, a car repair bill of a few hundred dollars may mean months of deprivation. Renting an apartment increasingly means paying one month's rent in advance and perhaps a security deposit as well and is often why poor people remain in substandard housing. In many states welfare programs make provision for such emergency expenses, but the unattached person who is not eligible for welfare may experience wide swings of fortune, with the downsides spent among the homeless.

The solution is to be found in extending the coverage of the social welfare system and incorporating provisions that would cushion against short-term economic difficulties. I will return to this point later.

What about the long-term or chronic homeless? Their critical characteristic is the high level of disabilities that both impair their earning capacity and reduce their acceptance by their families, kin, and friends. These are the people who are most strongly affected by shortages of unskilled positions in the labor force, lack of inexpensive housing, and declines in the economic fortunes of their families, kin, and friends. Under these unfavorable conditions, unattached persons with disabilities have increasing difficulty in getting along on their own. And as the living conditions of poor households decline, those disabled by chronic mental or physical illnesses or by chronic substance abuse are no longer tolerated as dependents.

Note that I am using the term disabled in this context to mark any condition that appreciably impairs the ability to make minimally successful connections with the labor market and to form mutually satisfactory relationships with family, kin, and friends. This definition goes beyond the usual meaning of disability to include a much wider set of conditions—for example, criminal records that interfere with employment chances or chronic problems with drinking, as well as physical and psychiatric impairments.

Let me emphasize that this interpretation is not "blaming the victim." It is an attempt to explain who become the victims of perverse macrolevel social forces. If there is any blame, it should be placed on the failure of the housing market, labor market, and welfare system, which forces some people—the most vulnerable—to become victims by undermining their ability to get along by themselves and weakening the ability of family, kin, and friends to help them. Of course blame can be assigned only where there is intent to harm or where bad judgment is exercised when clearly better options exist. In the case of the trends of the past two decades in poverty and homelessness, it is difficult to blame any set of persons or institutions.

We can now understand why we find so much disability among the homeless. The disabled are least able to negotiate successfully the labor and housing markets, to use the welfare system, or to obtain support from family, kin, and friends. Among the destitute, the disabled are the most vulnerable.

What Can Be Done?

I will now shift from diagnosis to treatment, outlining a set of public policy changes addressed to reducing homelessness in our society. The proposed policy changes are not instant remedies. Although homelessness in the larger sense will be with us for years and may never be totally erased, it is a realistic aspiration that no one in our society should involuntarily go without nightly shelter, even though that shelter may not fulfill all our ideas of a home. It is also a reasonable aspiration that almost all individuals and families should live in dwellings that fulfill the minimum safety and privacy requirements of the larger meaning of home.

It is useful to divide what needs to be done into two parts: policy changes addressed to the short-term problem of how best to ameliorate the condition of the current homeless, diminishing the suffering and pain that arises from their condition; and long-term policy changes designed to decrease the risk of becoming homeless.

Short-Term Remedies

Under short-term remedies I include those measures that can be taken without drastic overhaul of our current institutional structures. Homeless people have slipped through the loose weave of our existing social welfare safety nets. In a very short time, we can appreciably improve their condition by simply making it possible for them to obtain benefits for which they are already eligible.

Almost all the research on the homeless in the 1980s has shown that few of them participate in the welfare programs they appear to be eligible for by virtue of their financial plight and their disabilities. Few are receiving Social Security disability payments, food stamps, or AFDC payments or participating in the General Assistance programs of their states. In our Chicago Homeless Study, for example, almost all the homeless were eligible for General Assistance, and substantial minorities were eligible for one or another of the more generous benefit programs. However, only 22% were receiving GA payments, fewer than 7% were receiving Supplemental Security Income,[16] less than 7% were receiving payments from Social Security Disability Insurance, and a little more than 6% were receiving AFDC payments.

In part these low levels of participation reflect the fact that benefits from the programs let some people leave the homeless condition. This is so particularly for Social Security Disability Insurance (SSDI), which provides sufficient income (average payment in Illinois was $504 per month in 1986) to cover rent on the lowest level of the housing market. Hence some persons have been raised out of homelessness by the payments received and do not appear as subjects in the homeless studies. Of course, because SSDI eligibility depends on substantial previous employment, many of the long-term unemployed homeless are not eligible. Even so, many would be eligible for Supplemental Security Income (SSI) payments, a less generous program (average monthly payments in Illinois were $142 in 1985) for which disabled persons with meager employment records or none could qualify. Long-term unemployed persons earning less than $2,000 qualify for benefits under Illinois General Assistance, which provides more income ($154) than the median for all the homeless ($100). This may mean that by patching together intermittent jobs and benefit payments from General Assistance, some of the destitute find their way into SROs and rooming houses and thereby are no longer homeless. Indeed, as I showed in chapter 4, about a third of 1985 General Assistance clients lived by themselves, many of them presumably in SROs.

In part this low participation in benefit programs reflects the difficulty many

---

16. The Social Security Disability Insurance program provides payments for disabled persons who have a work history. Supplemental Security Income provides payment for those who do not. As table 7.1 shows, SSDI has clearly higher benefit levels than SSI.

homeless people experience in connecting with the welfare system and, once participating, remaining beneficiaries. Although applying for aid is not extremely difficult, the homeless often find it hard to negotiate several interviews, the submission of affidavits, and the other requirements of the application process. Their applications are easily rejected because they have little standing as citizens and hence are unlikely to make effective complaints. The homeless are especially vulnerable to being cut off when budget crunches lead welfare administration to look for people they may safely terminate.

The difficulty the homeless experience with the welfare system is dramatically shown in the fact that, among the Chicago homeless, more than 70% of those eligible for General Assistance have applied for benefits at one time or another, but most have been turned down or else accepted but later terminated. Similar experiences were typical of those among the Chicago homeless who were eligible for AFDC payments: of those eligible, almost all (96%) had applied for AFDC, but only 7% were receiving benefits; the rest had been turned down or had been accepted but later terminated. The reasons for termination given in the welfare records were overwhelmingly "technical" violations—failure to appear at appointments, failure to register at employment agencies, and the like.

The low level of welfare participation among the homeless can be effectively dealt with by the welfare agencies, without legislative changes. An aggressive outreach program to enroll all who are eligible in disability and public welfare programs would significantly raise the income of those currently homeless and enable some of them to find housing. In addition, the welfare agencies should review their practice of terminating benefits for technical reasons, making allowances for the difficulty homeless people have in meeting some of the requirements for continued participation. It is hard to keep an appointment if you have neither an appointment book (or its equivalent) nor a watch.

It is important to keep in mind that increasing welfare participation may ameliorate the condition of the homeless by providing them with more income, but unless benefit levels are changed, that additional income will not be enough to move them into conventional dwelling units or SROs. The clients in the Chicago General Assistance study who lived by themselves received aid from their relatives and friends and supplemented their benefits by part-time intermittent employment. (The issue of inadequate benefit levels will be discussed at length later in this chapter.)

Participation is also low in in-kind benefit programs such as food stamps and Medicaid. In many states Medicaid eligibility is tied to income-transfer programs, and hence participation rates will rise with increased enrollment in welfare programs. Other in-kind programs are more questionable: in particular, the food stamp program presents special problems. The program largely assumes that those receiving food stamps have cooking facilities, which simply is not true for the homeless. Of course it is possible to use the stamps to buy sandwich makings, milk, and other items that do not require cooking. But we need changes in our current food stamp programs that recognize the unique needs of the homeless. In particular, making it possible for food kitchens, shelters, and restaurants to accept clients' food stamps would substantially increase the practical utility of the stamps to homeless persons.

Similar changes are also needed in housing subsidies, such as those provided under section 8 of the Housing Act, to make it easier to use such subsidies in renting SROs or similar accommodations.[17]

A second short-term measure would be to move the most severely disabled from the shelters and the streets into total-care institutions. Many of the chronically mentally ill need an environment where they can be given highly supervised, supportive care. For some of the most impaired this may mean placement in mental hospitals. I realize that to civil libertarians this may sound like a step backward, but the principle is that the mentally ill should be treated in the least restrictive environment consistent with their ability to function without harming themselves and others. Living on the streets is certainly among the least restrictive environments imaginable, but it is not one that provides for any sensible regimen of medication and care. At least for the most deteriorated of the chronically mentally ill, whose behavior is self-destructive, institutionalization is probably the only alternative to early death.

Zealous guarding of someone's civil rights assuredly cannot mean leaving that person in a condition that poses immediate and considerable physical risk, else the concept of "civil rights" is stripped of all practical meaning. After several decades of deinstitutionalization and restricted institutionalization, we must also recognize that this recommendation may require expanding the mental hospital system, especially in states with insufficient capacity.

Implementing this recommendation requires two important changes in current policy. First, the chronically mentally ill should be released from hospitals only when there are strong assurances that supportive living arrangements are available. Second, it must be made easier to commit chronically mentally ill persons when they are unable to care for themselves outside an institution.

The first change means that a patient with a chronic mental illness should not be released unless there are kin who are willing and able to provide shelter or unless supervised living accommodations are available. To make such arrangements easier, I recommend that the patient be enrolled in disability payment programs before discharge and that the receiving household or non-hospital living accommodation be assigned a reasonable portion of the payments. The cost of such a program would not be excessive: assuming that about a third of the current homeless would eventually find their way into this program, annual costs would be about $600 million, positing monthly dis-

17. The rent vouchers issued by the Los Angeles Welfare Department to General Relief applicants, pending decisions on their applications, are a major source of income for the city's downtown SROs.

ability stipends of $500 a month to 100,000 chronically mentally ill homeless persons.

The second change involves making it easier for kin, social agencies, and the police to bring people who are acting in a bizarre or aggressive manner, are incoherent, or are neglecting to care for themselves to the courts for psychiatric evaluation and subsequent involuntary commitment if the complaints are sustained. Under present practices there are many incentives for the courts to "plea bargain" with such persons, trading voluntary (and limited) commitment for the more extensive procedure involved in involuntary (and usually longer) commitment. The extensive use of such plea bargaining in Illinois has led to the hospitals' serving as short-term residential accommodations where little therapy can be provided.[18] My recommendation is that patients, whether voluntarily or involuntarily committed, be treated the same when it comes to discharge, in line with the provisions noted above concerning support.

A third short-term measure is to maintain and possibly improve the financial support for existing shelters. I am ambivalent about this recommendation: the shelters are far from satisfactory, but some accommodations are clearly needed. The need for some housing clearly overrides whatever misgivings one may have about shelters. In many cities, even reasonable and conservative estimates show that homeless persons are twice as numerous as the existing shelter beds, and so the emergency shelter capacity needs to be expanded. But these dormitory shelters are far from satisfactory in the best of cases, and there is also the danger that a shelter "industry" may develop that acquires a strong stake in the permanent existence of what should be rightly construed as temporary emergency measures.

It is a safe bet that there are few large urban centers where shelter capacity comes close to being as large as the current number of homeless people. Yet there is some evidence that the shelters are not used to capacity: in Chicago we found that in the dead of winter (February 1986) the shelters were used only to 80% of capacity. Those shelters that anyone would judge as providing greater privacy and safety came closer to being fully used than the more open and less safe dormitory accommodations of the larger shelters. I believe it says something about the conditions of our shelters when one-third to one-half of the homeless are out on the streets and in public places in Chicago's winters while shelters go unused. It may also say something about the condition of the homeless that some shelters reject the most disabled as clients[19] and that some

18. A recent study of mental hospital patients in the Chicago area (Lewis et al. 1987) found that over 95% had been voluntarily committed, most after being brought before the courts on complaints signed by their kin or by the police. A person committed voluntarily can request release within ten days and must be discharged.

19. Almost all the shelter managers in Chicago refused admission to persons who were acting bizarrely, who were obviously drunk or under the influence of drugs, or who had "caused trouble" in the past. Although these policies are followed to safeguard the safety, peace, and rest of the other shelter residents, they have the unfortunate consequence of leaving the most severely disabled out on the streets.

of the homeless have justified fears about their personal safety within the shelters. A sensible policy may be to make subsidies for shelters proportional to their quality, thereby providing an incentive to upgrade them from dormitories to more private and safer accommodations.

Long-Term Policy Recommendations

In the long run, the reduction of extreme poverty and the reduction of homelessness are strongly linked. The extremely poor identified in previous chapters are the pool out of which both the short-term, episodic and the long-term, chronic homeless are recruited. The long-term reduction of extreme poverty can make it possible to reduce both forms of homelessness to acceptable minimums.

The message of the first part of this chapter is that the high level of extreme poverty experienced in the past decades is the outcome of structural failures in three major institutional sectors: the labor market, the housing market, and public welfare programs. Consequently, long-term solutions must address each of these sectors.

The Labor Market

The long-term reduction of extreme poverty obviously involves radically improving the labor market opportunities of young people, especially young minority males. It is equally obvious that this is not an easy task. There can be little doubt that the current crop of young homeless men is the harvest of two decades of catastrophically high unemployment for young minority males. Most of the homeless young men have not held steady jobs for five years or more, and some have never been employed. It is difficult to be optimistic about the chances of reintegrating long-term homeless men into the labor force. Reducing homelessness among young men in their thirties requires that we provide employment much earlier in their lives, in late adolescence and the early twenties.

The major thrust of our policies for reducing unemployment among minority youths has been a supply-side strategy, aimed at improving the quality of the labor they offer and thereby bettering their prospects in the existing labor market. Job-training programs attempt to accomplish this by teaching them the skills they lack. There have been several problems with our job-training programs over the past few decades. First of all, the programs have not been targeted well enough on young adults, improving the employment prospects of young men shortly after they finish their education. Second, given the experience with job training and supported work programs over the past two decades, it is hard to be sanguine about using such programs to compensate for the labor market's failure to provide jobs. Our experience does not support much optimism, since fairly extensive programs have been undertaken without much success.

Bear in mind that providing employment to young men will have important side-effects for other portions of the extremely poor population. For example, young women will benefit by the resulting improvement in the supply of men who may be worth marrying. Higher levels of employment will also lower crime rates, since arrests on criminal charges are highly concentrated among males aged sixteen to twenty-five. One of the few consistently upheld empirical findings in recent criminological research is the inverse relationship between employment and crime (Rossi, Berk, and Lenihan 1980). Employed men are less likely to engage in crime of all sorts, and persons released from prison who find jobs are less likely to become recidivists. And of course, the burden of support currently falling on parental households will be lightened.

Although the emphasis here is on young men, this does not imply that all the effort should go into that demographic group. Improving the job prospects for young women cannot help but bring improvements in the situation of the extremely poor. First of all, a majority of the extremely poor are women, most of whom are heading their own households. Providing employment may lower the proportion of very young women electing motherhood as an occupation. In any event, having job experience will make it easier for women to enter the job market after their children have matured. Third, a consistent finding in evaluations is that job-training programs have proved more effective in improving the long-term economic condition of women trainees.

Many of the job programs have been directed at changing the quality of the labor people can offer. There is little doubt that young persons who have been unsuccessful in entering the labor market are relatively poorly endowed with skills that are in demand. Yet these supply-side remedies have not been successful. On completing such programs, participants appear not to have any better chance of being employed or earning higher wages. Especially significant have been the experiences of the extremely impressive Supported Work Experiment conducted by the Manpower Development Research Corporation (1985). The experiment provided training in job deportment, job search, and job skills to drug users, released prisoners, and the long-term unemployed. Such training was accompanied by paid employment in environments that made increasing performance demands over time. In comparison with randomly selected control groups who did not experience the MDRC programs, male participants showed no detectable improvement.[20] Other evaluations of a variety of job training programs have led to similar dismal findings.

Complete disillusionment with job-training efforts is not justified. It may be possible to fine-tune programs so that they achieve their goals of connecting young persons effectively with job opportunities. For example, many of the programs have been aimed at those who have repeatedly failed to find jobs at

20. The experience with female participants has been more positive. Women participating in job training or supported work benefited significantly by being more likely to be employed and earning more after training.

ages beyond the earliest entry periods, typically the mid-twenties. The longer a person has been unemployed during the earliest period beyond labor market entry, the more difficult it may be to enter employment, whether one is trained or not. Programs aimed at those in their teens may be more effective.

Interventions dealing with the demand side of the labor market have also been disappointing, although they show some net public benefits. For example, the Comprehensive Employment Training Program (CETA) started under President Carter did not materially improve the subsequent labor market performance of its clients, although it did provide a significant number of jobs to the unemployed. CETA also augmented the labor supply available to local and state governments and made possible increased public services.

If the labor market cannot provide jobs for nondisabled young people, we may have to resort to public-sector employment. Indeed, some of the most popular welfare programs have been public employment programs—for example, the Civilian Conservation Corps of Great Depression days, the Job Corps, the Peace Corps, and Vista. Although the 1930s WPA (Works Progress Administration) did not get a good press at the time, we still enjoy some of the public facilities built by the program, including improved parks, city sidewalks, local libraries, and even the original terminals at New York's La Guardia airport.

At the moment the only public employment program that is widely available to young people is the armed forces, providing work and training opportunities that have been very attractive to minority young men and some minority women. We need to invent their civilian equivalents, involving jobs that produce transferable skills and also increase the quantity and quality of public facilities. I hesitate to recommend specific programs, but there is no dearth of urban public facilities that need augmenting and refurbishing, from our streets to our libraries and schools. There are also many public services that need additional personnel, ranging from public transportation to tax collection.

There are many potential advantages to public employment programs, especially in contrast to income maintenance. They are preferable in terms of human values in that they mitigate both the demoralizing effects of unemployment and the stigma of welfare. These programs provide earned income and job activities to people who would otherwise have neither. Their overhead might well exceed the corresponding cost of simple transfer payment programs, but there are benefits to participants that cannot be obtained through straight cash payouts: something productive to do with one's time and the consequent sense of self-worth.

Demography, it is said, is destiny. Likely demographic changes over the next decade include some with hopeful implications that will improve the chances of young men. The effects of the postwar baby boom that has flooded our labor markets with young people, depressing both their real wages and their employment prospects, will have subsided within the next four or five years. Beginning in the 1990s, there will be fewer young people entering the labor market, improving prospects for coming cohorts,[21] but without some intervention the problems of young minority males will persist.

The Housing Market

Recommendations concerning the housing market can be stated more optimistically. Clearly, the market has failed to meet the special needs of unattached poor persons. It is especially heartening to note the success of senior citizens' housing in removing that group from among the homeless (coupled with the rise in benefit levels for pensioners, as noted previously). A program of subsidized housing for younger unattached persons may provide similar benefits through preserving and upgrading existing housing as well as constructing new accommodations.

In at least one city, Los Angeles, a nonprofit corporation has been formed to purchase, rehabilitate, and manage SRO hotels that come on the market (Hamilton, Rabinowitz and Alshuler, Inc. 1987). How successful the Los Angeles corporation will be in providing clean, safe, and decent living space at reasonable rentals is yet to be seen.

Of course, preserving and upgrading SROs only keeps the inadequate stock of housing appropriate for unattached poor persons from being further depleted. Furthermore, SROs have not been paragons, their main attraction being price. To house such people properly, the size of that stock has to be increased and its quality raised.

In the past our society showed more concern for the housing problems of unattached persons. In the first part of this century the YMCA and YWCA built residential hotels in most cities to provide wholesome and "affordable" housing for unattached men and women.[22] Whether they or a functionally equivalent organization could do it again in this historical period is open to question. Most likely some form of government subsidy would be necessary. Furthermore, the Y hotels never aspired to dominate the housing market for unattached young adults: commercial SRO hotels and rooming houses provided most of that kind of housing. Our policies should also be directed at bolstering this segment of the urban housing stock.

In addition, it should become a matter of public policy to phase out emergency shelters as quickly as the housing programs can provide sufficient dwellings for unattached persons. Although the shelters vary widely in qual-

---

21. Of course, these demographic changes will improve the prospects for persons who will be young adults in the future. The currently demoralized young will have moved into their middle years in the next decade, posing a different set of problems for the future. Indeed, if the programs suggested in this chapter are successfully implemented, one may anticipate an increase in the average age of the extremely poor as those who are now in their twenties and thirties move into older age brackets.

22. Ironically, in many cities the Ys are phasing out their hotels, reluctant to serve as the "housing of last resort" for the mentally ill and nearly destitute aged.

ity, there are virtually none that come close to upholding common standards for minimally decent housing. Especially falling short are the mass dormitory shelters in our largest cities that offer no privacy, little security for persons or possessions, and little more than beds and sanitary facilities. The prospect that dormitory living for the unattached poor could become a fixed feature of our cities seems to me quite real: there are too many precedents for programs' living far beyond their usefulness because their organizational structures become self-serving bureaucracies with a greater stake in their own preservation than in fulfilling a function.

Public Welfare Programs

A final set of recommendations concerns eliminating the holes in our social welfare net. The present arrangements center on providing for those who suffer from the disabilities of aging or from recognized "traditional" disabilities—such as being blind or partially paralyzed—or who are children in families broken by death, desertion (before or after marriage), or divorce. Clearly these are the conditions that arouse most sympathy from legislators and presumably the public. We have not yet fully recognized that there are other forms of disability that are just as damaging to an individual's ability to participate fully in our society, especially in the labor force.

Chapter 6 presented ample evidence that chronic mental illness afflicts about one in three of the homeless. This disability is regarded somewhat ambivalently both by the public and by policymakers. In part, the very definition and diagnosis of mental illness are fuzzy at the boundaries, with honest disagreements about classification often arising among professionals. In part our ambivalence toward mental illness arises out of the long history of dividing the poor into the deserving and the undeserving, with the latter defined as those who do not want to work. The line between depression and "laziness" is often confusing. It is difficult to feel sympathy for the employment problems of someone who has a phobia against signing documents, but it is as much of a disability as a paralyzed hand.

In sum, in comparison with a paraplegic or quadriplegic, a chronically mentally ill person is not as easily recognized as disabled. Nevertheless, the disabilities resulting from psychotic thinking patterns or extreme depression are as real as those caused by physical shortcomings, precluding employment at any but the most routine jobs performed for the least demanding employers. For many of the chronically mentally ill, problems include routine maintenance of personal cleanliness, diet, and medication.

If we want to make it possible for the chronically mentally ill to live outside institutions in reasonably safe and decent homes, we need to ensure that they are more routinely included within the coverage of our disability support net. Chronic mental illness is recognized as an eligible disability in our two major disability income maintenance programs, Social Security Disability Insurance (SSDI) and Supplemental Security Income (SSI).[23] Indeed, one of the major premises of the deinstitutionalization movement that almost emptied our state mental hospitals was that SSDI and SSI would make it possible to support the discharged chronically mentally ill in a variety of community settings (Lamb 1984).

Although state mental hospitals and community mental health centers routinely attempt to get the chronically mentally ill enrolled under SSDI or SSI, their efforts often are unsuccessful. First, many of the chronically mentally ill escape the mental health care system. Among Chicago's mentally ill homeless, almost none were connected with either the disability programs or community mental health clinics. Second, procedures for establishing program eligibility are complicated and difficult to negotiate, frequently leading to failure for those who have difficulty keeping appointments, assembling necessary papers, and speaking for themselves. Third, because of the ambiguities surrounding the diagnosis of mental illness, chronic sufferers are among the most vulnerable of enrollees, most subject to termination when program administrators seek to cut back the rolls.

Enrollment in income maintenance programs, of course, will not cure chronic mental illness, although there is some evidence that the high levels of clinical depression seen among the homeless are situationally determined.[24] A steady source of income, however, may make it possible to rent housing, stabilize diet and health, and generally improve the quality of life. We need not wait upon the cure of mental illness to provide a decent standard of living for the chronically mentally ill.

Steady income will be most helpful to those whose mental illness is not the most severe. As touched upon in the section on short-term remedies, those who cannot care for themselves and whose illness leads them to follow self-destructive paths clearly need structured care that goes beyond income maintenance. For the most severely afflicted some form of institutionalization will clearly be needed.

Both SSDI and SSI do not recognize every disability as constituting eligibility, possibly following the lead of both public opinion and the convictions of policymakers. As seriously prevalent and as disabling as chronic mental illness among the homeless is long-term substance abuse. Thanks to the long-

---

23. SSDI is available for those who have a sufficient record of gainful employment and is almost as generous in payments as Social Security retirement. SSI is available to persons otherwise qualified who have an insufficient employment record. SSI provides only meager payments. (See table 7.1 for average payment levels for these two programs.)

24. The Chicago homeless who were enrolled in either General Assistance or AFDC had lower levels of depression than those who had applied and were denied. As usual, cause and effect are difficult to specify here. High levels of depression make successful negotiation difficult, and some steady source of income also may raise hopes.

term campaign pursued by Alcoholics Anonymous and similar groups, there is widespread acceptance of the notion that alcoholism is a disease. Our courts have gone so far as to decriminalize being drunk in public, recommending detoxification as a substitute for arrest.[25]

But have we gone far enough in recognizing long-term substance abuse as a chronic disability? It is time to consider including the more serious forms of alcoholism and drug addiction as disabilities that are eligible for SSDI and SSI participation. I recognize that this recommendation may appear to many to provide incentives for becoming careless in drinking and drug habits. After all, it is unlikely that anyone deliberately becomes a paraplegic to obtain a disability entitlement, but low-income heavy drinkers might not exercise the same care about their drinking if they knew the result might be a monthly disability benefit. Yet longtime chronic alcoholics or drug addicts are as disabled as any of the groups we have traditionally recognized. A long-term chronic alcoholic whose liver has been badly damaged and who suffers from brain seizures is surely no less disabled than a psychotic whose disordered thinking cannot support normal engagement with the world.

I have no specific recommendations about how to avoid building perverse incentives into our disability benefit programs.[26] I leave that difficult task to others. I suspect that chronic substance abuse needs a set of graduated treatments, as in the case of chronic mental illness. Some of the more deteriorated victims of substance abuse may require hospitalization while others need some less stringent form of structured environment.

Other aspects of our welfare system also need correction. Our society consistently underestimates the importance of income, especially to poor people, often mistaking the effects of poverty for personal deficiencies. Nothing seemed more dismal to the 1950s and 1960s researchers of Skid Row than the hopelessness of the old pensioners they found living there. Few if any advocated raising their benefits to ameliorate their living conditions. Yet as the value of old age pensions rose in the decade after this research, the drop in the number and proportion of aged persons among the homeless was the most dramatic change in that population. Of course raising the benefit levels most likely did not help the persons Bogue (1963) or Bahr and Caplow (1974) studied; but the next generation of aged men was spared the fate of becoming homeless.[27]

25. Thereby unwittingly contributing to the problem of street homelessness, as suggested in chapter 2.

26. There is some anecdotal evidence that the existence of shelters allows drug and alcohol abusers to channel most of their income into their addictions. A Chicago alcoholic who is receiving General Assistance payments of $154 a month can spend most of it on alcohol while being provided with a bed in an emergency shelter and meals in food kitchens.

27. The prevalent alcoholism among the old men on the Skid Rows may also have declined as a function of the increased living standards possible under the augmented benefit levels. Indeed, although we know that chronic alcoholism and poverty go hand in hand, it is not clear which is leading.

The lesson of what an upward turn in benefits accomplished for the aged may be used constructively in dealing with other categories of the homeless. Earlier in this chapter I presented evidence about the severe deterioration in our support for AFDC and General Assistance. We have allowed inflation to lower the real value of such payments to the point where recipients are not raised sufficiently above the level of destitution.

This deterioration in support for families and individuals undoubtedly helped to increase homelessness and certainly helped to change the composition of the homeless population. We created homelessness among families when we gave female-headed households barely enough money to pay the rent. We created homelessness when we placed on poor families the burden of supporting their unemployed adult members. We fostered long-term shelter residence when we failed to provide homeless single persons with enough income to rent better accommodations. All these changes helped to shift the age structure of the homeless downward and to increase the proportion of minorities among the homeless.

I propose three remedies for the welfare system. The first is relatively simple. We need to restore the value of the welfare dollar that has deteriorated through inflation over the past twenty years. This measure would restore the ability of many to cope effectively with the housing market.

My second recommendation has been suggested repeatedly over the past decades. Among the more senseless inequities in our current welfare system is the enormous variation in coverage and benefit levels among the fifty states. In part this variation reflects the relative prosperity among these jurisdictions, with the better-off states being the more generous. But there are also some glaring exceptions, prominent among them being Texas. Noting the concentration of the extremely poor in those regions where welfare programs are least generous, a great deal could be done to reduce extreme poverty by providing a nationwide standard so that benefit levels can be tied more realistically to prevailing price levels.

There is substantial evidence that the American public would favor such a move. In a 1986 national survey conducted by NORC, respondents awarded single-parent families hypothetical benefits several times those currently in place.[28] As shown in table 7.1, the average payment under AFDC was $325 a month in 1985. Survey respondents awarded $1,152 a month to AFDC eligible families, more than 3.5 times the current benefit level. The American public apparently understands inflation and its consequences better than our legislators of the past two decades.

Our current AFDC expenditures run about $15 billion annually. Countering the ravages of inflation over the past two decades would involve a 60% in-

28. The survey was conducted in 1986 on a national sample of adults, using an innovative measurement strategy in which succinct vignettes depicted single-parent families that were systematically varied in composition, age, and other characteristics. Respondents were asked how large weekly payments to those persons should be (unpublished data).

crease in the AFDC budget to $24 billion annually. Offsetting some of these costs are the savings that may be realized by the improved health of both mothers and children, the bolstering of the lower end of the rental housing market by firming up demand, and the increased expenditures for other consumer goods.

My third remedy is more difficult to accomplish because it entails subsidies for categories of families and individuals that we have not so far considered appropriate for public support. This recommendation is that we furnish support to families who subsidize their destitute unattached members. If it did not prove too unpopular a name, I would suggest a program entitled Aid to Families with Dependent Adults (AFDA). Whatever name might be applied, however, such a program would help poor families supply housing, food, and other amenities to adult members who cannot support themselves. This may take a variety of forms, including supplemental payments to families that share households with their dependent adult kin or splitting benefit payments, part to go to the host household and part to the recipient. For example, if the General Assistance payment to a destitute adult is, say, $300 a month, an additional payment should be provided directly to any primary kin providing a home.[29] To ensure that such payments would be worth more to poor households, they should not be tax exempt.

It is not easy to exaggerate the difficulties of defining and administering such a program. Our benefit programs have traditionally been addressed to persons either before maturity or beyond ordinary working years. Indeed, the very title of AFDC emphasizes that the benefits are for the sake of the children, deemphasizing that support is also being supplied for adults. This proposed program has as its target adults in their working years who do not have responsibility for children, a category toward which we have not acted with much generosity in the past. However, I believe that legislators and the public would feel sympathy for families who have taken on the support of dependent adults and favor a program that would help ease that burden.

As we saw in chapter 3, adult dependency is surprisingly extensive. In 1987 the Current Population Survey estimated there were some 4.9 million unattached (not currently married and without children) persons between the ages of twenty-two and fifty-nine who were neither students nor living on farms and whose 1986 incomes were under $4,000. Three million of them earned less than $2,000. The majority (60%) lived with parents or siblings, and the rest lived either alone (20%) or with nonrelatives (20%).[30] Many of these unat-

29. Earlier in this chapter I suggested that similar provisions can be attached to disability benefit programs, providing incentives to families to become host households to their chronically ill near kin.

30. The Current Population Survey counts only parents, children, and siblings as relatives. More distant kin such as grandparents and aunts or uncles are classified as nonrelatives. Many of these unattached adults classified by the CPS as living with nonrelatives may thus have been living with kin.

tached adults were only temporarily destitute: in March 1987 (when the survey was conducted), a third were employed.

If we set the eligibility requirements of the program so that an unattached adult must have an income under $4,000 for at least eighteen months before becoming eligible and take into account that as many as 1 million would likely be eligible for benefits under disability programs, then approximately 2 to 2.5 million people might qualify. Assuming benefits that amounted to $6,000 a year ($500 a month), the benefit payments potentially would amount to $12 to $15 billion annually. This estimate assumes that all eligible persons will be covered. However, a program of this sort can expect to cover only half to three-quarters of those eligible, with actual costs ranging from $6 to $12 billion. The net cost would be offset to some degree by the increased tax liability of the host households. More prosperous households would pay increased taxes that would offset payments received to the extent of their marginal tax rates.

A crucial point of my proposal is that the benefits be divided between the unattached person and that person's family if they share a household. The first problem to be encountered is defining which kinship relationships constitute "family": certainly parents and children would qualify, as would siblings. More distant kin, such as grandparents, parents' siblings, and so on, are all problematic. I suggest that family be narrowly confined to parents, children, and siblings, including step or foster versions. A second difficulty surrounds how to split and deliver the payments; about this I have no recommendations. I am sure that experts in the design of payment systems could come up with sensible solutions.

A third problem is deciding at what age a person becomes an adult. Surely our society recognizes that many people in their late teens and early twenties are in a period of trial-and-error sorties into the labor market and that many are still in training for their eventual occupational roles. I suggest that full-time students be ineligible for payments and that eligibility start at twenty-five years of age. I have no strong argument for that starting point compared, say, with twenty-six or twenty-seven. The main point is that there be general consensus about when a person should become self-supporting.

Finally, there is the problem of how to avoid perverse incentives. For example, the benefit system should encourage dependent adults to find jobs, possibly by tapering off payments rather than abruptly terminating them when they become employed. The program also ought not to discourage people from forming new households, though it should aim at their not simply becoming beneficiaries of some other program. Certainly a program of this sort would be difficult to administer and subject to abuse, but if we abandoned all programs on that basis we would accomplish nothing.

A Matter of Choices

The policies and programs outlined in this chapter are costly, involving considerable additional public expenditure.[31] Whether these proposals receive any consideration in a period of increasing federal deficit spending clearly depends whether the social problems they address are seen as serious enough to warrant such fiscal commitment. There are many claims on the tax revenues, and the ultimate fate of any proposal to spend more on the homeless depends on how these claims are evaluated comparatively.

I cannot judge how these proposals may fare or even be certain any of them will gain the attention of policymakers. Nonetheless, I am certain of the following. First, the problem of extreme poverty and resultant homelessness is as serious as the poverty among the aged in the 1960s that fueled the changes in Social Security. The presence of homeless persons is a disgrace in a society that claims to be humane. Second, the costs will be at least partially offset by the benefits. For example, the cost of lowering unemployment among young people may be at least partially offset by the taxes they will pay and by the reduction in female-headed households. Third, public officials are not currently ignoring extreme poverty and homelessness; tax dollars are being spent now, and more may be appropriated under existing programs or their extension. The proposals set forth here are designed to substitute for the present patchwork of programs; hence the critical consideration is what additional funds would be needed.

Summary and Conclusions

I have attempted to summarize what we have learned about homelessness and extreme poverty from the social research of the past several years and to convey what that knowledge implies about possible solutions.

The resurgence of extreme poverty and homelessness in the past two decades should remind us that the safety nets we initiated during the Great Depression and augmented in the 1960s are failing to prevent destitution. The Reagan administration did not succeed in dismantling any significant portion of the net, but it made the mesh so coarse and weak that many fall through. Those who are disabled by minority status, chronic mental illness, physical illness, or substance abuse are especially vulnerable. All the very poor suffer, but it is the most vulnerable who fall to the very bottom—homelessness.

The social welfare system has never been very attentive to unattached, disaffiliated men, and now it appears to be as unresponsive to unattached females. Likewise, the social welfare system does little to help families support ·

---

31. Although I have made some estimates throughout this chapter of the costs of some of the specific programs, the total cost of all the programs combined is difficult to calculate. It may be greater or smaller depending on how inclusively the programs are defined. Some of the programs, housing in particular, are difficult to estimate without knowing how much is needed.

their dependent adult members. Many of the homeless of the 1950s and early 1960s were pushed out or thrown away by their families when they passed the peak of adulthood; many of the new homeless are products of a similar process, but this one commences at age twenty-five or thirty rather than at fifty or sixty.

As a consequence, homelessness now looms large on our political agenda, and there is anxious concern about what can be done. I have suggested a number of measures to reduce homelessness to a more acceptable level. These include compensating for the failure of our housing market by fostering the retention and enlargement of our urban low-income housing stock, especially that appropriate for unattached persons; reversing the policy that has put personal choice above institutionalization for those so severely disabled that they are unable to make decisions that will preserve their physical well-being; enlarging our conception of disability to include conditions not purely physical in character and, in particular, recognizing that chronic mental illness and chronic substance abuse are often profound disabilities; restoring the real value of welfare payments to the purchasing power they had in the late 1960s; and extending the coverage of welfare benefits to include long-term unemployed, unattached persons.

There is considerable public support in the United States for a social welfare system that guarantees a minimally decent standard of living to all. Homelessness on the scale currently being experienced is clear evidence that such a system is not yet in place. That homelessness exists amid national prosperity without parallel in the history of the world is likewise clear evidence that we can do something about the problem if we choose to. I have stressed that public policy decisions have in large measure created the problem of homelessness; they can solve the problem as well.

Annotated Bibliography of the Combined Homeless Studies and Studies on the Extremely Poor

The research listed in the first section of this appendix comprises the empirical studies of the homeless whose findings are summarized in chapters 4–6. Studies in the second section provided data on the domiciled extremely poor.

Studies of Homeless Populations

Baumann, Donald J., Charles Grigsby, Cheryl Beauvais, and D. Franklin Schultz. 1986. *The Austin homeless.* Final report to the Hogg Foundation for Mental Health. Austin: University of Texas.
Site: Austin, Texas
Date of data collection: August 1984
Method: Homeless persons in Austin, Texas, were located in known areas of habitation as pointed out by the police department and key-person informants. The homeless were identified by appearance and interviewed. Searches of other areas of the city were also conducted; 500 homeless persons were interviewed.

Brown, Carl, Steve MacFarlane, Rob Parardes, and Louisa Stark. 1983. *The homeless of Phoenix: Who are they and what should be done?* Prepared for the Consortium for the Homeless. Phoenix: South Community Mental Health Center.
Site: Phoenix, Arizona
Date of data collection: Summer 1982, March 1983, winter 1983
Method: Three separate interview studies of the Phoenix homeless are reported, each being treated as a separate study. (1) Phoenix Study A: Conducted in summer 1982, the first study by the Phoenix Community Mental Health Center was an unsystematic set of interviews with people in the soup lines of the Salvation Army, mainly to determine the proportion who were chronically mentally ill. (2) Phoenix Study B: In the March 1983 study, 195 homeless persons were interviewed in depth and another 1,264 answered a short eight-item questionnaire. Respondents were picked out of food-kitchen lines, and every tenth person was asked to participate in the in-depth study. (3) Phoenix Study C: In the winter 1983 study, interviews of adults in homeless families were conducted in motel rooms rented by the Salvation Army for homeless families and in transient camps consisting of

cardboard shelters and other shacks erected on vacant lots in the city center. All persons were enumerated in the camps, and some were interviewed.

Chaiklin, Harris. 1985. *Report on the homeless: The service needs of shelter care residents.* Baltimore: School of Social Work and Community Planning, University of Maryland.

Site: Baltimore, Maryland

Date of data collection: 1983 and 1984

Method: Two surveys are reported. A 1983 survey is based on 271 interviews with soup-kitchen users, interviewed as they were leaving one of the three major Baltimore soup kitchens. A 1984 survey was undertaken of half of the residents in nineteen Baltimore shelters; 263 interviews were undertaken with shelter residents. Both surveys are reported as having about 20% refusal rates.

Chicago Coalition for the Homeless. 1983. When you don't have anything: A street survey of the homeless.

Site: Chicago, Illinois

Date of data collection: 1983

Method: Interviews were undertaken with persons who appeared to be homeless at locations known to be frequented by the homeless. Interviewing was done in daylight hours, and interviewers approached everyone who appeared to be homeless; 82 interviews were collected.

Crystal, Stephen. 1982. *New arrivals: First time shelter clients.* New York: Human Resources Administration.

Site: New York City

Date of data collection: 1982

Method: Interviews with all new applicants for shelter during a one-month period in 1982; 681 interviews.

Crystal, Stephen, and Merv Goldstein. 1982. *Chronic and situational dependency: Long term residents in a shelter for men.* New York: Human Resources Administration.

Site: New York City

Date of data collection: 1981

Method: Interviews with all men who had been in residence at the Keener Men's Shelter for over two months; 128 men were interviewed.

Crystal, Stephen, Susan Ladner, and Richard Towber. n.d. Multiple impairment patterns in the mentally ill homeless. Unpublished manuscript, Human Resources Administration.

Site: New York City

Date of data collection: 1983

Method: Interviews with a large sample (7,568) of residents in New York City municipal shelters. Little detail on selection of respondents.

Farr, Rodger K., Paul Koegel, and Audrey Burnham. 1986. A study of homelessness and mental illness in the Skid Row area of Los Angeles. Los Angeles County Department of Mental Health.

Site: Los Angeles, California

Date of data collection: 1985

Method: Based on an enumeration of residents in shelters, people fed in food kitchens, and those accommodated in drop-in centers. Subsamples were undertaken with a sample of 379 homeless persons drawn systematically from these groups. Homelessness was defined as being without a steady place to sleep for thirty days or more.

Fischer, Pamela J., Sam Shapiro, William R. Breakey, James C. Anthony, and Morton Kramer. 1984. Mental health and social characteristics of the homeless: A survey of mission users. Paper presented at 1984 meetings of the American Public Health Association. Johns Hopkins University School of Public Health.

Site: Baltimore, Maryland

Date of data collection: Winter 1980–81

Method: Four "mission" shelters in Baltimore were sampled, with a one in five systematic sample taken; 51 interviews were obtained. Data from shelter residents were compared with results of a large epidemiological study of the general population in the Baltimore area.

Freeman, Richard B., and Brian Hall. 1986. Permanent homelessness in America. Unpublished manuscript, National Bureau of Economic Research, Cambridge, Mass.

Site: New York City

Date of data collection: 1985

Method: Data were collected by Brian Hall, who interviewed 210 shelter residents, 101 homeless families in welfare hotels, and 205 people living on the streets. The appendix describes the survey procedure as "not a Census Bureau-style random design" but an effort to cover the homeless. The city was divided into five regions: Penn Station, Grand Central Station, and Times Square; Lower West Side; Lower East Side; Upper West Side and Upper East Side; and Central Park. Hall approached people who showed at least one of the following characteristics: being poorly dressed or ragged, pushing a supermarket cart, carrying a bag of belongings, or collecting cans, as well as "anyone with a mental illness." He also visited soup kitchens and shelters, dividing interviews evenly between family shelters and others. He claims an 81% response rate. Methods used were judgmental, including setting quotas for interviews among various sources.

Hamilton, Rabinowitz and Alschuler, Inc. 1987. *The changing face of misery: Los Angeles' Skid Row area in transition, housing and social services needs of Central City East.* Los Angeles: Community Redevelopment Agency.

Site: Los Angeles, California

Date of data collection: 1986

Method: The study is based on a comprehensive study of the fifty-block Los Angeles Skid Row area. The universe of area residents was divided into three strata: missions and shelters; high-density indoor and outdoor public places, as identified by experts; and other locations that are not dwelling units. Shelter residents were selected for interview using systematic samples of all nine cooperating shelters. Each shelter was visited in the evening after beds had been allocated. Researchers attempted to interview 135 residents and completed 129 interviews. High-density areas were identified by key-person informants as places where the homeless were known to congregate at night. Researchers attempted 75 interviews in the high-density congregating places and managed to complete 64. The third stratum was studied by taking a sample of blocks "faces" in the remainder of the fifty-block area (sidewalk and adjacent area on one face of a block). Interviewers, accompanied by off-duty police escorts, approached 525 persons in their dead of night fieldwork, identifying 242 as homeless and finishing interviews with 216.

LaGory, Mark, F. J. Ritchey, and Jeffrey Mullis. 1987. *The homeless of Alabama: Final report of the Homeless Enumeration and Survey Project*. Birmingham: Department of Sociology, University of Alabama.

Site: State of Alabama and Birmingham, Alabama

Date of data collection: 1987

Method: Three studies were reported in this source: (1) a count of persons in shelters in each of the eight Alabama metropolitan statistical areas on 11 February 1987; (2) a matching count, also on 11 February 1987, of homeless persons found outside shelters in a three-hundred-square-block area of Birmingham; and (3) a survey of 150 street and shelter homeless in Birmingham conducted in the spring of 1987. Basic demographic information was collected in the two February 1987 counts. The Birmingham interview surveys collected more detailed socioeconomic and psychological data. The sampling plan for the interview survey was not discussed in detail. (The first two studies are combined and treated as one for our purposes, and the third is treated as a separate study.)

Lee, Barrett A. 1988. Homelessness in Tennessee. Unpublished paper prepared for edited volume now in press. Vanderbilt University, Nashville.

Sites: Chattanooga, Memphis, Knoxville, and Nashville, Tennessee

Date of data collection: 1986–87

Method: Interviews were conducted with homeless persons in the four cities using a standard questionnaire. Homeless persons both in shelters and in public places were counted (in the dead of night), and subsamples were interviewed. Sampling plans varied: in Nashville a quota sample was used, yielding 117 interviews; in Knoxville researchers interviewed everyone they could find, 258 persons. In Chattanooga 186 persons were interviewed, although the sampling method was not specified, and in Memphis 543 were interviewed, consisting of everyone coming to the Salvation Army shelter in a two-month period.

Morse, Gary, Nancy M. Shields, Christine R. Hanneke, Robert J. Calsyn,

Gary K. Burger, and Bruce Nelson. 1985. Homeless people in St. Louis: A mental health program evaluation, field study and followup investigation. Unpublished report, State of Missouri Department of Public Health.
Site: Saint Louis, Missouri
Date of data collection: 1983–84
Method: The researchers undertook to sample shelter residents, selecting roughly equal numbers of males and females residing in thirteen Saint Louis shelters; 248 persons were interviewed.

Mowbray, Carol T., et al. 1984. Mental health and homelessness in Detroit: A research study. Michigan Department of Mental Health.
Site: Detroit, Michigan
Date of data collection: 1983–84
Method: Two studies are reported: (1) Based on a screening of the records of patients in a mental hospital to identify homeless persons, interviews were undertaken with 124 persons so identified. (2) A random sample of 75 homeless persons was obtained among residents of four large Detroit shelters. Interviews included a health-status examination by a nurse plus a self-report psychological symptom scale along with an interview about socioeconomic background.

Philadelphia Health Management Corporation. 1985. Homelessness in Philadelphia: People, needs, services.
Site: Philadelphia, Pennsylvania
Date of data collection: 1983–84
Method: Several substudies were conducted to provide data for this report. The two studies I used consist of 97 interviews with clients of one shelter and administrative records pertaining to 3,691 admissions to that shelter over a year's time. In addition, interviews were undertaken with shelter providers. Research assistants were also assigned to the same shelter as participant observers.

Piliavin, Irving, and Michael Sosin. 1987–88. Tracking the homeless. *Focus* 10, 4: 20–24.
Site: Minneapolis, Minnesota
Date of data collection: 1985–86
Method: This study is based on a sample of 339 homeless persons in Minneapolis approached through food kitchens, shelters, and day shelters. The homeless people in the sample were followed up with additional interviews after six and twelve months.

Robinson, Frederic G. 1985. *Homeless people in the nation's capital*. Washington, D.C.: University of the District of Columbia, Center for Applied Research and Urban Policy.
Site: Washington, D.C.
Date of data collection: 1985
Method: Based on a direct enumeration of homeless persons in Washington, D.C., on 31 July 1985. (1) Enumeration of the street homeless was

accomplished by dividing the city into thirty-seven districts (corresponding to Advisory Neighborhood Councils). Each was assigned a team consisting of at least two people, one with experience in working with the
homeless (shelter managers, counselors, etc.). Enumerators worked between 9:30 P.M. and 3:30 A.M., traveling on every block in their districts.
Each team covered its assigned area and counted as homeless anyone sleeping on the sidewalks, streets, or other public places, sleeping in a car, sub-
way entrance, bus kiosk, or train station, or seen entering an abandoned
building. (2) Counts of shelter residents were taken from the shelters'
monthly occupancy reports, supplemented by direct reports from several
shelters that do not report to the District of Columbia Commission on
Homelessness.

In addition, District of Columbia police stations and hospitals were tele-
phoned to determine the number of homeless people there on the night of
the count.

Adjustments were made to take into account homeless persons who were
not observable from the street. Using "shelter assistants" as informants, a
team was formed to conduct an intensive search of all places within one of
the districts. The team counted people on the streets (112) and was led
to locations within buildings where the shelter assistants claimed about
280 persons were hidden. The ratio of the homeless observed on the streets
to the hidden homeless was used to adjust the street counts taken in all the
districts.

Ropers, Richard. 1985. The rise of the new urban homeless. *Public Affairs
Report* 26, nos. 5 and 6.
Site: Los Angeles, California, and Dallas, Texas
Date of data collection: 1983 and 1984
Method: Two studies are reported. The Los Angeles study was based on
interviews with homeless persons located in shelters in Santa Monica, Ven-
ice and Downtown. A total of 283 interviews were collected. Sampling
method used was not discussed. The Dallas study collected 104 interviews
with homeless persons in the Dallas Salvation Army "sit-up" shelter (homeless people are allowed to sleep in chairs). Sampling procedures used are
not discussed.

Ropers, Richard, and Marjorie Robertson. 1984. Basic shelter research proj-
ect. Psychiatric Epidemiology Program, University of California at Los
Angeles.
Site: Los Angeles, California
Date of data collection: 1983
Method: This study is based on interviews conducted with residents of a
large shelter in Los Angeles. Although 243 men were approached for inter-
viewing, only 107 interviews were completed.

Rossi, Peter H., Gene A. Fisher, and Georgianna Willis. 1986. *The condition of the homeless of Chicago.* Amherst, Mass., and Chicago: Social and Demographic Research Institute and NORC.

This is the Chicago Homeless Study cited in the text. See appendix B for a detailed description.

Roth, Dee, Jerry Bean, Nancy Lust, and Traian Saveneau. 1985. *Homelessness in Ohio: A study of people in need.* Columbus: Ohio Department of Mental Health, Office of Program Evaluation.

Site: State of Ohio

Date of data collection: 1983–84

Method: Twenty Ohio counties were randomly selected for study. Key persons in each county identified locations where the homeless could be found. Details of how sampling was accomplished and interviews were taken are not given. All told, 139 homeless persons were interviewed outside shelters and 979 within shelters.

Schaffer, David, and Carol W. Caton. 1984. Runaway and homeless youth in New York. Report to the Ittleson Foundation, Division of Child Psychiatry, New York State Psychiatric Institute.

Site: New York City

Date of data collection: 1983

Method: This report is based on an interview survey of 175 youths in New York City shelters for runaways. The sampling method used is not described.

Schutt, Russell K., and Gerald R. Garrett. 1985. A report on the homeless: New guests at the Long Island Shelter. Unpublished report, Department of Sociology, University of Massachusetts at Boston.

Site: Boston, Massachusetts

Date of data collection: 1984

Method: Analysis of administrative records kept at the Long Island Shelter on all unduplicated admissions to the shelter during 1984.

Schutt, Russell K., and Gerald R. Garrett. 1986. Homelessness in Boston in 1985: The view from Long Island. Unpublished report, Department of Sociology, University of Massachusetts at Boston.

Site: Boston, Massachusetts

Date of data collection: 1985

Method: Interviews with 203 persons systematically sampled from those admitted to Boston's Long Island Shelter during 1984.

Snow, David A., Susan G. Baker, and Leon Anderson. 1986. The myth of pervasive mental illness among the homeless. *Social Problems* 33 (5 June): 407–23.

Site: Austin, Texas

Date of data collection: 1985

Method: This study used two sources of data: a haphazard sample of 164 homeless persons interviewed on the streets; and a sample of 767 names from the rosters of homeless persons served by the Austin Salvation Army shelter over a fourteen-month period. The second sample was not interviewed, tabulations being made of administrative data linked via name and Social Security number with administrative data obtained from social service agencies, the police, and hospitals in Austin.

Solarz, Andrea. 1985. An examination of criminal behavior among the homeless. Paper given at the 1985 meeting of the American Society for Criminology. Department of Psychology, Michigan State University.

Solarz, Andrea, and G. Anne Bogat. n.d. When social support fails: The homeless. Unpublished paper, Department of Psychology, Michigan State University.

Site: Not given in publication

Date of data collection: 1985

Method: Both these papers refer to the same study but deal with different topics. The study was based on interviews with 125 homeless in shelters in a "midwestern city." Sampling procedures used are not discussed.

Struening, Elmer L. 1987. *A study of residents of the New York City shelter system.* New York: New York State Psychiatric Institute.

Site: New York City

Date of data collection: 1985

Method: This study is based on a systematic sample of residents in New York City shelters; 832 residents were selected and interviewed in sessions that averaged eighty minutes.

Woods, William K., and Edward L. Burdell. 1987. *Homelessness in Cincinnati.* Cincinnati: Applied Information Sources.

Site: Cincinnati, Ohio

Date of data collection: 1986

Method: This study is based on a survey of shelter residents conducted by students at Mount Saint Joseph College and a survey of shelters in Cincinnati and adjacent Kentucky counties by Applied Information Sources; 801 interviews were undertaken. Shelter sampling methods are not discussed.

Wright, James D., and Eleanor Weber. 1987. *Homelessness and health.* New York: McGraw-Hill.

Site: Nineteen urban centers

Date of data collection: 1985–88

Method: Data were gathered from all persons receiving medical care at sixteen of the nineteen medical clinics for the homeless supported by the Robert Wood Johnson Foundation and the Pew Memorial Trust. The clinic sites included most of the country's major cities and every region. Data were obtained on the presenting symptoms of each of the more than 60,000 persons seen at the clinics over a two-year period. Detailed socioeconomic data were obtained from a randomly chosen subsample of 1,637 persons seen at least twice at the clinics in sixteen cities. Clinic personnel filled out a questionnaire concerning each client sampled.

Studies on the Extremely Poor

Chicago General Assistance Study

The tabulations in this volume concerning General Assistance clients were obtained from the data files of a study of 400 General Assistance clients who had been approved for eligibility during March 1984. Most were new clients, but a good proportion were returning to the rolls. All were interviewed at the General Assistance offices. In addition, follow-up interviews with 355 were obtained six months later in August 1984.

The full results of the study are reported in Matthew Stagner and Harold Richman, *General Assistance Profiles: Findings from a Longitudinal Study of Newly Approved Recipients* (Springfield: Illinois Department of Public Aid, 1985).

Chicago AFDC Study of Clients

The tabulations concerning Chicago residents on the rolls of Aid to Families with Dependent Children were obtained from data files of a study of AFDC recipients enrolled in the program for at least one month during May 1984 to May 1985. The sample was selected from the administrative records of the Illinois Department of Public Aid, with oversampling of male and Hispanic recipients; 1,000 recipients were selected, and 737 were interviewed.

A report of the main findings can be found in Matthew Stagner and Harold Richman, *Help-Seeking and the Use of Social Service Providers by Welfare Families in Chicago.* (Chicago: Chapin Hall Center for Children, University of Chicago, 1986).

Chicago SRO Residents Study

The data on residents of Chicago SRO hotels came from a 1985 study on a sample of SRO hotels. The researchers first enumerated every SRO hotel in Chicago, starting with a diverse set of lists and verifying the status of hotels by phone. All in all 185 interviews were completed, a completion rate of over 70%.

A report on the major findings of the study can be found in Charles Hoch and Diane Spicer, *SROs, an Endangered Species: Single-Room Occupancy Hotels in Chicago* (Chicago: Community Organization Shelter Organization and Jewish Council on Urban Affairs, 1985).

Chicago Urban Family Life Study

Tabulations on poor families in Chicago were based on data from the Chicago Urban Family Life Study, of which William J. Wilson is the principal investigator. This study sampled households living in census tracts where more than 20% of the families fell at or below the poverty line according to the 1980 census. Households in which there were parents between ages nineteen and forty-five were sampled. Unfortunately, because of the restrictions placed on the sample the data were of limited usefulness as a source of information about the extremely poor segments of Chicago.

The Current Population Survey

The Current Population Survey is a quasi-longitudinal sample survey based on monthly interviews with about 55,000 households. Households are queried for eight months and then replaced with additional sampled households. Data appearing in this book are based on tabulations made by the author using public-use tapes distributed by the Inter-University Consortium on Political and Social Research at the University of Michigan. See United States Department of Commerce, Bureau of the Census, *Current Population Survey March 1987, Technical Documentation* (Washington, D.C.: Government Printing Office, 1987).

The Design of the Chicago Homeless Study

Sampling Strategy

An efficient sampling strategy for dealing with the homeless must take into account the special characteristics of that population as discussed in chapter 3. Such a strategy would reduce to a minimum the task of screening to find homeless persons, thereby conserving scarce resources. It would also concentrate efforts on areas where the homeless tend to congregate in relatively large numbers. Three procedures were devised to maximize efficiency in the Chicago Homeless Study (Rossi, Fisher, and Willis 1986), as follows:

1. We divided the survey into two parts: a survey of homeless persons housed in shelters specifically dedicated to supplying sleeping places for them, and a survey of homeless persons found on the streets, in public places, and in all other places to which the public has access. On any given night, some (though not all) homeless persons use the shelters provided for them, and very few if any persons with homes do so. A survey of shelter dwellers appeared to be an efficient way of getting at that component of the homeless population who used shelters. The survey of "street homeless" was to be conducted by making a thorough search of a sample of census blocks in Chicago, with the searchers entering all places on those blocks to which they could gain access. All persons encountered were to be interviewed to determine whether they were homeless.

2. We chose a survey time during the twenty-four-hour day for the street homeless survey that maximized the separation between homeless persons and those with homes. The overwhelming majority of those with homes are in their dwellings sleeping from 1:00 to 6:00 A.M. A survey taken during that period of persons outside dwellings would minimize the screening of persons with homes.

3. We concentrated the survey effort on places where the homeless were known to congregate. Homeless people are not distributed uniformly through a city but concentrate in specific locations. By obtaining some knowledge about this distribution, our survey efforts could be made more efficient.

Adapted from the technical appendix to Rossi, Fisher, and Willis (1986) as written by Gene A. Fisher of the Social and Demographic Research Institute at the University of Massachusetts, Amherst.

These approaches reduced the cost of screening for homelessness and also provided unbiased estimates of the major components of the homeless population and opportunities to gather rich data on their characteristics.[1]

The severity of homelessness most likely varies with the seasons, which affect both the size and the composition of the homeless population. Hence a survey taken in the summer may not represent the same conditions as a survey taken in the winter. The Chicago Homeless Study was initially designed as a set of three surveys, each to be done in a different season, but because the operations were more expensive than originally estimated, only two were conducted, a fall survey from 22 September to 4 October 1985, and a winter survey from 22 February to 7 March 1986. Both surveys were based on the same general design, but the winter survey contained modifications suggested by the experience of the earlier phase and also included several topics that went beyond the concerns of the earlier survey.

The Shelter Survey

The shelter survey was envisaged as a relatively conventional operation, involving no particularly different or more difficult procedures than the usual survey of the members of any residential institution such as a college, hospital, or military unit. As is usual with surveys of residential institutions, the main difficulty was the "political" one of obtaining the cooperation of those who control access—in this case shelter operators. Shelter operators were asked to furnish NORC with complete lists of shelter occupants, to provide access to those we wanted to interview, and to designate someplace in the shelter where interviews could be conducted in privacy. Fortunately we had the cooperation both of the Chicago Mayor's Task Force on the Homeless and the Illinois Department of Public Aid,[2] and hence the NORC interviewing staff could cite trusted sources that would vouch for their goodwill and authenticity when approaching shelter managers.

To sample sheltered homeless persons properly, we needed as complete a listing as possible of all the shelters that provided sleeping places primarily for homeless persons. From several knowledgeable sources,[3] NORC obtained a complete list of all shelters, then we surveyed them by phone to ascertain whether each was still operating and whether the shelter was oriented primarily toward homeless persons per se or had some other primary function.[4]

1. Similar but not identical approaches were used to estimate the sizes of the Washington, D.C., and Boston homeless populations. See appendix A for descriptions of those two studies.
2. The Illinois Department of Public Aid generously provided part of the funds for both fall and winter surveys of the Chicago Homeless Study.
3. The sources included the Mayor's Task Force on the Homeless, the Illinois Department of Public Aid, Chicago Catholic Charities, and Travelers Aid Society.
4. Some of the places on our initial lists were shelters for persons who may or may not have been homeless but who were in special categories. For example, some places were primarily de-

Table B.1   Chicago Shelter Universe and Shelter Samples, Fall and Winter Surveys

	Fall	Winter
A. Shelter Universe and Samples		
Eligible shelters in universe	28	45
Universe bed capacities	1,573	2,001
Shelters drawn in sample	22	27
B. Details of Winter Shelter Sample		

Shelter Size Classification	Number in Universe	Number in Sample	Occupant Sampling Ratio
Large (37 or more beds)	17	17	0.25
Medium (18–33 beds)	12	6	0.50
Small (under 18 beds)	16	4	1.00

Note: Shelters were drawn with probabilities proportionate to size, with residents sampled disproportionately within shelters to form a self-weighting sample. Sampling ratios for the phase two sample are given in panel B.

In the fall survey (phase one) the listed universe of eligible shelters in Chicago consisted of twenty-eight units with a total capacity of about 1,600 beds. The winter (phase two) shelter universe contained many more shelters, forty-five, and a correspondingly larger bed capacity, about 2,000, as the social services of Chicago apparently responded to the greater shelter needs. (See table B.1 for details on the sample of shelters.)

The shelter surveys were planned as two-stage probability samples: the first stage consisted of a probability sample of shelters; the second consisted of a systematic sample of shelter inhabitants drawn within each of the shelters chosen. In the winter survey, twenty-two shelters were selected from the universe of twenty-eight. The shelter sample consisted of all of the large shelters (more than 5 beds) and a one-in-three randomly selected sample of smaller places. Within the large shelters, one in three shelter dwellers was selected systematically for interviewing,[5] and within the smaller shelters all persons

---

toxification units. Others were set up primarily to serve battered women. Reasoning that such special-purpose shelters were similar to other special-purpose units that may also serve homeless persons—such as hospitals and jails—we excluded them from the universe of homeless shelters. Among the shelters excluded in phase two (the winter survey), three were for the chronically mentally ill (bed capacity 44), six were for battered women (total capacity 146), and five were detoxification units (bed capacity 101). The remaining excluded places turned out not to provide sleeping accommodations. The combined bed capacity of shelters excluded in phase two was 291. (Comparable information on the phase one experience unfortunately was not collected.)

In retrospect, excluding these shelters was probably a judgment error. Many, if not most, of their residents would be judged homeless under our definition. A better decision, aided by incisive questioning, would have been to screen out the nonhomeless among their residents.

5. The actual selection was made by taking every third name (after a random start) on rosters containing the name of every person registered as spending the night in the shelter. The rosters were supplied by the shelter operators.

were selected. This sampling strategy led to an overall sample of one in three shelter dwellers.

In the winter survey, a larger sample of shelters was taken and the sampling ratio within shelters was correspondingly reduced, as described in panel B of table B.1.

The two shelter surveys served as the basis for fairly precise estimates of the total sheltered homeless population. The interviewers obtained from the shelter operators a complete list of all persons being sheltered on the nights of the surveys,[6] thus yielding a complete count of the sheltered homeless on those nights. The sums of such counts, added together over all the shelters in each of the samples and properly weighted to take into account that a fraction of the smaller shelters were in each sample, form the bases for fairly precise estimates of the nightly average numbers of homeless persons in shelters during the survey periods.

Persons selected to be interviewed in the shelters were offered $5 as payment and taken off to a private spot for the fifteen- to twenty-minute interview.

The Street Survey

Surveying homeless persons who were not in shelters was more difficult. Even in the dead of night, homeless persons are not easy to identify. Nor are they found only in places that are easy to discover. The strategy we settled on was to make a thorough search of a sample of all places besides dwellings where people might shelter for the night. The number of homeless people we actually located was then used to make projections of the total number of such persons in the city, as described later in this appendix.

The "places" we sampled were census blocks, usually identical to square residential or commercial blocks as conventionally understood but also including open places, parks, railroad yards, or vacant land. Census blocks are divisions of the entire area of a city, including all land whatever its use. For the city of Chicago, the 1980 census defined approximately 19,400 blocks.

Since we expected—and experts agreed—that homeless persons would tend to concentrate in particular localities, the blocks in our sample were stratified by how likely it was that homeless persons were to be found there. To obtain that information we needed to tap the intimate knowledge of some organization that was acquainted with the "dead of night" conditions on each block. A few organizations do have the coverage that makes such knowledge possible, including the police and fire departments, public utilities, and other organizations operating round the clock.[7]

---

6. Sometimes the counts actually referred to the previous night, when the shelter was surveyed in the early morning after the night's residents awoke. However, in all cases the total shelter counts and the occupants interviewed referred to the same night.

7. Should the experts we consulted not have really known where the homeless were likely to be found, the overall design of the survey would have suffered some small loss in precision (i.e.,

NORC was fortunate in obtaining the cooperation of the Chicago Police Department, which assigned the task of rating each of the blocks in Chicago to community relations officers in the city's police precincts. The blocks were rated on a scale ranging from zero probability of finding homeless persons on that block to "high-density" blocks in which five or more homeless persons were likely to be found. The community relations officers consulted with officers on each of the beats in their precincts to obtain the ratings, as well as relying on their own acquaintance with the area.

In addition, the resulting classification of Chicago blocks was reviewed by several knowledgeable groups, including members of the Coalition for the Homeless, the Chicago City Planning Department, and officials of Catholic Charities. The final classification of Chicago census blocks is shown in table B.2. Note that the vast majority (94%) of Chicago blocks are classified as having a very low probability, and only 6% as having some significant chance, of having homeless persons there in the dead of night. As anticipated, Chicago's homeless were said mainly to be found in a small number of neighborhoods.

Within each density classification, blocks to be sampled were picked randomly.[8] To further enhance the efficiency of the street survey, low-density blocks were clustered into units of five contiguous blocks in the fall survey and three in the winter survey and then sampled as clusters.

Because the fall survey results had large standard errors, the sample for the winter survey was enlarged, especially in the low-density stratum. Special attention was paid to blocks with especially high densities, such as railroad stations, airports, and bus stations. In addition, a subsample of high-density blocks was also searched in the early night hours, 6:30 to 10:30 P.M. to test how far our choice of the dead of night might have systematically excluded homeless persons who managed to negotiate the temporary sharing of someone's dwelling and hence were missed in our regular late-night search.

To protect interviewers, NORC hired off-duty Chicago police officers to escort interviewers, preceding them into abandoned buildings, open hallways, and other such places that might be dangerous.

A week or so before launching each survey, NORC supervisors visited all the sample blocks, marking on an outline map of each block special features such as alleys, abandoned buildings, or restaurants. Copies of these maps and special instructions were furnished to each interviewing team.

On the assigned survey night, each block in the sample was canvassed by teams of NORC interviewers between 1:00 and 6:00 A.M. At least two teams

---

larger standard errors than with simple random sampling), but this would not have produced biased estimates of the homeless population. On the other hand, if the experts were knowledgeable (as we believe they were), the precision of the survey would be increased.

8. Note that the blocks searched were *not* picked by the Police Department, whose only role was to provide a classification. The blocks searched were chosen by a strictly random procedure.

Table B.2   Street Survey Sample Design

	A. Stratified Random Block Sample[a]		
	Census Block Classification and Sample Sizes		
Prior Density Classification[b]	Universe Number of Blocks	Fall Sample Size	Winter Sample Size
High density	295	49	49
Medium density	806	49	49
Low density[c]	18,308	70	147
Total	19,409	168	245
	B. Additional Blocks Surveyed in Phase Two		

"Superblocks"
With the help of knowledgeable persons from the Mayor's Task Force on the Homeless, seven locations were identified as places with exceptionally heavy nighttime concentrations of homeless persons. These "superblocks" included Union Station, the Greyhound Bus Station, several stations on the elevated train line, and similar locations.

"Dusk blocks"
To evaluate the contention that our "dead of night" street searches missed significant portions of homeless persons who found temporary accommodations with other persons and who could be found on high-density streets during the evening hours, seven of the high-density blocks were randomly chosen and searched on an alternate evening between 6:30 and 10:30 P.M.

[a] Phase one and phase two samples were drawn independently.
[b] Prior classification was accomplished with the help of community relations officers of the Chicago Police Department and modified with the help of other knowledgeable persons.
[c] Low-density blocks were sampled in clusters of five blocks in phase one and three blocks in phase two.

of interviewers, each consisting of two interviewers escorted by two off-duty police officers, visited each of the chosen blocks. A night's survey assignment ordinarily would consist of several blocks. The teams assigned to work together drove to their location in cars furnished with mobile telephones so they could call supervisors at NORC for any reason.

The teams were instructed to walk around each block, go down any alleys or passages, and enter each structure that allowed public access (that did not have a locked door or gate) and to query each person they encountered. Interviewers were specifically instructed to look in parked cars or trucks, to check all-night movies, restaurants, and bars or other places open to the public, and to enter every structure on the block, proceeding as far into each as possible, including searching open basements, roofs, hallways, and any other place they could gain access to without destroying property or taking undue risks.

The police escorts were asked to determine whether particular locations were safe enough for an interviewing team to enter. In a few cases, they said they were not.

The interviewers were instructed to interview each person they encountered using a short "screening" schedule. Everyone they met walking, sitting, or lying down, whether inside a structure or outside, in a car, van, or truck, or riding a bicycle was to be approached for screening. Sleeping persons were to be gently awakened and then asked for an interview. In all cases the interviewing teams were to announce their purpose, assure the person approached that no harm was intended, and identify themselves and their escorts.[9]

The screening interview was to determine whether the person encountered was homeless. Each was offered $1 for responding to the screening questionnaire. If the person was determined to be homeless according to the definition described below, the interviewer proceeded with a longer interview, offering an additional $4 in payment. The longer interview schedule was identical to the one used with shelter occupants.

On blocks where they found too many people to handle easily, the assigned interviewers were instructed to count everyone present and systematically choose persons to be approached, to get as representative a sample as possible. Given the hour when the interviews took place, there were only a few times this sampling procedure had to be used: there simply are not many places in Chicago where the streets are crowded during the dead of night. Supervisors were in touch with the interviewing teams through their mobile telephones. This arrangement made it possible to assign additional interviewers when the original teams encountered too many people to handle or when other problems arose.

The interviewing assignments were arranged so that each night's locations were a random subsample of blocks. Teams alternated nightly between interviewing in shelters and participating in block searches.

Sampling Experience

The worth of a sample design rests primarily on how well it conforms to the requirements of the statistical inference models it was based on. Of almost equal importance is how faithfully the sampling plan is carried out. Especially critical for samples of human populations is the sample completion rate, or how many of those designated to be sampled are interviewed. The relevant data for both the shelter and street surveys in both phases are given in tables B.3 and B.4. All the completion rates are well within the acceptable range for sample surveys. Indeed, considering that the homeless are a difficult population to interview, the completion rates must be regarded as exceptionally high.

Cooperation was obtained from over 95% of the shelter operators in the fall survey and more than 85% in the winter survey. Within shelters, 83% in the fall and 78% in the winter of the sampled residents cooperated by giving interviews. About half of the residents who did not complete interviews refused to

---

9. The escorts were identified as off-duty Chicago policemen who were present to protect the interviewers, not to harass the interviewee. As in other places, Chicago police are usually recognized despite the absence of uniforms or insignia.

Table B.3   Shelter Survey Sampling Experience

	Fall	Winter
A. Shelter Universe		
Eligible shelters in universe	28	45
Shelters drawn in sample	22	27
Sampled shelters agreeing to participate	21	23
Shelter completion rate	(95.5%)	(85.2%)
B. Shelter Resident Sample		
Eligible residents in sampled shelters	934	1,183
Eligible residents selected in sample	320	317
Sample residents interviewed	265	248
Resident completion rate	(82.8%)	(78.2%)
Uninterviewed sample shelter residents		
Unavailable for interview[a]	41	19
	(12.8%)	(6.0%)
Refused interview	14	49
	(4.4%)	(15.4%)
Interview breakoff before completion	0	1

[a]"Unavailable" means that person was not in the shelter at the time of the survey (at work, temporarily absent, etc.) and hence was not asked for an interview. Callbacks were attempted on all unavailables: the cases shown here are those with whom callbacks were not effective in retrieving the interviews.

cooperate; the other half were unavailable for interviewing. The uncompleted interviews consist of persons who were absent from the shelters at the time of interviewing but were shown on the rosters as present during the reference period of the survey.[10] Some were on their jobs, on errands, or absent for some other reason.

Table B.4 contains the sampling experience for the street survey. All the blocks designated in the sample were surveyed. A total of 318 persons in the fall and 289 in the winter were approached to be screened as to their eligibility for interviewing on the main questionnaire. At this stage of screening, 25% and 13%, respectively, in the two surveys refused to answer the screening questionnaire, leading to completion rates of 73% and 82%.[11] Some of the persons approached simply ignored the interviewers; others misinterpreted their request, and still others refused to answer. Clearly, to be approached on the street in the dead of night for an interview is not a "normal" experience, and some people were not confident the approach was legitimate. Neverthe-

10. The initial number of uncompleted interviews in phase one was considerably larger. However, NORC made strong efforts to interview the absent persons at times convenient to them, drastically reducing the number of persons missed. That so many of the missing respondents were found again at the same shelters suggests that some large portion of the shelter population consists of regular residents who return night after night.

11. Completion rates and refusal rates do not add to 100% because a few persons broke off the screening interview before completion (four in phase one and five in phase two), and a few others could not be screened (two in phase one and nine in phase two).

Table B.4   Street Survey Sampling Experience

	Fall	Winter
A. Block Universe and Sample		
Blocks in universe	19,409	19,409
Blocks selected in sample	168	244[a]
B. Street Search Experience		
Persons encountered and approached for screening[b]	318	289
Persons encountered *and* screened	232	238
Screen completion rate	(73%)	(82%)
Persons who refused screening interview	80	37
Screen refusal rate	(25%)	(13%)
Screen interview breakoff	4	5
Person encountered unable to be screened	2	9
C. Main Questionnaire Experience		
Persons screened and eligible for main interview	23	30
Completed main interview	22	28
Completion rate	(96%)	(93%)
Refused main interview	1	0
Interview refusal rate	(4%)	(0%)
Interview breakoff before completion	0	2

[a] Note that 245 blocks were selected for the block sample. However, one of the blocks selected "did not exist" and hence was not searched.

[b] An "encounter" consists of any person present on a block or in any of the public access places on a block who was walking, sitting, standing, lying down, sitting in a parked car or truck, or riding a bicycle.

less, more than three out of four did agree to answer the questions put to them.[12]

All told, 23 persons in the fall survey and 30 persons in the winter survey were found to be homeless. Of these, 96% in the fall survey and 93% in the winter survey agreed to answer the main questionnaire, leading to an overall completion rate of more than 90%, far exceeding that obtained in the usual sample survey.

Although many people familiar with the homeless had warned us repeatedly that they were difficult to interview, the NORC interviewing teams did not find it nearly as difficult as expected.

Analysis Sample

The sample sizes resulting from the fall and the winter surveys are small: 22 and 28 interviews, respectively, with the street homeless and 265 and 248 in-

12. Note that in the usual survey uncompleted cases consist mainly of persons who were never approached, generally because they were repeatedly not at home when the interviewers called. In the street survey, almost every person encountered was approached; hence uncompleted interviews consist primarily of outright refusals.

terviews with shelter residents. Especially small were the two street samples. To augment the sample sizes, we considered using additional street interviews from the pretests and nonsample interviews from the street and shelter surveys. The nonsample interviews in the fall survey and the winter survey arose in two ways. Some shelter residents who were not chosen in the samples of their shelters slipped in among those who were selected and were interviewed (and paid $5) inadvertently; and in the winter survey we chose a set of "superblocks" consisting of places where street people were known to congregate.

All told, some 159 additional street and shelter resident interviews were available. Using analysis of variance and discriminant analysis to compare the nonsample residents with their sample counterparts, we found no significant statistical differences on a wide variety of characteristics, such as age, gender, or employment. To be sure, the shelter sample differed in significant ways from the street sample, but nonsample street interviews were not discernibly different from the sample ones, and nonsample shelter residents were not noticeably different from their sample counterparts. This fortunate finding justifies our merging the pretest and nonsample interviews with the shelter and street samples.

The final merged sample consists of 722 cases—166 street interviews and 556 shelter interviews. Note, however, that the merged sample is not used for the projected estimates of the size of the Chicago homeless population presented in chapter 3: only the sampled homeless counts are used in those estimates.

Estimating the Size of the Chicago Homeless Population

Estimates of the homeless population were made separately for each survey, for each component of the survey (street and shelter samples), and for each substratum of the street and shelter samples. The general procedures used were the same for each subsample. An average number of homeless people per unit sampled (shelter or census block) was computed and multiplied by the total number of units in the substratum the sample was drawn from. This projection is the population estimate for the substratum.[13] The standard error of the population estimate is obtained by multiplying the standard error of the mean number of homeless per unit sampled by the total number of units in the substratum.[14]

Substratum estimates were combined in the following manner: substratum estimates of population size were added together to form stratum estimates

13. This procedure is equivalent to the conventional and perhaps more familiar procedure of multiplying each homeless person in the subsample by the inverse of the probability of being selected to estimate the homeless population in each substratum.

14. The standard error of the mean is the standard deviation of the sample divided by the square root of the sample size.

(estimates of street and shelter populations), then stratum estimates were added to form a total estimate. Estimates of the standard errors of the strata and the total population were obtained by adding the squares of the estimated standard errors for each substratum and taking the square root of the total.[15]

Street Samples

As I explained earlier, it was not always possible to screen every person encountered in the block searches. Some ignored the interviewers; others misinterpreted the request; still others simply refused to answer; and a few broke off the interview before their residential status could be determined. In the fall survey, 103 of 144 encounters (72%) in the high-density stratum, 104 of 142 encounters (73%) in the medium-density stratum, and 25 of 32 encounters (78%) in the low-density stratum were adequately screened.[16] In the winter survey, the percentages adequately screened were high density, 84%; medium density, 86%; and low density, 76%.

The conventional method of incorporating missing information into the sample design is to inflate the estimated mean number of homeless per block/cluster by the degree to which the blocks/clusters in each stratum were underscreened.[17] The estimated standard errors of the mean are inflated in the same way. The multipliers used in the fall survey are high density, $144/103 = 1.398$; medium density, $142/104 = 1.365$; and low density, $32/25 = 1.280$. The multipliers used in the winter survey are high density, $208/174 = 1.195$; medium density, $22/19 = 1.158$; and low density, $59/45 = 1.280$.

The estimates of the homeless population on the streets or in public places for the fall survey and the winter survey are shown in table B.5. The computation procedures described above were used to make the estimates. The mean homeless per block/cluster in each substratum is multiplied by the multiplier and then by the number of blocks/clusters in the substratum to obtain the population estimate. Similarly, the standard error of the mean is multiplied by the multiplier and then by the number of blocks/clusters to obtain the standard

15. Standard errors are measures of the average distance from the mean. As such they follow the laws of Euclidean geometry and in particular the Pythagorean theorem—that the distance from one point to another in multidimensional space is the square root of the sum of squared distances along each dimension. In this case each substratum is a separate dimension.

16. That is, enough information was obtained during the screening interview to make an objective determination of the respondent's homeless status.

17. This procedure assumes that the probability that someone is homeless, given that the person is encountered, is the same as the probability that someone is homeless given that the person is encountered and adequately screened and that this probability remains constant throughout all the blocks/clusters in the substratum sample. Under these assumptions, the probability that someone is homeless given an encounter is estimated by the ratio of the number classified as homeless to the number adequately screened. This estimate is multiplied by the total number of encounters to obtain an estimate of the total number of homeless people in the substratum sample. The multiplier is then computed as the ratio of the estimated total number of homeless to the number of screened homeless.

Table B.5   Computation of Estimates of Homeless Population from the Street Subsamples

Stratum	Mean per Block/ Cluster	Standard Error of the Mean	Multiplier	Number of Blocks/ Clusters	Population Estimate	Standard Error of the Estimate
Fall estimates						
High density	.102	.060	1.398	295	42	25
Medium density	.306	.098	1.365	806	337	108
Low density	.214	.155	1.280	3,662	1,004	726
Total					1,383	735
Winter estimates						
High density	.571	.400	1.195	295	202	141
Medium density	0.0	0.0	1.158	806	0	0
Low density	.041	.029	1.280	6,103	326	229
Total					528	269

Table B.6   Estimates of the Homeless Street Population That Incorporate Interviewer Assessments

Stratum	Fall Survey		Winter Survey	
	Population Estimate	Standard Error	Population Estimate	Standard Error
High density	98	40	281	181
Medium density	378	95	0	0
Low density	1,004	726	653	316
Total	1,480	734	934	364

error of the population estimate. Clusters were used as the sampling unit in the low-density stratum. The cluster size was five blocks in the fall survey and three blocks in the winter survey.

We made an additional set of estimates of the homeless population on the streets and in public places, using interviewer assessment of the truthfulness of the respondents' answers to the screening interview. In a few cases (9 in the fall survey and 13 in the winter survey) the interviewer felt on the basis of appearance or answers or both that the respondent really was homeless. The estimates obtained by incorporating interviewer assessments are shown in table B.6.

Using interviewer assessments increases the estimate by 7% in the fall survey and 77% in the winter survey. The sharp increase in the winter survey occurs because two additional cases were added in the low-density substratum, where each case has a weight of 125 (before prorating nonscreened cases).

Although interviewer assessments suggest that our estimates of the homeless population, based solely on screening criteria, may be slightly low (amounting at most to an undercount of 406 homeless in the winter survey), the accuracy of these assessments cannot be determined. Using them will probably lead to an overestimation of the number of homeless. Hence, our final estimates, shown in table B.5, are based strictly on the responses made to the screening questions. I present the estimates shown in table B.6 only as one way to assess the extent of downward bias inherent in the use of survey data.

Shelter Samples

Estimates of the shelter population were derived from shelter rosters during the survey periods. A master list of shelters was drawn up, and substrata were based on shelter size. In the large size substrata the enumeration was complete. In the smaller size substrata, population estimates were projected from samples of varying sizes.

Two substrata were used in the fall survey, consisting of nineteen large shelters and nine smaller shelters, the latter having fewer than 20 beds. The sample consisted of all nineteen shelters in the large size substratum, and three of the nine shelters in the small size substratum. Three substrata were used in the winter survey. The large substratum (37 or more beds) numbered seventeen shelters, all of which were enumerated. The medium substratum (18 to 33 beds) numbered twelve shelters, six of which were enumerated. The small substratum (fewer than 18 beds) numbered sixteen shelters, of which four were enumerated. To complete the estimation of the shelter population in the winter survey, NORC conducted a telephone survey to obtain counts during the survey period from seven of the Chicago's nine warming centers that had not been included in the master list of shelters from which the substratum samples were drawn.[18]

The Fall Survey

Only one estimate needed to be made of the homeless population residing in shelters. Of the twenty-eight shelters identified at the time of the survey, all but nine were fully enumerated, giving a count of 919 occupants. The remaining nine shelters were small, each having fewer than 20 beds. Three of these were sampled. The sample had a mean of 4.67 occupants per shelter. The standard error of the mean (adjusted for a finite population) was 1.453. Consequently the estimated occupancy of the nine small shelters was $9 \times 4.67 = 42$ homeless; and the standard error of the estimate was $9 \times 1.453 = 13$. There is no standard error for the nineteen larger shelters, because they were fully enumerated. Thus the estimate for the homeless population staying at shelters is $919 + 42 = 961$, with a standard error of 13.

18. The Chicago Park District opened its buildings to homeless persons whenever the temperature fell below twenty degrees Fahrenheit. These buildings had no sleeping accommodations, but they were heated and provided shelter when the temperature was so low that there was serious danger of hypothermia. On the phase two nights when these "warming centers" were opened, NORC supervisors called each center to ascertain the number of persons being accommodated.

The Winter Survey

Of the seventeen shelters sampled from the first substratum, one with a 50-bed capacity refused to participate. The shelter reported to the City of Chicago Department of Human Services that all its beds were full on the night it was scheduled to be surveyed. Combining this information with the enumeration data, a total of 1,151 adults were found in this substratum. This estimate has no sampling error, because all shelters in the substratum were enumerated.

There was one refusal in the second shelter substratum. Its report filed with the city stated that 8 of its 30 beds were occupied. A second shelter, Lincoln Park, delayed participation, but at length its occupancy was found to be 26 out of 30 beds. The mean of the six shelters sampled in this stratum (half of the total) was 14.17 with a standard error (adjusted for a finite population) of 2.2466. The mean and standard error were multiplied by 12, the total number of shelters in this stratum, to obtain a population estimate of 170 and a standard error of 27.

Two of the four shelters sampled in the third substratum refused to participate in the survey, but both filed reports with the City of Chicago Department of Human Services stating that they were filled to capacity (16 beds and 10 beds, respectively) on the night they were to be sampled. Of the two remaining shelters in the sample, the first had 5 occupants and 13 beds; the second, with 5 beds, was empty. The mean number of residents per shelter was 7.75; the standard error of the mean (adjusted for a finite population) was 2.9660. The population estimate is 124; the standard error of the estimate is 47.

There were nine warming centers in operation during the field period of the winter survey. Two of these, Wellington Street and The Port, were included in the shelter listing, and Wellington Street was included in the shelter sample. Occupancy estimates for the seven warming centers not on the list of shelters were obtained by telephone calls from NORC to the warming centers each night of the field period and by information furnished by the City of Chicago Department of Human Services. The two sources were in fairly close agreement. In general, the estimates obtained by NORC's calls were used.

Since estimates were available for a seven-day period, a nightly mean and standard error for each of the seven warming centers was computed. The means of the seven centers were then combined to form the estimate of the number of homeless in warming centers at any given night during the field period. That mean was 48. Similarly, the squares of the standard error of the mean for each warming center were added together, and the square root of the sum was used as the estimate of the sampling error of the grand mean. The standard error was estimated at 6.

The estimate of the total homeless population in shelters during the winter survey was obtained by combining the estimates from the various substrata, as shown in table B.7.

Table B.7   Estimates of Homeless Population in Shelters, Winter 1986 Survey

Shelter Substratum	Population Estimate	Standard Error
Large shelters	1,151	0
Medium shelters	170	27
Small shelters	124	47
Warming centers	48	6
Shelter total	1,492	55

Capture/Recapture Estimates

In the original design of the study we contemplated using the capture/recapture method (Seber 1973) to estimate the homeless population. We abandoned this approach because the homeless population is not "closed"; that is, there are many transitions into and out of the homeless state between the survey periods. Still, the capture/recapture method can be applied if one has a separate estimate of the percentage surviving from one phase of the survey to the next. The number of homeless "captured" in both surveys is inflated by the reciprocal of the survival rate. The percentage of the fall survey homeless that was "recaptured" is assumed to be the same as the percentage of the total homeless population "captured" in the winter survey. Accordingly, the total population size at the time of the winter survey is estimated by dividing the number sampled in the winter survey by the percentage of the fall survey homeless who were also surveyed in the winter survey.

Of the 287 subjects who were given sample design interviews in the fall survey, 24 (8.36%) were given sample design interviews in the winter survey. If this percentage is inflated by the reciprocal of the survival rate (estimated at .619 from the duration of the current episode of homelessness), the result is 13.51%. The number of design interviews in the winter survey ($N = 276$) is divided by the inflated percentage of recaptures from the fall survey to get an estimate of $276/.1351 = 2,043$ homeless in the winter survey, with an estimated standard error of 411. The closeness of this estimate to the survey-based estimate greatly increases our confidence in the survey methodology, but the larger standard error associated with the capture/recapture method is a further argument for retaining the conventional area sampling approach we have adopted.

References

Anderson, Nels. 1940. *Men on the move.* Chicago: University of Chicago Press.

————. 1923. *The hobo: The sociology of the homeless man.* Chicago: University of Chicago Press. Reprinted 1975.

Bach, Victor, and Renée Steinhagen. 1987. *Alternatives to the welfare hotel.* New York: Community Service Society.

Bahr, Howard M., ed. 1970. *Disaffiliated man: Essays and bibliography on Skid Row, vagrancy and outsiders.* Toronto: University of Toronto Press.

Bahr, Howard M., and Theodore Caplow. 1974. *Old men: Drunk and sober.* New York: New York University Press.

Bahr, Howard M., and Gerald Garrett. 1976. *Women alone.* Lexington, Mass.: Lexington Books.

Baxter, Ellen, and Kim Hopper. 1981. *Private lives/public spaces: Homeless adults on the streets of New York City.* New York: Community Service Society.

Blumberg, Leonard, Thomas E. Shipley, and Stephen F. Barsky. 1978. *Liquor and poverty: Skid Row as a human condition.* New Brunswick, N.J.: Rutgers Center of Alcohol Studies.

Blumberg, Leonard, Thomas E. Shipley, Jr., and Irving W. Shandler. 1973. *Skid Row and its alternatives.* Philadelphia: Temple University Press.

Bogue, Donald B. 1963. *Skid Row in American cities.* Chicago: Community and Family Study Center, University of Chicago.

Boston Emergency Shelter Commission. 1978–79. *Making room for Boston's homeless.* Boston: Emergency Shelter Commission.

————. 1984. The October Project: Seeing the obvious problem. In *HUD report on homelessness.* Joint Hearing before the Subcommittee on Banking, Finance and Urban Affairs and the Subcommittee on Manpower and Housing of the Committee on Government Operations, 98th Cong., 2d sess. Washington D.C.: Government Printing Office.

————. 1986. *Boston's homeless: Taking the next step.* Boston: Emergency Shelter Commission.

California Department of Housing and Community Development. 1985. *A study of the issues and characteristics of the homeless population in California.* Sacramento: California Department of Housing and Community Development.

Chicago, Department of Planning. 1985. Housing needs of Chicago's single, low income renters. Manuscript report.

Clements, Sylvia. 1984. The transformation of the wandering poor in nineteenth century Philadelphia. In *Walking to work: Tramps in America, 1790–1935,* ed. E. H. Monkonnen. Lincoln: University of Nebraska Press.

References

Comstock, George W., and Knud J. Helsing. 1976. Symptoms of depression in two communities. *Psychological Medicine* 6:551–63.

Crouse, Joan M. 1986. *The homeless transient in the Great Depression: New York State, 1929–1941.* Albany: SUNY Press.

Crystal, Stephen. 1982. *New arrivals: First time shelter clients.* New York: Human Resources Administration.

Crystal, Stephen, and Merv Goldstein. 1982. *Chronic and situational dependency: Long term residents in a shelter for men.* New York: Human Resources Administration.

Cuomo, Mario M. 1983. 1933/1983—never again: A report to the National Governors' Association Task Force on the Homeless.

Dohrenwend, Barbara S., Bruce P. Dohrenwend, Bruce Link, and Itzhak Levav. 1983. Social functioning of psychiatric patients in contrast with community cases in the general population. *Archives of General Psychiatry* 40:1174–82.

Dohrenwend, Bruce P., Patrick E. Shrout, Gladys Egri, and Frederick S. Mendelshon. 1980. Nonspecific psychological distress and other dimensions of psychopathology. *Archives of General Psychiatry* 37:1229–36.

Easterlin, Richard A. 1987. The new age structure of poverty in America. *Population and Development Review* 13, 2:195–208.

Farr, Rodger K., Paul Koegel, and Audrey Burnham. 1986. A survey of homelessness and mental illness in the Skid Row area of Los Angeles. Los Angeles County Department of Mental Health.

Florida, Statewide Taskforce on the Homeless. 1985. Final report: Florida's homeless, A plan for action.

Freeman, Richard B. 1988. The magnitude and duration of homelessness. Paper presented at the February meetings of the American Association for the Advancement of Science, Boston.

Freeman, Richard B., and Brian Hall. 1986. Permanent homelessness in America. Unpublished manuscript, National Bureau of Economic Research, Cambridge, Mass.

Freeman, Richard B., and Harry J. Holzer, eds. 1986. *The black youth employment crisis.* Chicago: University of Chicago Press.

GAO. *See* United States General Accounting Office.

Hamilton, Rabinowitz and Alschuler, Inc. 1987. *The changing face of misery: Los Angeles' Skid Row area in transition, housing and social services needs of Central City East.* Los Angeles: Community Redevelopment Agency.

Hoch, Charles, and Diane Spicer. 1985. *SROs, an endangered species: Single-room occupancy hotels in Chicago.* Chicago: Community Shelter Organization and Jewish Council on Urban Affairs, 1985.

Hombs, Mary Ellen, and Mitch Snyder. 1982. Homelessness in America: A forced march to nowhere. Community on Creative Non-Violence, Washington, D.C.

Hope, Marjorie, and James Young. 1986. *The faces of homelessness.* Lexington, Mass.: Lexington Books.

Hopper, Kim. 1987. The public response to homelessness in New York City: The last hundred years. In *On being homeless: Historical perspectives,* ed. Rick Beard. New York: Museum of the City of New York.

HUD. *See* United States Department of Housing and Urban Development.

Jackson, Kenneth M. 1987. The Bowery: From residential street to Skid Row. In *On being homeless: Historical perspectives,* ed. Rick Beard. New York: Museum of the City of New York.

Katz, Michael B. 1975. *The people of Hamilton, Canada West.* Cambridge: Harvard University Press.

———. 1986. *In the shadow of the poorhouse.* New York: Basic Books.

Kozol, Jonathan. 1988. *Rachel and her children: Homeless families in America.* New York: Crown.

Lamb, H. Richard, ed. 1984. *The homeless mentally ill: A task force report of the American Psychiatric Association.* Washington, D.C.: American Psychiatric Association.

Lee, Barrett A. 1980. The disappearance of Skid Row: Some ecological evidence. *Urban Affairs Quarterly* 16, 1:81–107.

Lewis, Dan A., Tom Pavkov, Helen Rosenberg, Susan Reed, Arthur Lurigio, Zev Kalifon, Bruce Johnson, and Stephanie Riger. 1987. *State hospitalization utilization in Chicago.* Evanston, Ill.: Center for Urban Affairs and Policy Research, Northwestern University.

Link, Bruce, and Dohrenwend, Bruce P. 1980. Formulation of hypotheses about the true prevalence of demoralization in the United States. In *Mental illness in the United States: Epidemiologic estimates,* ed. B. P. Dohrenwend, B. S. Dohrenwend, M. S. Gould, et al. New York: Praeger.

Lynd, Robert A., and Helen M. Lynd. 1929. *Middletown.* New York: Harcourt, Brace.

———. 1937. *Middletown in transition.* New York: Harcourt, Brace.

McMurry, Dan. 1988. Hard living on Easy Street. *Chronicles* 12, 8:15–19.

Manpower Development Research Corporation. 1985. *Summary of findings of the National Supported Work Demonstration.* Cambridge, Mass.: Ballinger.

Maryland Department of Human Resources. 1986. *Where do you go from nowhere?* Baltimore: State of Maryland, Health and Welfare Council of Central Maryland.

Piliavin, Irving, and Michael Sosin. 1987–88. Tracking the homeless. *Focus* 10, 4:20–24.

Radloff, Lenore Sawyer. 1977. The CES-D scale: A self-report depression scale for research in the general population. *Applied Psychological Measurement* 1:385–401.

Ricketts, Erol B., and Isabel Sawhill. 1988. Defining and measuring the underclass. *Journal of Policy Analysis and Management* 7, 2:316–25.

Robert Wood Johnson Foundation. 1983. Special report 1.

Robinson, Frederic G. 1985. *Homeless people in the nation's capital.* Washington, D.C.: University of the District of Columbia, Center for Applied Research and Urban Policy.

Rossi, Alice S., and Peter H. Rossi. 1989. *Of human bonding: A life course perspective on parent-child relations.* Hawthorne, N.Y.: Aldine-DeGruyter.

Rossi, Peter H. 1987. No good applied research goes unpunished. *Social Science and Modern Society* 25, 1:73–80.

Rossi, Peter H., Richard A. Berk, and Kenneth J. Lenihan. 1980. *Money, work and crime: Experimental evidence.* New York: Academic Press.

Rossi, Peter H., Gene A. Fisher, and Georgianna Willis. 1986. *The condition of the homeless of Chicago.* Amherst, Mass., and Chicago: Social and Demographic Research Institute and NORC.

Schubert, Herman J. P. 1935. *Twenty thousand transients: A year's sample of those who apply for aid in a northern city.* Buffalo, N.Y.: Emergency Relief Bureau.

Seber, George A. F. 1973. *The estimation of animal abundance and related papers.* London: Griffin.

Sosin, Michael, Paul Colson, and Susan Grossman. 1988. *Homelessness in Chicago: Poverty and pathology, social institutions and social change.* Chicago: Chicago Community Trust.

Spradley, James P. 1970. *You owe yourself a drunk: An ethnography of urban nomads.* Boston: Little, Brown.

Stagner, Matthew, and Harold Richman. 1985. *General Assistance profiles: Findings from a longitudinal study of newly approved recipients.* Springfield: Illinois Department of Public Aid.

―――. 1986. *Help-seeking and the use of social service providers by welfare families in Chicago.* Chicago: Chapin Hall Center for Children, University of Chicago.

Sutherland, Edwin H., and Harvey J. Locke. 1936. *Twenty thousand homeless men: A study of unemployed men in Chicago shelters.* Chicago: J. B. Lippincott.

Tucker, William. 1987. Where do the homeless come from? *National Review,* 25 September, 32–43.

United States Conference of Mayors. 1988. *The continuing growth of hunger, homelessness and poverty in America's cities: 1987* (authors Lilia M. Reyes and Laura Dekoven Waxman). Washington, D.C., United States Conference of Mayors.

United States Department of Commerce, Bureau of the Census. 1984. *1980 census of population: Persons in institutions and other group quarters.* Pub. PC80-2-4D. Washington, D.C.: Government Printing Office.

United States Department of Housing and Urban Development (HUD). 1984. A report to the secretary on the homeless and emergency shelters. Office of Policy Development and Research, Washington, D.C.

United States General Accounting Office. 1987. *Non-cash benefits: Methodological review of experimental valuation methods indicates many problems remain.* Washington, D.C.: Government Printing Office.

United States Public Health Service. 1982. *The national ambulatory medical care survey, United States: 1979 summary.* Series 13, no. 99. Hyattsville, Md.: National Center for Health Statistics.

Wallace, Samuel E. 1965. *Skid Row as a way of life.* Totowa, N.J.: Bedminster Press.

Weissman, Myrna M., Diane Sholomskas, Margaret Pottenger, Brigitte A. Prusoff, and Ben Z. Locke. 1977. Assessing depressive symptoms in five psychiatric populations: A validation study. *American Journal of Epidemiology* 106:203–14.

Wickendon, Elizabeth. 1987. Reminiscences of the program for transients and homeless in the thirties. In *On being homeless: Historical perspectives,* ed. Rick Beard. New York: Museum of the City of New York.

Wilson, William J. 1987. *The truly disadvantaged.* Chicago: University of Chicago Press.

―――. 1988. *Urban Family Life Project: Detailed progress report.* Chicago: Urban Family Life Project, University of Chicago.

Wiseman, Jacqueline O. 1970. *Stations of the lost: The treatment of Skid Row alcoholics.* New York: Prentice-Hall.

Wright, James D., and Julie Lam. 1987. Homelessness and low income housing supply. *Social Forces* 17, 4:48–53

Wright, James D., and Eleanor Weber. 1987. *Homelessness and health.* New York: McGraw-Hill.

Index

Index

Woods, W. K., 220
Works Progress Administration, 25, 202
Wright, J. D., 54, 161, 182, 220, 242

YMCA, 203
Young, J., 8, 240
YWCA, 203

DATE DUE

DEMCO 38-296